Fraud and Corruption

Foreword by Christopher Flint*

The increasing pressure being applied to corporate business, whether through the Sarbanes-Oxley legislation, UN or EU directives, consumer watchdogs or increasingly inquisitive accounting procedures, is beginning to have a positive effect. It is forcing corporate business to introduce more effective controls to prevent and reduce the incidence of fraud and corruption. However there is still much to be done as illustrated by the collapse of a number of conglomerates, with hapless shareholders and stakeholders taking the brunt of the personal greed of senior directors. The extent of fraud and corruption within the business community has been assessed as a multi-billion-dollar industry and the need for increased vigilance is probably greater now than ever. No part of the corporate business structure is safe from predatory attacks. These attacks come in a variety of guises including the use of fictitious invoices, false payment instructions, leaking of price-sensitive information, transfer of knowledge to competitors in exchange for a bribe, illegal trading of company shares, sale of company property, or alterations of bank account details to divert payments to an employee's account amongst others.

Nigel Iyer and Martin Samociuk have produced an exceptionally detailed handbook on ways and methods to identify fraud and corruption within corporate organisations. Their explanation of the various procedures which could be adopted to prevent fraud and its companion corruption is extensive and based on considerable investigative experience. They have also incorporated an innovative corporate case novel called *The Tightrope* which demonstrates the nature of fraud and corruption as well as the challenges in actually doing something about it and the determination needed to secure a lasting solution. The novel is based on an amalgamation of hundreds of incidents of corporate fraud and corruption and the authors' quite exceptional range of experiences. This gives strong credence to the many sensible and innovative prevention methods that they recommend.

Fraud and Corruption is essentially a reference book. Its aim is to recognise the sheer scale of the cost of fraud and corruption to business. Through raising awareness and by introducing appropriate training for the management of incidents the author's argue that significant improvements can be achieved if cognisance is taken of the behavioural and transactional 'red flags' by which fraudulent and corrupt behaviour can be identified within corporate business. The book has a range of detailed and useful Appendices which provide the basis of training for senior managers, team leaders, supervisors, and line managers in the

---

*Christopher Flint is a founder member of the European Institute of Corporate Security Management (www.eicsm.org) and the former head of security of Cadbury Schweppes Plc. A number of EICSM members kindly provided comments on *The Tightrope*.

form of workshops, practical training scenarios and a system for measuring fraud and corruption resistance.

This book could appear rather daunting through its sheer size and depth of detail but that is also its strength. For a business however, which is serious to ensure that its own defences to fraud and corruption (both internally and externally) are sufficiently robust, it is an essential addition to the library of the chief financial officer and the risk manager. It will help them to put in place awareness programmes to recognise the risks, prepare appropriate policies and implement a business strategy. Each of these processes is carefully described.

Nigel Iyer and Martin Samociuk are to be congratulated on producing this exceptionally well researched and relevant handbook with its uncompromising message to corporate businesses to mend their anti-fraud and corruption fences and use the helpful and easy to follow workshop material. There is little doubt that shareholder scrutiny will not tolerate any indifference to this corporate threat. As the authors contend it is about: *'measuring how good an organisation is at doing things in practice, not just fulfilling legal and other requirements on paper.'*

If corporate businesses take heed of the advice offered they will have taken a significant step in controlling the cost of fraud and corruption, and importantly, in establishing a reputation for financial scrutiny and control. Not least this would make shareholders a lot happier.

Fraud and Corruption

Prevention and Detection

NIGEL IYER AND MARTIN SAMOCIUK

GOWER

Published by
Gower Publishing Limited
Gower House
Croft Road
Aldershot
Hants GU11 3HR
England

Gower Publishing Company
Suite 420
101 Cherry Street
Burlington VT 05401–4405
USA

Nigel Iyer and Martin Samociuk have asserted their right under the Copyright, Designs and Patents Act 1988 to be identified as the authors of this work.

British Library Cataloguing in Publication Data
Iyer, Nigel K.
    Fraud and corruption : prevention and detection
    1. Corporations – Corrupt practices 2. Fraud – Prevention
    I. Title II. Samociuk, Martin
    364.1'63

    ISBN-10: 0566086999

Library of Congress Cataloging-in-Publication Data
Iyer, Nigel K.
    Fraud and corruption : prevention and detection / by Nigel K. Iyer and Martin Samociuk.
    p. cm.
    Includes bibliographical references and index.
    ISBN-13: 978-0-566-08699-1 (alk. paper)
    ISBN-10: 0-566-08699-9 (alk. paper)
    1. Corporations--Corrupt practices. 2. Fraud. I. Samociuk, Martin. II. Title.

HV6768.L94 2006
658.4'73--dc22

2006018454

Typeset in 9 point Stone Serif by IML Typographers, Birkenhead, Merseyside
Printed and bound in Great Britain by TJ International Ltd, Padstow, Cornwall.

Contents

List of Figures

List of Tables

Acknowledgements

Nigel Iyer would like to thank his wife, children and parents for their patience and support in writing this book. Martin Samociuk would like to thank his wife Karen for her enthusiastic help and support, particularly in developing many of the drawings and diagrams.

Both authors are grateful to their clients and contacts as well as to colleagues in the Hibis group, without whom the development of this book would not have been possible, and for the hard work put in by Jonathan Norman and the staff at Gower.

We wish to thank our friends at Det Norske Veritas for recognising the importance of Resistance to Fraud and Corruption as part of their worldwide rating and certification programs. We would also like to thank the Securities Industry Research Centre of Asia-Pacific ('SIRCA') for their kind permission to use content from the authors' publication 'Fraud Resistance: a Practical Guide'.

Using 'The Tightrope' in Training and to Raise Awareness

A common feature in many cases of fraud and corruption is that there were obvious indicators or red flags which should have raised suspicions. However honest employees either did not notice them or, if they did, they ignored them because they did not understand their significance.

That is why organizations which have suffered from fraud have realized that one of the most important preventive measures is for all employees to be empowered to prevent fraud and corruption through effective training and awareness programmes.

We believe that the anatomy of a fraud that's presented in *The Tightrope* will be a very useful tool for training and raising awareness right across your organization. It provides a highly readable and very realistic picture of how fraud and corruption can develop and the kind of signals that employees might pick up, if they are alert to them.

To help you use *The Tightrope* in your training or to raise employee awareness of fraud and corruption, Gower will supply a free version of this part of the book, as a pdf file, to anyone who has purchased a copy of *Fraud and Corruption*. You may use the pdf to share *The Tightrope* with people right across your organization, whether in a formal training session or as part of internal communication, that's entirely up to you.

The only caveat is that we ask that you respect the authors' copyright and moral rights and do not circulate the material to anyone outside of your organization nor that you amend or adapt the text that is provided in any way.

To obtain your copy of *The Tightrope* as a pdf, simply contact our marketing team by post or e-mail, including your contact details: Name, Job Title, Organization, Address and e-mail address and we will send you a copy on CD ROM.

The Marketing Department,
Gower Publishing,
Gower House,
Croft Road,
Aldershot,
Hampshire,
GU11 3HR,
UK.
e-mail: marketing@gowerpublishing.com

1 *The Greatest Unmanaged Risk*

Corporate fraud and corruption are arguably the greatest unmanaged commercial risks of the day. But are management taking fraud and corruption seriously enough by making prevention integral to their business strategies? Many executives would argue that they are, after having spent the last couple of decades implementing extensive corporate governance and control frameworks which are supposed to do just that. Furthermore, these frameworks are regularly reviewed by internal and external auditors, lawyers, risk managers, compliance officers, audit committees and non-executive directors.

However, in spite of tougher legislation and vociferous corporate rhetoric in recent years, not that much has changed in the world of fraud and corruption. Reports of major frauds and bribery scandals are just as prevalent now as they were twenty years ago.

Could this be your organisation?

An email arrives at head office alleging that certain directors have been buying personal items on the company's account and that some of the marketing expenses are not genuine. Furthermore, people who have spoken up are being quietly dismissed. It's not the first email of this kind and rumours to this effect have been circulating for a while. However, financial results in the region are strong and local management resents interference. The tone of the emails is increasingly angry and some of the claims about fraud and corruption are hard to believe.

You are one of seven recipients of this email. You are not directly responsible for the division concerned and it is easier to close your eyes to unsubstantiated claims by assuming that they cannot be true.

What you are unaware of is that if enough resources were actually dedicated to uncovering the whole truth then you would find that many of the allegations are in fact true and just the tip of an iceberg. In reality profits are declining, losses are being systematically hidden in the books, some managers have covert ownership in business partners via offshore companies, property frauds are taking place and bribes are being paid in violation of the code of conduct.

You may think that this sort of thing would never occur in your organisation, but are you sure? At first glance, any organisation may appear to have procedures and controls in place to prevent fraud and corruption, but when examined through the sharp eyes of a criminal, it quickly becomes evident that many different methods of fraud and corruption could easily succeed. And when you are in business, fraudsters, corrupt employees and corporate psychopaths are always looking to find a way round your controls if they can.

If you would like to find out if your organisation's defences are in fact a paper tiger, and if you wish to prevent fraud and corruption, to detect cases as early as possible and to put the lost profits back then this book is most definitely for you.

Overkill in bureaucracy and legislation

In recent years there have been improvements in reporting requirements and a greater level of awareness, but a lot still has to be done to prevent the recurrence of fraud and corruption. Rather than making the prevention of fraud and corruption central to their management style, many executives still tend to rely on the belief that people are honest. During numerous workshops over the past twenty years, we have been repeatedly told by employees in both large and small organisations that despite all the focus on controls, they can easily spot ways to defraud the organisation. The reason they haven't done it is because they are honest. Sadly, the spate of recent corporate collapses and the fact that investigators around the world continue to prosper shows that there are plenty of dishonest people around.

So much time and effort has gone into creating corporate responsibility agendas, defining corporate governance and internal controls frameworks, and implementing risk management strategies that very little time has been left to get to grips with the actual risks of fraud and corruption, the way criminals think and the methods that they use. Fraud and corruption differ from many other risks in that they are aggressively perpetrated against the company by intelligent people who are continuously looking, covertly, to identify and target new loopholes for new opportunities. That is why it comes as a distressing shock to management and employees alike when a fraudster or corrupt individual is uncovered; the honest people find it very difficult to believe that dishonest people will affect their organisation.

Extensive efforts have been made around the world to improve laws and definitions to ensure that legal processes are capable of adequately punishing fraudsters, corrupt employees and corporate psychopaths. Up until now we have not seen the same effort made by organisations in detecting attempts and preventing them succeeding in the first place.

Furthermore, the overkill in bureaucracy and legislation is something which international criminals understand only too well. Provided they can stay one step ahead by using the latest tools and technology and are able to move money around offshore destinations, they face very little prospect of being caught. Even if the money is traced and they are facing charges, they usually can afford lawyers who have the capability and resources to win the war of attrition against government prosecutors.

A way of making money is to stop losing it

Once the opportunity to stop losing huge sums of money is recognised at the board level, there are effective measures which can be put in place to prevent fraud and corruption. Even for multinational organisations, the solution to the problem has to come from within because there is little help from governments or regulators on an international level.

Tackling fraud and corruption on an international level is always difficult as it takes so long to get agreement as to how to go about it. Even agreement on the definition of fraud and corruption is nowhere near an international standard. There are dozens of definitions of fraud and corruption in use around the world.

This book is aimed at helping commercial organisations boost profits by increasing resistance to fraud and corruption. Therefore we have adopted the widest and simplest definitions and classifications of fraud and corruption along the lines of 'any unethical act done by anyone, which diminishes the value of the organisation'.

For the definition of fraud, we are using:

- 'an intentional act by one or more individuals among management, those charged with governance, employees, or third parties, involving the use of deception to obtain an unjust or illegal advantage' (International Auditing and Assurance Standards Board, 2004).

For the definition of corruption we are using:

- 'the abuse of public or private office for personal gain' (which is adapted from a World Bank definition by Huther and Shah in 2000 and the simplest we could find to apply to the commercial sector).

Therefore for practical purposes and to cover as many forms of inappropriate commercial behaviour as possible our definition of fraud and corruption covers:

- any form of theft in the widest sense.
- deception in reporting
- corruption and bribery in the widest sense.

and any other form of dishonest or unethical activity which eats into profits or harms reputation or the organisational culture.

It still may take years to reach international agreement on the definitions of fraud and corruption and on what it costs organisations and economies. Rather than waiting for precise international definitions to materialise we propose that organisations start tackling the problems by gaining a better understanding of the fraud and corruption risks that they face and then developing a much greater level of resistance to them.

Whether you are an employee, a manager or an executive director it makes sense to pay more attention to the behavioural aspects of fraudsters, corrupt employees or corporate psychopaths, rather than being blinded by accounting, legal or procedural issues.

Even were you to look at the potential fraud and corruption risks in your own job function, you should be able to see that there are ways to bypass the controls. If you cannot, then we hope to open your eyes to the world of possibilities of committing fraud or indulging in corrupt behaviour which exist. It is only once you have recognised the potential, that you can do something to prevent fraud and corruption.

Our aim with this book is to provide the practical solutions which create value and improve resistance to fraud and corruption. The story, called the Tightrope, included in this book, is based on an amalgamation of real-life experiences. Many of the corporate issues raised by fraudsters, corrupt employees and corporate psychopaths are illustrated there.

2 *Fraud and Corruption Demystified*

The true cost of fraud and corruption

There is a wealth of academic and empirical research which demonstrates the extent and effect of corporate fraud and corruption. For example, research by the Association of Certified Fraud Examiners (2002, 2004, 2006) in the US across a wide range of industries has repeatedly indicated that:

* fraud and corruption are widespread problems that affect practically every organisation
* the typical organisation loses 5 per cent of its annual revenues to fraud and corruption.

These US reports use the term occupational fraud and abuse to describe fraud and corruption stating that nearly half the incidents were detected by a tip-off rather than by active monitoring and control.

Corruption all over the world is a well-known and major problem. The word corruption features regularly in news bulletins and current affairs programmes. In some industries, for example construction, corruption can be found at every stage of the process, project and supply chain (Stansbury, 2005). It can involve major multinational companies, banks, government officials and trade unions

Recent national surveys on the cost of corruption tend to confirm the scale of the problem. In 2003 the World Bank Director for Global Governance, Daniel Kaufmann, said that a rough but conservative estimate of the cost of corruption to the global economy was 5 per cent of the world economy or about $1.5 trillion per year (Kaufmann, 2003).

However, the mounting piles of research, surveys and statistics are of little value in organisations if board executives and senior managers are reluctant to take fraud and corruption seriously.

Many senior executives believe either that their organisation is so much better than others that the likelihood of fraud and corruption is low, or alternatively that since there have not been many problems in the past then there cannot be any. They wait for a tip-off, and as a result, are often waiting whilst the damage is being done.

Once executives have experienced the effects of a major fraud or corruption scandal there is very little need to convince them to invest in preventing a reoccurrence. They also realise that their past inaction has led to significant losses. Because these losses eventually come off the bottom line, every dollar lost reduces net income by the same amount. If the profit margin of the organisation is say 10 per cent, then to recover the lost income requires 10 times the revenue to be generated. Hence to recover a $10 million loss requires $100 million of extra revenue.

In most cases the hidden indirect costs such as constraints on expansion and development, damage to reputation and employee morale greatly outweigh the direct costs.

Finally the costs of investigation are not to be taken lightly. If a case is complicated and involves the international movement of funds, then the investigation costs can be very complex. It is not unusual to spend $1 million on investigating a $10 million fraud. If it involves international money movement and offshore tax havens, this can cost from 30 per cent to 100 per cent of the amount lost.

Probably the single largest, and most ignored, cost element of fraud and corruption is the cost of all the on-going cases which have not been discovered and which are being carried by the organisation.

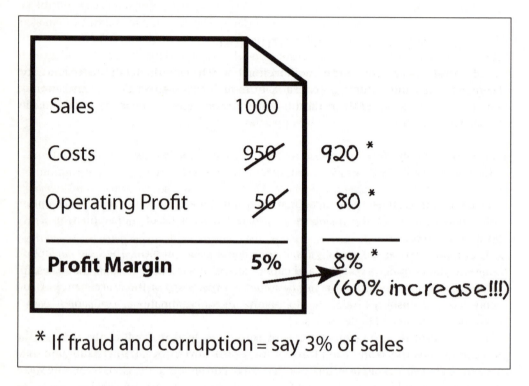

Figure 2.1   Hidden costs

Unfortunately, managers rarely set out to look for hidden costs (see Figure 2.1) caused by fraud and corruption and tend to ignore the warning signs.

Example

A multinational company recruited a new superstar to bring in fresh ideas to its management training schemes and gave him a free rein and a reasonable budget. The new manager immediately brought in some purportedly world-renowned management consultants. In order to be able to afford these consultants, it was necessary to displace (or make redundant) some of the employees in the training department.

It was subsequently discovered that the consultants (which were actually three front companies, all sharing the same remote farmhouse address) used low-paid sub-contractors to do the actual work. At least 80 per cent of the $2 million invoiced was discovered to be fictitious and *the owner of the front companies had, amongst other things, settled the new internal training manager's divorce payment as a reward for his cooperation. Worse still, he had been involved in a similar scheme in his previous job. In a post-mortem, it was estimated that at least 200 other senior managers had the same possibilities of abusing their budgets without this being detected by the routine internal controls. It was discovered later when a fraud and corruption health check was performed on major suppliers and their invoices that some simple tests would easily have detected this case and a number of similar incidents.*

Given the speed at which business is done today, invoice approval and budgetary control are inadequate to prevent misuse of organisational funds. The average time taken by managers to check an invoice or payment instruction prior to approving it is about 15–45 seconds, with only a cursory glance if they believe that someone else has previously looked at it and given it the OK. Quite often, the person authorising the payment does not understand the underlying transactions which generated it. In spite of this, signatures and segregation of duties continue to be one of the main anti-fraud controls for many organisations. Fraudsters have realised that this opens up sizeable opportunities which can be exploited.

Example

A manager with a severe gambling problem used a ballpoint pen containing erasable ink to make out a spurious cheque to a genuine payee. He waited until his director had an office full of people before knocking on the door and requesting an 'urgent' signature. The director verified that the cheque was made out to the expected payee and signed it without querying the supporting documentation. After this the manager rubbed out the payee name, inserted his own name and cashed the cheque. He used this technique to raise dozens of cheques over a number of years and obtained more than $5 million. The fraud only came to light when he went on holiday as a guest of the betting agency and a colleague discovered how he had been hiding discrepancies in the books.

This simple example illustrates why it is so difficult to measure the hidden cost of fraud and corruption. On the face of it, controls are working as they are supposed to, but in reality they are a comfort blanket concealing numerous opportunities.

Who are the perpetrators?

Fraud and corruption take place because an individual, or group:

- sees an opportunity to make money or obtain other benefit
- is motivated to act
- believe they can get away with it.

If asked to think about it, most honest people are usually able to spot opportunities to commit fraud or make money through corrupt relationships. They can also usually work out a method whereby they believe they will not get caught. However, because they are honest, they believe that they will never take advantage of that opportunity. That is until the day when their circumstances change in a way that provides them with the motivation.

At the opposite end of the scale to those who believe they are honest we find the professional fraudsters, organised criminals and corporate psychopaths. These people have such a pronounced desire for money that they always have a motivation to steal. They actively seek out opportunities and continuously test the system so that they know they can get away with it.

There are circumstances where corruption is considered acceptable too. For example, some people and companies feel that paying bribes in countries like Angola, Brazil, Indonesia or India, which they perceive to be corrupt cultures, is acceptable and legal.

Employer pressure can make questionable business practices seem acceptable. In the 1990s, it was accepted practice for analysts in certain investment banks in the US to provide misleading advice to investors in order to promote the shares of favoured corporate clients, or for short-term traders in some mutual funds to make profits to the detriment of long-term shareholders, providing they did it in the name of making profit for the company.

But even in the absence of the sort of pressure and factors described above, what is it then that motivates seemingly honest employees to commit fraud or take a bribe?

If you ask a group of people whether they are honest, the answer is nearly always 'Yes'. However, if you then ask them to answer certain questions as honestly as they can, they begin to realise that their perception is not always so clear-cut. Try and answer the questions in Table 2.1 below.

Table 2.1   Perception of honesty

Question	Have you ever?	Your answer (Y/N)			
1	Used unlicensed software or illegally copied music?				
2	Knowingly not paid your bus or train fare?				
3	Taken items of office stationery or equipment to use at home?				
4	Knowingly inflated a private insurance claim?				
5	Paid tax-free cash to a builder, plumber, electrician, etc?				
6	Knowingly exceeded the speed limit?				
7	Added things that you shouldn't have to your travelling expenses?				
8	Claimed a benefit you know you really should not have?				
9	Told a white lie about your qualifications?				
10	Deliberately not paid parking fines?				
11	Taken and not declared a gift from a supplier or customer?				
12	Paid a bribe to get a contract?				
13	Stolen anything?				
14	Submitted personal expenses such as golf club membership or private entertainment as a company expense?				
15	Channelled company purchases or services through another company in which you or family members have a personal interest?				
16	Under-declared or omitted items from your tax return?				
17	Brought items through customs which you should have declared?				
	YOUR SCORE	YES	___	NO	___

If you answered the questionnaire honestly, how many did you answer 'yes' to?

Of the many hundreds of times that we have asked these questions to audiences, there have been very few instances when someone answered 'No' to all the questions. In these cases, it was almost always because the persons thought that by answering 'Yes', they would implicate themselves, so they were just protecting their backs. Also, in some cultures people find it embarrassing to answer 'Yes' to this type of question so again they will take the easier route by saying 'No'.

There have been numerous occasions where people have answered 'Yes' to five or more questions and yet still thought of themselves as fundamentally honest.

The number of times when someone answers 'Yes' depends on the person's attitude to risk taking. For example, it is common to find that senior managers, particularly a chief executive officer (CEO), will answer 'Yes' to more than five questions, whereas more cautious individuals such as accountants or human resource managers will usually answer 'Yes' to less than five.

Nearly everyone bends the rules, but just how far you go depends on your own personality and view of the risk of getting caught. CEOs are natural risk takers and hence seem to be willing to bend the rules more than others.

Some companies also recognise that employees may bend the rules, for example, by taking the odd pen or piece of stationery home. Such practices are accepted, providing that they do not develop into wholesale removal of boxes of materials to sell privately. Then, a minor bending of the rules becomes a more serious fraud.

Whichever path people take to migrate from bending the rules to more serious dishonesty depends on whether they are ever faced with a set of circumstances that alters the threshold above which they are basically honest, to a level where they can justify to themselves that fraud is acceptable.

For example, let's suppose a person has children, and is also the owner of a password to access the company's payment systems. If a criminal group kidnapped the children and told the person they would be returned in exchange for giving them the password, so that the criminals could commit a fraud, it would probably be sufficient pressure for the person to cooperate.

There has also been a lot of discussion and analysis as to whether certain remuneration schemes have had the unintended consequence of motivating senior executives to commit fraud. It has been very common in the past for executives' remuneration to be tied to targets based on a company's earnings and share price. Executives who meet their targets can expect higher base salaries, huge cash bonuses and allocation of a large number of share options. There is thus a very strong incentive to meet the targets, and some executives have resorted to dubious or fraudulent practices in order to meet them. It is a little naïve for the people who decide on remuneration to assume that some CEOs, who by their very nature are innovative problem solvers, will not at least consider all possible ways of meeting their targets, including creative accounting. It is also naïve to assume that massive remuneration is the key to developing honest, ethical business practices and people.

At a number of fraud and corruption seminars when discussing opportunity and motivation, audiences were asked: 'In general, who has the greater opportunity to get involved in fraudulent or corrupt acts, those at the bottom of the organisation or those at the top?'

The almost unanimous answer was that people at the top of the organisation had the greater opportunity. The follow-up question, dealing with the motivation, was: 'What do people with power and money want most?' The immediate answer was 'more money!' or 'more power and more money', immediately dispelling any myths that upwardly spiralling director's remuneration packages provide any deterrent whatsoever to fraud and corruption.

In another example, management bonuses were calculated as a percentage of operating profits for the year gone by, but paid out and charged as a cost the subsequent year. Although any bonus is simply a salary paid in arrears, management established the practice of charging the bonus to financial expenses, that is, after operating profit was calculated. Thus by perpetrating a simple reporting fraud management were able to slightly increase the bonus paid to them.

A popular example of senior executive dishonesty is described in the book *Freakonomics* and its so-called 'bagels test' (Levitt and Dubner, 2005): when a basket of bagels was placed in corporate offices along with an honesty box for payment, it was discovered, almost inadvertently, that more often than not executives higher up the corporate ladder cheated more than ordinary employees.

Another common misconception is that the main losses through fraud occur because of dishonest employees. In our experience, losses in the core business are attributable to a number of perpetrators – fraudulent suppliers, business partners and customers, competitors, professional criminals – as well as dishonest employees. Once some of these groups start working together, fraud and corruption are much harder to stop.

Furthermore, corruption of disgruntled or naïve employees by third parties is a growing problem, whether it is by a dishonest supplier wanting to corrupt a purchasing manager, or a criminal group wanting to persuade an operator in a bank's payment centre to assist in making high-value funds transfers.

The point is that nearly everyone employed by, involved in or associated with an organisation could be a potential fraudster (see Figure 2.2).

Although most organisations have a business ethics policy, fewer have a comprehensive program for raising the awareness of employees about threats from unethical or dishonest third parties. There have been many cases where con artists, posing as customers, have convinced, for example, honest employees in a call centre to reveal confidential information about a customer, or a back-office person to move money out of a customer's account. In these cases, it usually comes as a complete shock to the employees that they have been duped, when they believed they were only helping the customer. That is why even companies with very good controls can still suffer from fraud: because their own honest employees choose to bypass the controls in favour of providing better customer service.

The corruption of individuals is a gradual, almost unnoticeable process. Usually employees do not realise that they have crossed the lines between acceptable and unacceptable business behaviour, and between the unacceptable business behaviour and criminality. Employees committing frauds often live in dream worlds, where they do not have any perception of the criminality or seriousness of an offence, or the heavy penalties for corruption. For example, where bribes have been received, employees will believe they have been given a gift in exchange for doing a favour for a third party, which is to the benefit of their company.

When discovered, the employees will often claim that they had done nothing wrong because there was no company policy defining acceptable or unacceptable behaviour. In some cases, the area is so grey that it is impossible to secure a conviction for the wrongdoing.

Figure 2.2   Who commits fraud?

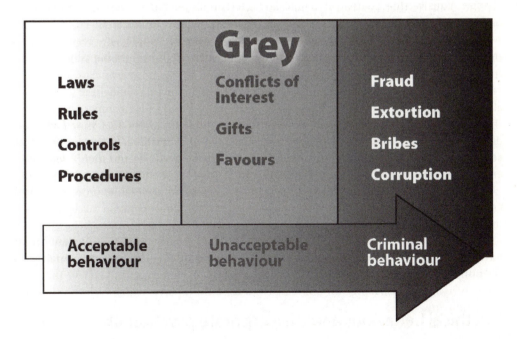

Figure 2.3   Shades of grey

As shown in Figure 2.3, the progression from acceptable to unacceptable to criminal behaviour can be a seamless transition for some employees because they do not see, or they ignore, where the line is.

In the high technology IT and telecom industry, we have regularly observed that as many as 20 per cent of employees were running their own separate IT businesses on the side, without the knowledge of their employer. Once the businesses were started, the employees used some of the time, equipment and knowledge that they had at work to prepare for the time when they would resign.

Dishonest employees will start to steal as soon as they can see a way round the controls. Honest employees will be drawn in as the dishonest culture develops. As well as corrupting permanent employees, criminal groups now actively seek to place their own person in a company as a temporary employee or contractor.

Example

The main board of a multinational organisation appointed a new management team at a subsidiary which had been grossly under-performing. The new management received a tip-off from a young former employee that fraud was rampant throughout the organisation.

A covert investigation uncovered a multi-million dollar fraud involving almost the entire sales force with payments moving upwards to a senior manager reporting to the new directors. It came out during the trial that honest employees were actively encouraged to join in the frauds or were intimidated to leave the company for example by having their cars smashed up. In the end 14 people were convicted, with a large number of other employees and managers being dismissed.

Fraud and corruption are dynamic, and new opportunities present themselves as the company changes. Equally, thresholds are dynamic; an honest employee today could become dishonest tomorrow. Unfortunately however hard an organisation tries to create an ethical, honest working environment, it has absolutely no control over an employee's personal life or motivation so it is very difficult to predict or measure when this is likely to happen.

Example

An IT manager in a Scandinavian bank changed from being honest, hard working and potential senior management material to a fraudster within the space of 12 months. His new girlfriend was addicted to heroin and managed to get him addicted as well. Despite the fact that he had taken fraud prevention courses and knew all about avoiding detection, he was so desperate for money that he simply started crediting his girlfriend's account using false internal vouchers which were quickly detected.

Even though employees may be honest today, prudent managers should prepare for the eventuality that one of their employees, suppliers or other third parties becomes dishonest in the future.

Unethical behaviour and the corporate psychopath

At the top of a company, the pressure exerted by a dishonest CEO and/or CFO (chief financial officer) can motivate other managers and employees to participate in a major fraud. Such frauds can have catastrophic effects and, once started, are hard to stop.

Most people look upwards for their behavioural role models. Where an organisation is plagued by fraud and corruption, we can often trace the root cause to undesirable, unethical attitudes near or at the top.

Management-initiated frauds can spread rapidly through an organisation, particularly if rumours of unethical behaviour being perpetrated by senior management begin to circulate amongst the middle and lower layers of the organisation. This leads to a lack of interest in controlling the business and an increasing temptation to join in with similar, albeit smaller frauds. In some cases, employees also are allowed to develop their own fraudulent businesses.

Example

In a large company there were initial indications that certain branch managers were colluding with suppliers to provide overpriced and fictitious services. Further probing revealed that several employees were running their own companies on the side and were invoicing their employer (and their customers) for work done in company paid time. A divisional director was found to be earning more than his actual salary through director's emoluments from his (undeclared) side business.

When the employees were interviewed, they said senior management were aware of everything they had done from the beginning.

What emerged afterwards was considerable management involvement in fraud and corruption including patterns of hidden ownership of businesses, falsification of records, concealment of losses and deliberate overcharging of customers. It was only when the managing director was removed that the organisational culture could be changed.

It is also important that senior management do not encourage attitudes such as 'well if they can do it, so can I' or give out signals which either encourage the rest of the workforce to act unethically or stimulate frustration and resentment because certain privileged members of the management can get away with whatever they want.

Example

The Managing Director of a company was concerned about huge levels of theft from the stores. At his request, an investigation was carried out and it was discovered that over three-quarters of the workforce had been involved in petty theft of some kind.

In the examination of what triggered this, one of the workforce referred to an incident when the managing director was seen by many of the employees leaving on a Friday evening with a large bale of toilet paper (taken from the stores) under his arm. His wife had asked him to buy some, but as he was working late and had no time, he helped himself – meaning to replace it the following afternoon.

The story spread; if the managing director took such blatant liberties, why couldn't everybody else?

Even where the senior executives are reasonably honest, they can be pressured by external factors to adopt fraudulent and corrupt business practices which then percolate down the organisation. Establishing an honest culture throughout the organisation requires leaders who are perceived to behave ethically at all times, in their professional and private lives.

We do not believe it possible to draw up a personality profile of the typical fraudster that could be used to pre-empt a fraud. In over 25 years, we have investigated fraud and corruption at all levels in organisations, involving both male and female employees, and have not found any set of personality traits that one could use to accurately predict whether someone was going to become a fraudster.

However, there seem to be some general personality trends which suggest that some types of people are more disposed to participate in certain types of fraud than others. For example, experience has shown that in financial markets, it is extremely rare to find employees who work in a back-office area colluding to commit a fraud. There have been numerous incidents where back-office staff have committed solo frauds which have been concealed for long periods of time or colluded with external criminal groups to effect high-value, smash-and-grab type frauds, but there has to be a unique combination of circumstances for two honest people who work alongside each other to both suddenly develop the motivation to commit a fraud.

On the other hand, there have been some notable incidents where front-office traders have colluded to commit fraud. They develop traits which make them good at their job, such as a focus on short-term profits, the ability to take large risks, and so little empathy for others as to border on arrogance and greed. Unfortunately, sometimes it also seems to be easier for them to rationalise and collude once they find an opportunity to make money even if it means committing a fraud.

Example

In Operation 'Wooden Nickel', the FBI arrested 47 foreign exchange traders in New York who had colluded to defraud customers by quoting off-market rates and passing the profit down the chain to a bank account where the money could be withdrawn in cash and distributed amongst the participants, usually a few thousand dollars cash on each deal. Given the sizeable salaries and bonuses which these traders were earning, it may appear surprising to the layman that they were prepared to risk their careers and livelihoods for comparatively small sums of money.

Some CEOs and senior directors are hired because they achieve results by being ruthless, decisive, aggressive risk takers who are totally fixated on the bottom-line profit. There is nothing intrinsically wrong with this because improved profit is still what the shareholders and stock markets want to see. However when these senior officers are surrounded by weak fellow directors and management they may begin to treat the company and its assets as their own. At this point they find it hard to see anything wrong with running up large personal expenses which the company pays for, having work done on their homes by company contractors, or treating their employees as an entourage of personal servants. Indulging in business practices which are maybe fraudulent and corrupt is seen as acceptable, as long as they are making large profits for the company.

Example

In 2000, L Dennis Kozlowski, CEO of US conglomerate Tyco International, told Business Week that his 1999 pay packet of $170 million, including $130 million from the exercise of stock options, was justified because he had created wealth for Tyco shareholders to the tune of $37 billion (Reingold 2000).

He used the phrase 'I created' which implied that none of the other 180 000 Tyco employees had created anything.

In 2005, he was convicted of looting Tyco after being found guilty of several counts of fraud and falsifying business records. It was revealed that Kozlowski had lavishly indulged himself like an emperor with excesses such as a $2.2 million birthday party for his wife, a $6000 shower curtain for their $31 million apartment, and an ice sculpture looking like Michelangelo's David complete with a vodka-peeing appendage (not covered by a fig leaf).

To assist honest employees to spot and take action against these sorts of excessive behaviours, there is increasing focus on a personality type known as the 'corporate psychopath' (Clarke 2005). These individuals can reach the highest levels in an organisation and can wreak untold damage, even leading to corporate collapse. Interestingly there is very little to distinguish this type of person from those in the upper echelons of organised crime.

A Canadian psychologist, Dr Robert Hare, developed the Psychopathy Checklist-Revised or PCL-R (Hare 1993) which uses 20 personality traits in order to identify clinical psychopathy. He subsequently identified the following eight traits to try to define corporate psychopaths:

- glib and superficially charming
- grandiose sense of self-worth
- pathological liar
- very skilful manipulator
- lack of remorse
- displays shallow emotions
- callous and lacks empathy
- fails to accept responsibility for his or her own actions.

He emphasised that the checklist cannot be used by untrained people and that a person displaying some of the characteristics is not necessarily a corporate psychopath: there needs to be a cluster of related symptoms. Nevertheless when one looks at the character of some of the CEOs and other directors who have caused corporate collapses, it raises the question as to whether an evaluation by a qualified psychologist would produce a diagnosis of psychopathy in any of them.

Corporate psychopaths have an overwhelming urge to obtain the power and status that having a lot of money brings. They desire influence and power over their colleagues, make plans over long periods of time, and lie, deceive and manipulate as necessary to commit their frauds, without feeling any remorse. They enjoy humiliating staff without making it obvious that they are behind it and can change their stories so skilfully that it can leave employees confused and wondering if they have stumbled into a room full of smoke and mirrors.

Very few people actually see the real persona. Most usually see the executive as a 'cuddly gruff teddy bear' who has to be tough to do their job, or as a suave, charming and intelligent person. Only those few who are on the receiving end of the psychopath's attention catch a glimpse of what is lurking below the surface.

Following the spate of corporate collapses in the last few years, there has been a drive for organisations to implement whistle-blowing policies to provide a route for employees to report suspicions about dishonest board directors. There is a legal requirement in some countries which have adopted whistle-blowing legislation, for the whistle-blower to receive a guarantee of protection from any adverse reaction by the company or directors following their disclosure, providing that the disclosure was not malicious.

In spite of improvements in legislation it is still a brave employee who raises issues when the CEO or another board member is in focus. Employees working for an executive who is a corporate psychopath usually find it very difficult to come up with solid proof even if suspicions are raised about behaviour or lifestyle, or if there is evidence in transactions or documents. The corporate psychopath is an expert at manipulating situations, evidence and people and has built up a powerful network of supporters, both executive and non-executive. Employees who raise concerns are usually sidelined, but not in a manner where they could successfully argue that they had been unfairly discriminated against as a result of them blowing the whistle. At worst whistle-blowing can be a fatal exercise.

Example

In early 2003, a 31-year-old technical manager with the National Highways Authority of India wrote a letter to the Prime Minister's Office complaining about corruption in a major construction project which he was involved in. His request for anonymity was ignored and the letter was widely circulated, including to his superiors at the highways authority. In November 2003, he was shot dead whilst travelling home. The case raised international concerns and eventually resulted in the implementation of a scheme authorising a Central Vigilance Commission to protect whistle-blowers and act on their complaints.

Global business and justifiable fraud and corruption

Increasing globalisation has meant that companies have set up operations in parts of the world where ethical environments are totally different from those in their own country. For example, it has been common practice in countries such as Nigeria, Indonesia and Russia to make facilitation payments to government officials in order to reduce or remove bureaucratic interference in the business. In some industries, particularly the construction industry, there is such competitive and political pressure to win contracts, that the problem of fraud and corruption is endemic. There are numerous examples of major international projects which have been awarded where large kickbacks and bribes have been paid to gain contracts and have not produced any significant benefit when complete (Bosshard 2005).

Fraud and corruption have been so deeply embedded in international business and politics for years that there has been little incentive for board directors to treat prevention as part of a business strategy. If the organisation is making large profits, then providing that directors can show to the stakeholders that the level of visible fraud is low, shareholders are happy. It is one of the failings of the capitalist system that directors are remunerated by their ability to maximise profits for the benefit of shareholders, which can lead to sharp practice in order to achieve them, and then to fraud and corruption.

When fraud and corruption are not adequately recognised in the organisation or even at the senior management level then sometimes the boundaries as to what is acceptable and what is not can become blurred. In the absence of effective risk analyses, there is a significant difference in most organisations between the perception of the risks at the board level and the actual risks which could occur. For example the CEO and fellow directors may have set a business strategy where either deliberately or inadvertently fraud and corruption become part of the way that new business is obtained. In other cases, it may be because the risk assessment process is so weak that significant fraud and corruption risks which exist throughout the organisation are not brought to the attention of the board.

Some companies have a policy which allows local managers to make small facilitation payments to local officials (for example, to speed up the processing of a customs clearance), but which prohibits larger bribes to government officials (for example, to win a large contract or to gain approval for large-scale importations at very low duty rates). Unfortunately, local management ignores the policy, with the tacit approval of top management, because they believe that is the only way that they are going to win contracts.

Thus, a fine and ambiguous line is taken on what is acceptable, where directors are seen as condoning some forms of practice that would be seen as unethical in the home country and turning a blind eye to more serious violations. However, when senior management is seen to allow bribes to be paid for obtaining contracts, they greatly increase the risk that employees will follow their example and engage in corrupt practices of their own.

Example

At the start of a two-day workshop in South America for a major manufacturing and sales facility, the previously taboo subject of agency payments (bribes) to offshore destinations was discussed. Initially many participants said that this was commonplace in the country they were selling to, and this was the only way of doing business if they wanted to make significant sales.

However, when the fraud profile was produced, all agreed that the potential damage to the reputation of the whole corporation, the risk that many of the payments were taken by people connected with the company, as well as the ethics of this practice were too high. At the end of the workshop, the financial director told his senior management team that now that they were aware of what was going on, a policy decision had been taken to review and eliminate such payments. He went on to say: 'In our country, the role models (politicians) have a bad name. However, why should we accept this type of behaviour in our company?'

In some instances, the directors do not understand the sophistication of the people they are dealing with. The directors may be willing to take large risks and bend ethical rules in order to get the business going, believing that because they have been successful in one country, the same tactics will work in another. This is not always the case.

The following illustrates the naïve approach often taken when doing business in developing economies:

Example

The Western European company utilized a loophole in international law and transferred the ownership rights to materials so that further production could take place in a former Soviet Union country. A complex set of legal documents was supposed to ensure that the transfer of title scheme was watertight and that the company would regain ownership when production was completed.

Nominee front companies were set-up, based in tax havens such as Jersey and the Cayman Islands. However the company's lawyers did not see at the time how this would make any difference as long as they had sufficient assurances that these front companies were actually controlled by the same people in charge of the production. The lawyers also did not see it as their business to challenge why money was being paid into offshore companies and bank accounts.

Two years later, at a point when the company had just transferred the title for approximately €100 million worth of goods, they discovered that one of the offshore companies in the chain was controlled by criminals who had stolen the goods and funds. In the end an accounting loss of over €150 million was provided for in the company's accounts which also stated that there was only a moderate hope of any recovery.

Another problem is that it is difficult for middle managers, who are under pressure to produce results, to get behind the facade of a charming, sophisticated business partner about whom very little is known. This is particularly true where they are dealing with corporate psychopaths who do not play by the rules and who are quite willing to do anything to further their own aims. Even if they wished to do so, the pressure to close a deal may outweigh caution, and they may be without resources and have limited sources of information. As a result, investing in joint ventures may be fraught with risks about which senior management is completely unaware.

As the world shrinks in terms of travel and human contact and business cultures get closer, good and bad business practices circulate. We have seen several cases where Western European country managers, having spent a couple of years overseeing the payment of bribes in certain Pan Pacific countries, have been tempted to take some of the money for themselves. Once back in their home (or another) country, with their perceptions of right and wrong clouded, they have repeated this behaviour again (and again).

Sometime, without completely realising it, management and employees convince themselves that certain frauds are in fact beneficial for the company. In addition to the payment of bribes to win contracts, common examples include:

- smoothing or the inflation of sales figures and assets, often justified as necessary so as not to destabilise the market;
- hiding bad debts or obsolete stock;
- price fixing or the establishment of cartels;
- circumventing export embargoes;
- submitting lower valuations to avoid customs duties;
- avoiding VAT and other taxes;
- overcharging of clients;
- obtaining subsidies and grants on false or partly false premises;
- moving funds into and around offshore destinations to avoid taxes, smooth profits and more.

All of the above increase profits and shareholder value, and are sometimes seen as justifiable frauds which need to be perpetrated in the best interests of the company, its shareholders and employees.

Experience has shown that such attitudes are short-sighted and if such practices persist they often lead to widespread fraud, corruption and – in the worst case – corporate collapse. Sometimes a company may be reluctant to really enforce its code of conduct when this is likely to have a seriously adverse affect on profit. However, when enforcement of the code of conduct happens, longer-term benefits may outweigh short-term loss of profits. The two real examples of company X and company Y demonstrate very different ways of dealing with breaches in the code of conduct:

Example

Company X

In Company X it was discovered that very substantial bribes were paid into offshore accounts in order to secure oilfield development contracts in a Middle Eastern country for the European company. After a while the details of the transaction were leaked to the press and the chief executive was caught by surprise when asked by a television reporter to explain the nature of the payments. He vehemently denied any bribery on the part of the company. Subsequently he made the claim that his company's code of conduct which explicitly forbid any form of bribery and which he himself had signed off, was not possible to apply in all countries, such as the Middle Eastern county in question. Within a matter of days he had been removed from the post of chief executive and both he and the company itself were the subject of several long-drawn-out national and international enquires into malpractice and corruption. Company X had to also pay a number of heavy fines.

Company Y

As part of a number of frauds which included colluding with suppliers, a senior marketing director in Company Y was the ringleader of a secret, illegal cartel involving competitors and subcontractors. The cartel ensured that they had a trusted insider at every major customer, and the insider would receive a small commission when overpriced contracts were awarded. The cartel would divide the spoils, usually to the advantage of the ringleader – the losers were the customers, and often the general public.

The largest beneficiary for a number of years had in fact been Company Y itself. However, the company reported this case to the authorities (with full knowledge of the consequences) and publicly stated that any breaches in the code of ethics would not be tolerated. This honest and open statement enhanced the company's reputation and gained it immediate favourable publicity. Although the company had to face a long and drawn-out enquiry into whether it knew of the cartel, it was, after five years able to prove its innocence in this matter and thus avoid any fines.

Profit can be made in many ways, including using unethical and criminal methods. If a company believes in ethical profits, then it cannot afford to turn a blind eye to unethical profits, even if top management was responsible. This is not easy in some industries, where it is very difficult to win contracts unless bribes are paid.

What's being done to stop fraud and corruption?

Over the past twenty-five years there has been a huge emphasis on business ethics, corporate governance, risk management and more recently corporate responsibility. However these initiatives do not appear so far to have succeeded in bringing about a marked decrease in corporate fraud and corruption.

As communications become global an individual country can no longer be seen as an island of seclusion, untouched by fraud and corruption. Even countries which were regularly perceived to be honest such as Finland and Iceland have been tainted.

In some countries the reaction to fraud and corruption has been reflected in stronger regulations covering corporate governance and financial reporting, in the belief that longer prison sentences and larger monetary fines will prevent such collapses in future.

Each time there has been a major management fraud there has been mass public outcry, a wealth of new legislation and even more copious guidelines.

The Lockheed bribery scandal led to the creation of the Foreign and Corruption Practices Act of 1977. The savings and loans frauds in the USA in the 1980s led to the founding of the Treadway Commission who in turn laid down in 1992 some of the most far-reaching and comprehensive principles of internal control in their 'COSO report' (Committee of Sponsoring Organisations of the Treadway Commission, 1992). The Bank of Credit and Commerce International crash of 1991 was eventually followed by a more stringent code of conduct and corporate governance guidance. The Enron, WorldCom and other incidents in effect led to the US Congress passing the Sarbanes Oxley Act of 2002.

Some would say that the sheer overload of documentation, legislation and controls that exists makes it easier for a criminal to spot loopholes and slip through the net.

Some progress has been made in understanding the psychology of fraudulent and corrupt individuals, what motivates them and the methods they use. However the results of this work have not quite reached the executive boardrooms. For example, ask any executive whether they believe that they have good corporate governance, risk management and controls in place to prevent fraud and corruption and they will usually answer yes. Then ask them what fraud and corruption risks they are trying to prevent. The usual answer, which we have received on numerous occasions, is that they are not sure. And yet, those same executives will readily admit that preventing fraud and corruption is something they are required to do.

Establishing corporate governance and corporate responsibility frameworks is only part of the battle to prevent fraud and corruption. Equally important is to understand what risks you are facing, to have the ability to detect incidents and to be able to deal with them.

Fraudsters and corrupt individuals are, by nature, deceptive and will do their utmost to cover their tracks. Consequentially the true extent of fraud and corruption is never known. Whilst scandals appear almost every day in the world press, most corporate managers and directors are blissfully unaware about the acts of fraud and corruption taking place in their own organisation. This knowledge gap primarily occurs because of a lack of training and awareness. Most MBA core programs pay little attention to the prevention of corporate fraud and corruption, give or take the occasional token mention at business ethics lectures. The same goes for graduate and other training programs aimed at budding executives. Although some changes are afoot they will take some time to ripple through to the upper management. It is likely that the majority of today's and tomorrow's generation of business managers have received little training in an area which could be critical to the survival of the business.

Some positive results as far as corruption and bribery is concerned are stemming from the efforts of non-commercial organisations, such as Transparency International, the Organisation for Economic Co-operation and Development, and the World Economic Forum. For example, in January 2005 at the World Economic Forum meeting, 62 major multinational companies signed a support statement to the 'Partnering Against Corruption Principles' (see initiatives on www.weforum.org) derived from Transparency International's Business Principles for Countering Bribery. They call for two fundamental actions:

- a zero-tolerance policy towards bribery;
- the development of a practical and effective implementation programme.

At the highest level the fight against corruption is endorsed by the United Nations (UN Global Compact Principle 10, 2004). External corporate responsibility indexes such as the FTSE4Good series (FTSE4Good, 2006) are also becoming popular with investors and analysts.

Initiatives like these are a start and although still too narrow, they help to create a climate where fraud and corruption has to be recognised at the top of organizations. This should eventually lead to senior managers feeling that the prevention of fraud and corruption is their responsibility.

Winning the war

From the tone in the previous sections, you may now believe that the fight against fraud and corruption is a hopeless cause. However, the situation is not quite as desperate as it may seem. Preventing fraud and corruption is a route to greatly improved profitability, stronger reputation and competitive advantage. A fundamental rule is to know your enemy. Too many criminals and fraudsters have succeeded because they were able to operate unknown, unseen and unchecked.

Although the majority of organisations have realised that prevention of fraud and corruption should be an important element of a corporate strategy, there are gaps in their knowledge about fraudsters and the way that they operate. The key areas where improvements can be made are:

- establishing a clear, visible and credible tone at the top aimed at eliminating fraud and corruption;
- investing time in understanding where fraud and corruption takes place by conducting profiling workshops right across the organisation and then taking action to eliminate the gap between what employees know as reality and what executives believe to be the case;
- encouraging all employees to participate actively in the fight against fraud and corruption, including training all staff to be aware of the red flags which might indicate fraudster and corruption;
- employing techniques which are successful at continuously monitoring and identifying the red flags of fraud and corruption;
- systematically measuring the organisation's resistance to fraud and corruption rather than testing the completeness of controls.

The purpose is to take senior management from a position where they are ignorant of the risks of fraud and corruption to a point where they can be reasonably confident that they recognise where it could strike.

The timing has never been better. Shareholders and other stakeholders are increasingly demanding an end to the excesses of the last couple of decades as well as better performance. As a result, non-executive directors and audit committees are taking a much closer look at their own roles and responsibilities as far as risk management, and at the performance and remuneration of CEOs and other executives.

Summary of key points

- The typical organisation loses up to 6 per cent of its annual revenue to fraud and corruption, most of it hidden in the accounting figures.
- Everyone has their own individual perception of honesty and level of how far they are willing to bend the rules.
- Nearly everyone employed by or associated with an organisation could be a potential fraudster, given the motivation.
- An organisation has little control over someone's personal life outside of work, and the factors which might motivate a person to consider fraud or corrupt behaviour.
- An ethical culture in an organisation can be rapidly undermined if the executive directors do not follow their own code.
- Appointing a corporate psychopath to run a company can have catastrophic consequences.
- Organisations where the executive directors sanction fraudulent or corrupt behaviour in the interests of improving profits and shareholder value often suffer from widespread internal fraud and corruption.
- Increasing legislation, regulations, documentation and controls have greatly increased the compliance burden on organisations, but appears to have done little to decrease the incidence of fraud and corruption.
- A route to greatly improved profitability, stronger reputation and competitive advantage is to set a clear, visible and credible tone at the top, obtain a detailed understanding of the fraud and corruption risks and then measure your resistance to them.

3 Recognising and Respecting the Risk

Tone at the top

The tone set at the top of an organisation is the single most important factor in determining how resistant that organisation will be to fraud and corruption. By tone we mean the cultural, ethical and behavioural patterns, both visible and subliminal, which permeate the whole organisation.

The board of directors in consultation with key managers should establish the anti-fraud and corruption strategy in agreement with the non-executive directors. An independent audit committee should be responsible for overseeing the effectiveness of the implementation of that strategy.

Although all organisations have their own individual ways of establishing and reflecting the tone at the top, the starting point for many organisations is to issue a code of conduct and a fraud and corruption policy endorsed by the board of directors. These are discussed in more detail later. Figure 3.1 below shows a typical hierarchical document structure which is used.

WHAT ARE WE PREPARED TO ACCEPT?

Publicly listed corporations often expend a considerable amount of effort in implementing the principles of good corporate governance and corporate responsibility as a way of demonstrating to shareholders and other stakeholders that they are serious about preventing fraud and corruption. However, these actions in isolation do not necessarily lead to less fraud and corruption if:

- the directors are too blindly focussed on cost-cutting and efficiencies in order to improve cost to income ratios; and if they have no mechanism in place to evaluate the effect of reducing headcount on controls or on employee morale – both of which can have a significant effect on fraud and corruption risks;
- the CEO is overly focussed on risk taking rather than risk management and is perceived as someone who prefers profit and good news to hearing stories about losses and potential disasters;
- the directors and senior managers see the code of conduct primarily as a way of putting a gloss on their activities to satisfy the stakeholders and not having issues raised: for example, where they are using third parties to make illicit payments to government officials in other countries to progress the business.

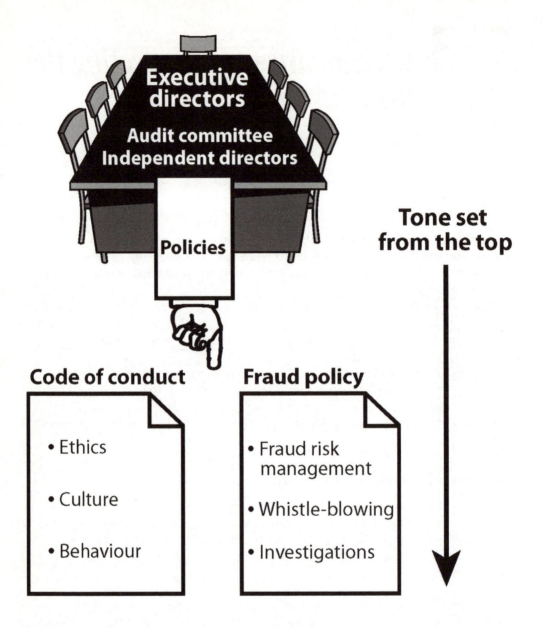

Figure 3.1   Tone at the top

So the first major step for you is to establish whether the directors are going to implement the fraud and corruption risk management strategy for cosmetic purposes or because they really do want to use it to prevent fraud and corruption.

If it is the latter, you should define their fraud and corruption risk management objectives. These can be divided into primary objectives and a number of secondary objectives flowing from them, as shown in Table 3.1.

You should then establish the level of risk that they are prepared to carry, often referred

Table 3.1   Fraud and corruption risk management objectives

Primary objectives	Secondary objectives
• create an environment for fraud and corruption prevention	• recover losses
	• protect honest employees
• build a fraud- and corruption-resistant organisation	• comply with fiduciary requirements
• reduce the hidden cost of fraud and corruption	• meet regular and industry expectations
• enhance shareholder value	• protect corporate reputation
• ensure business continuity	

to as their 'risk appetite'. This is a tolerance level which can be applied to the risks of fraud and corruption.

For example, most retail operations accept that having an open-counter environment when selling clothes to the public will result in stock shrinkage which is caused either by employee or customer theft. If the level of shrinkage is around 1 per cent, this is considered tolerable ('risk tolerance'), but if the level rises to 5 per cent then this is unacceptable and measures have to be taken to reduce the risk, such as using in-store detectives, electronic tags and closed-circuit television. So although the company accepts that some theft will occur, that is it has an 'appetite', it is concerned to ensure that the risk tolerance is within certain limits.

Similar situations exist in financial institutions which have credit card operations. They are all experiencing a certain level of fraud. The current level of fraud, whilst high, may be considered to be acceptable compared to the cost of new technology solutions to reduce the risks.

In some cultures, the term fraud and corruption appetite could be interpreted to mean the amount of fraudulent behaviour that is considered to be acceptable business behaviour. So rather than trying to prevent fraud and corruption, senior management encourages kickbacks and payoffs in order to obtain business and maximise profits, but takes extra precautions to disguise them from the auditors as 'security' or 'marketing consultancy' fees. This is clearly not what we mean by appetite here. If the directors of an organisation are serious about preventing fraud and corruption, then the strategy must start at the top and the directors must include themselves in the risk management process. In other words the culture of a company is only as honest as its senior executives.

It is relatively easy to establish an appetite when losses can be quantified. However in most cases, the situation is different when looking at corporate fraud and corruption because losses are usually hidden and unexpected. Recent cases have shown is that there is a chicken-and-egg situation at the top of most organisations as far establishing a risk appetite in that:

• the board has a responsibility to decide on the risk appetite but to do so, it needs an accurate analysis of the risks of fraud and corruption;
• an accurate analysis is very difficult with standard risk self-assessment methodologies

because most honest line managers usually grossly underestimate the potential for fraud. They assume that because they are honest, that others around them are also honest. Also, they do not have any statistics or historical loss figures to provide guidance;

• the audit committee has a responsibility for actively overseeing the effectiveness of implementation of the fraud risk-management strategy and for arranging and reviewing an annual fraud and corruption risk assessment covering the board and senior management. Yet few organisations evaluate the fraud potential of individuals at the board level.

For example, following corporate scandals such as Enron and WorldCom, the US Congress introduced much more stringent reporting and compliance requirements for any organization which has a US presence, by enacting the Sarbanes-Oxley Act of 2002 (SOX). This requires that CEOs and CFOs implement internal controls and certify annually that all frauds, involving anyone who has a significant role in those controls, have been reported to the auditors and audit committee. The associated sentencing guidelines provide for severe penalties including heavy fines and up to 20 years imprisonment for a CEO or CFO who deliberately falsifies the certification.

As a result, those organisations which have to comply with the act have expended a great deal of effort on process mapping and evaluating controls effectiveness to reduce the risk of financial misstatement.

Yet this does not seem to have addressed the principal reason why the act was brought into being, that is, corrupt and fraudulent behaviour by dishonest executives. So far, all that SOX compliance work seems to have enabled is that a CEO and CFO can sign off that their organisation complies with SOX. Recent research has suggested that very few organisations have profiled the fraudulent and corrupt practices which a dishonest chairman, CEO or CFO could become involved in should they be acting alone or in collusion.

Furthermore SOX did not herald any new thinking in terms of how to implement good corporate governance. This subject has been debated for a long time. Early examples of good corporate governance codes can even be found in ancient Greek and Babylonian writings. More recent work such as the COSO report in the 1990s provided much of the good corporate governance guidance now embraced by SOX.

It remains to be seen how effective some of the new measures contained in SOX will be in preventing serious management fraud and corruption in the future.

Essence of an anti-fraud and -corruption strategy

An anti-fraud and -corruption strategy should be implemented by all companies and organisations. Apart from the obvious reasons, there is increased pressure from national and international legislative bodies and other pressure groups such as non-governmental organisations. Also new laws, such as the requirements of SOX, have made such a strategy mandatory for many large corporations.

However, as with any major new initiative, if it is going to be of long-lasting benefit it needs to be well planned and to be constructed on solid ground. Otherwise the programme will simply get bogged down in bureaucracy and political points scoring. To succeed it is important that certain fundamental issues are addressed first. These prerequisites are:

- Senior management and the board should already have recognised the risk and extent of fraud and corruption. They should have the determination to tackle the problem in the face of resistance, and should be convinced that the anti-fraud and -corruption strategy is an important way of adding value and effectively governing their organisation.
- The tone at the top must be both genuine and credible. Nobody expects instant sainthood from management, but they should be seen to be aspiring to reach the corporate values, which they themselves have described in the company code of conduct.
- There should be a determination to ensure that the policies of the company covering business ethics, anti-fraud and -corruption reflect the tone at the top and are known and supported by everyone.
- There should exist a documented understanding of the fraud and corruption risks which are faced by the organisation in the form of a risk map or profile.
- At least one senior executive on the management board should be responsible for implementing, supporting and, if required, driving home the programme.

If these conditions are met, then the anti-fraud and -corruption strategy has a good chance of success.

An effective strategy involves treating the identification and reduction of fraud and corruption as a separate element integrated with other elements, such as credit and market risk, in a business risk-management strategy. The fraud and corruption risk-management strategy should consist of six elements as shown below in Figure 3.2.

Figure 3.2   Fraud and corruption risk management strategy

Together they are designed to manage the risk of fraud across the whole organisation, starting at the top with the directors, who have the broad picture of where the high risks are likely to be, down to individual operating units which have detailed fraud profiles.

Table 3.2 below illustrates where we believe current fraud and corruption risk management strategies can be enhanced.

Table 3.2   Current and desired fraud and corruption risk management strategies

Element	Typical governance	Desired strategy
Tone at the top	• focus on corporate governance • based on historical loss figures	• set the tone from the top down with a code of conduct and a fraud and corruption policy
Understand the risk	• main focus on audit to ensure that all the controls are in place • generic fraud risk analyses	• a detailed understanding of the potential methods of fraud and corruption by job function, including executive directors and senior managers
Reduce the risk	• implementation of controls to reduce generic fraud risks	• implement preventive controls for specific methods of fraud and corruption • factoring fraud and corruption risk effects into strategic business decisions
Monitor and detect red flags	• detection in specific areas such as credit card or cheque fraud, but not across the organisation	• training of all staff to identify early warning signs (red flags) • a pro-active detection strategy for specific methods of fraud and corruption
Manage incidents	• a reactive response to individual incidents of fraud and corruption	• a response plan and incident management team • awareness of key issues in managing investigations
Enhance resistance	• map the process and measure the effectiveness of individual controls: ignores the human factor	• measure the resistance of the organisation to fraudulent and corrupt individuals

Describing and ranking the methods of fraud and corruption (in a fraud and corruption profile) allows directors to manage the risks in a holistic way. They can decide whether they are going to accept the risk of a particular type of fraud occurring, or whether (and how) they want to transfer or reduce it. The fraud and corruption profile becomes an input to the overall risk-management strategy. Chapter 4 describes how a fraud and corruption profile should be developed.

Making directors (who are indifferent or incompetent) aware of the severe fraud and corruption risks which could impact the organisation could take them from a position of ignorance to a position of negligence, if they do not do anything subsequently to reduce the risks.

The objective is not to eradicate fraud and corruption – a zero tolerance for fraud and corruption is unrealistic: simply being in business carries an inherent risk of fraud and corruption.

The aim is to prevent high-impact frauds and reduce the hidden costs of fraud, whilst implementing the minimum number of controls to enable the business to function efficiently. At the same time, it is possible to design and implement procedures to follow up on those frauds which do occur.

Fraud and corruption are dynamic, and fraudsters respond quickly to changes in companies and their control environments: a fraud and corruption risk management strategy should enable organisations to dynamically adapt their defences.

POLICIES

A healthy and ethical organisational culture from the top down is a cornerstone of effective fraud and corruption prevention. A strong ethical stance by directors will directly influence the threshold for employees to commit fraud – by reducing their motivation. It will send a message throughout the organisation that dishonest or corrupt business practices will not be tolerated.

As stated earlier, most organisations communicate the tone at the top to employees by means of two policy documents:

- code of conduct (or business ethics policy)
- fraud and corruption policy.

The purpose of the code of conduct is to change and influence the attitudes and behaviour of employees, contractors and others. Codes of conduct vary in length and scope; they depend on the size and nature of the organisation. Some simply contain short statements that the company and its employees do not engage in illegal practices, bribery, corruption, or improper or illicit relationships. Others are much wider ranging, covering issues such as respecting the laws of all countries, human rights, workplace practices and culture, respect for the environment, and open and transparent business relationships.

Codes of conduct have become much more important in recent years. Many large companies are now by law required to have one.

A fraud and corruption policy is used to communicate how an organisation views fraud. Again there are no standard policies. The policy normally includes:

- an introduction explaining where the policy fits into the organisation's overall risk management strategy and to whom the policy applies
- a statement about the board's policy regarding fraud and corruption and its intention to prosecute offenders
- definitions of fraud and corruption
- responsibilities for prevention and detection of fraud and corruption
- risk management
- procedures to be followed on the discovery of fraud and corruption
- post-investigation follow up.

A sample fraud and corruption policy is provided in Appendix 1.

A very important point to remember is that policies in themselves, whilst being a vital part of the strategy, are not the most important part. The most important part is the application of the policies across the organisation. For example, the 65-page Enron Code of Ethics issued by Kenneth Lay, its Chairman and Chief Executive Officer in 2002 was a very comprehensive document which obviously applied to honest employees lower down the organisation, but not to some top executives.

Therefore rather then spending an inordinate amount of effort on creating comprehensive and lengthy policy documents which no one reads, it makes much more sense to create short documents which everyone understands and applies.

The code of conduct and the fraud and corruption policies should be consistent with all the other policies which form part of the risk management strategy, such as:

- recruitment screening (describes the reference checks and level of screening required for new employees)
- Internet and email use
- anti-money laundering
- information and IT security
- whistle-blowing
- operational risk reporting
- insider trading.

It is important to ensure that the definitions of fraud and corruption in the various documents are consistent.

Implementing the strategy

Whilst the board sets the strategy, senior management should be responsible for implementing the fraud and corruption risk management strategy, and for managing the risks. This should include risk assessment, reduction and detection. Detailed responsibilities should be included in the key performance indicators of the executive managers.

ROLES AND RESPONSIBILITIES

Once explicit non-executive and executive support has been given to fraud and corruption risk management, it is important to choose a team of people, primarily from key corporate functions, who will be responsible for driving the programme home.

Roles and responsibilities should be adequately defined right across the organisation. Often the tasks of preventing, detecting and even investigating fraud and corruption can fall between the responsibilities of various staff functions and line management. For example, the following can all have an interest:

- corporate management
- internal audit
- corporate security
- corporate risk management

- corporate responsibility
- financial control
- human resources
- legal
- central procurement
- specialist fraud teams, for example, investigating cheque, credit card or Internet banking fraud.

Without a clear and comprehensive fraud and corruption risk management mandate, these functions often fail to work together and responsibilities become fragmented.

As a result, critical actions to prevent fraud and corruption, such as identifying specific risks, detecting red flags, awareness training or ensuring compliance with ethics policies are not addressed at all.

Typical candidates to champion the programme include corporate security, operational risk management, internal audit, legal, compliance, the CFO's office as well as corporate responsibility and human resources as shown in the Figure 3.3.

There is no single function which does the job better than any other. Often a team approach with strong coordination is the most productive. In most companies the

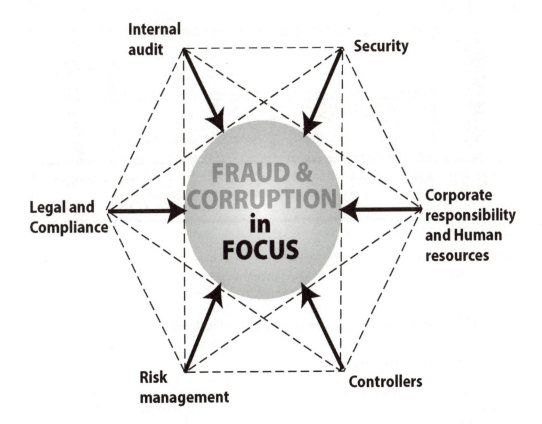

Figure 3.3   Programme champions

effectiveness of these functions in the fight against fraud and corruption is often very dependent on the personality and style of the head of the function.

Roles and responsibilities should be clearly defined in the organisation's policies and the strategy should also include the most important participants in the fraud and corruption risk management strategy, that is, the employees. It is no good just having some employees involved. Ideally all persons in an organisation should have a role in the prevention and timely detection of fraud and corruption.

To achieve this, some organisations have made it a mandatory requirement that all employees must read the fraud and corruption policy and they are then tested that their understanding meets a pass level. This is followed up by fraud awareness briefings.

External third parties such as suppliers, business partners and customers should also be made aware of the policies.

Implementing a programme to engage employees and third parties in the prevention of fraud and corruption is discussed further in Chapter 5: Upfront Prevention and Detection.

Figure 3.4 shows how an anti-fraud and -corruption programme could fit within the organisation.

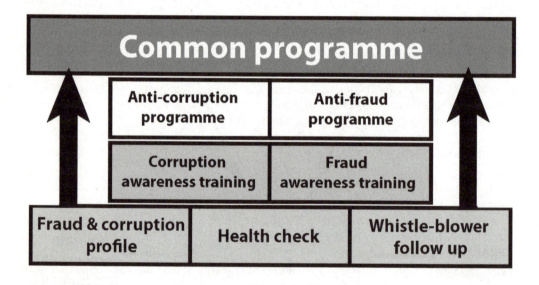

Figure 3.4   Anti-fraud and -corruption programme

Internal champions and their responsibilities

ROLE OF THE BUSINESS FUNCTION

The business function plays a front-line role in the prevention and detection of fraud and corruption. Managers set the tone for employees regarding compliance with laws, policies and procedures. Managers are also responsible for implementing risk management strategies and for managing the risks. This includes analysing risks and putting in place mitigating controls to reduce unacceptable risks. Whether or not these responsibilities are defined in key performance indicators and included in evaluation of job performance can have a significant effect on fraud and corruption risks.

ROLE OF OPERATIONAL RISK MANAGEMENT

Many financial institutions are finding that the rapidly developing field of operational risk management is a logical place to embed the management of fraud and corruption risks. Operational risk is defined as 'the risk of loss resulting from inadequate or failed internal processes, people and systems or from external events' (Basle Committee on Banking Supervision, 2003). Operational risk management is the process of identifying and managing those risks in a systematic and consistent manner. This is important for financial institutions because under the new Basle Capital Accord, banks now have to allocate economic capital for operational risks. Those that can demonstrate improved risk-management practices will be able to set aside less capital for operational risk.

The operational risk function is responsible for collating and disseminating information relating to risks in areas such as:

- internal and external fraud
- employment practices and workplace safety
- clients, products and business practices
- damage to physical assets
- legal and regulatory compliance
- business disruption and system failures
- execution, delivery and process management.

Operational risk management defines the framework which business units will use to analyse risks in a consistent manner across the organisation. They prepare periodic reports on the nature and status of identified risks and on follow-up and disposition to senior management and the board, which can then refine its risk appetite accordingly.

However, even large banks have tended to regard operational risk management as something which needs to be done to satisfy regulatory requirements rather than as an essential strategic element in managing the business more efficiently. As a result, they have underestimated the long-term effect of failures of operational risks such as compliance or of major frauds or anti-trust actions. All these have been shown to have a major long-term impact on shareholder value (Dunnett, Levy and Simoes, 2005).

The operational risk function has an important role to play by firstly collating and then disseminating information relating to fraud and corruption risks. Managing operational fraud and corruption risks can prevent sizeable losses, fines and damage to reputation.

Identified fraud and corruption risks should be included in a register containing other operational risks. Operational risk management should implement a reporting and escalation policy so that fraud losses and failed attempts can be collated. Summary reports of incidents and the follow up activity to improve controls to prevent a recurrence should be provided to senior management and the board of directors. Regular reporting of information to senior management and the board of directors will assist in the proactive management of fraud and corruption risks.

Operational risk management can also implement periodic measurement processes to ensure compliance with the reporting and escalation policy and to ensure that key fraud and corruption risks which reflect the current situation have been identified and captured.

Because operational risk management looks across the organisation and has a direct reporting line to the board, the problem of the silo approach to fraud by senior management discussed earlier is overcome, as is the problem of business units only assessing risks in known loss areas.

ROLE OF INTERNAL AUDIT

Internal audit can provide an alternative channel of communication outside management control. This reduces the temptation for senior managers to hide things from the board, since the board will find out anyway (if it is important enough). Internal auditors can communicate with the board directly, normally informing management of their intentions in order to provide a fair opportunity to comment. Internal auditors who have poor access to the board can also communicate via the external auditors. Internal auditors provide a natural channel of communication for potential whistle-blowers.

ROLE OF CORPORATE SECURITY

As with internal audit, corporate security can provide a channel of communication outside the formal management control lines.

It is often the case that the responsibility for preventing and investigating fraud and corruption is a shared one, with corporate security and internal audit sharing a large part of the burden. How it is shared will depend on the culture in the company and the personalities and skills of the people in the respective departments.

ROLE OF LEGAL AND HR DEPARTMENTS

The legal and human resources departments also have a key role to play in the prevention and investigation of fraud and corruption both from the point of view of compliance with existing laws, regulations, company policy and procedure, and also in terms of protecting the rights of the people concerned.

Legal and human resources can also, like the other key departments involved, play a significantly proactive role in understanding the risks involved.

THE GROWING ROLE OF CORPORATE RESPONSIBILITY

The subject of corporate responsibility has climbed the corporate agenda in recent years (Mackenzie and Mallon, 2005). As a function, Corporate Responsibility tackles seemingly diverse issues such as human and labour rights abuses, environmental damage and corruption. The underlying requirement for an ethical tone at the top is also a principle for good corporate governance, as is the goal of preventing irresponsible behaviour by companies, their officers and employees. By working together with other internal champions, Corporate Responsibility can help keep the company honest.

External stakeholders – their role and influence

It is also important to ensure that external stakeholders such as the external auditors, customers, suppliers, law enforcement agencies, external regulators and where possible, pressure groups and the public in general, are supportive of the organisation's anti-fraud and -corruption strategy.

Some stakeholders, such as external audit, suppliers and customers, can play an important role in fraud prevention and detection, others less so.

EXTERNAL AUDIT

The International Standard on Auditing ISA 240 defines the external auditor's responsibility in respect of fraud and error in the financial statements. This standard has also been widely adopted in various forms by internal auditors and public sector auditors. Although it reiterates that the primary responsibility for the prevention and detection of fraud lies with management, the measures laid down and suggested in the standard aim to ensure that the auditor has a greater chance of picking up and reporting material fraud. The auditor should aim to be 'professionally sceptical' and the audit should include some tests aimed at detecting fraud.

Furthermore, the enactment of SOX and the consequent adoption of Public Company Accounting Oversight Board (PCAOB) Auditing Standard Number 2 (PCAOB, 2004) in the US placed a requirement for external auditors to incorporate detection routines into annual audit programmes so that there is a reasonable expectation of detecting material misstatement in the financial statements arising from fraud. The rules encourage organisations to use a control-centric approach whereby processes are documented and then controls are tested to determine whether they are effective at mitigating risk.

However, recent research in the US (Leech and Gupta, 2005) has suggested that there is widespread confusion in the interpretation and implementation of the regulations. One of the points made by the researchers is that there has been too much focus on controls, and not enough on first identifying and assessing the fraud risks. They suggest that the control-centric approach should be changed to a residual risk approach where the board is provided with an assessment based on how the controls mitigate identified fraud risks.

The fundamental basis for a fraud and corruption risk management strategy should be to first understand the fraud risks which confront the organisation.

Once the fraud and corruption risks have been identified, the auditors can design tests to detect whether fraud is occurring.

However, we believe that the scope, definitions and methods of external auditing still make it difficult for auditors to detect fraud and corruption. The first signs usually are found in the details, and most auditors who work verifying transactions and talking with relatively junior staff are junior auditors themselves. Without sufficient training and experience, they are likely to miss the subtle indicators of fraud. Audit managers and partners review staff auditors' work and try to understand the big picture. It is usually not possible for them to justify time spent looking at transactions, or profiling senior management and verifying third parties as checks on the possibilities of fraud.

Many of the tests which need to be done to detect the early warning signs of fraud and corruption are usually not part of the audit programme. However, senior management and shareholders often live in the belief that someone is constantly policing the company for fraud. We believe that if external audits are to be more effective in detecting fraud and corruption, auditors need to receive substantial training in how to detect specific methods of fraud using techniques such as those described in Chapter 5: Upfront Prevention and Detection.

SUPPLIERS AND CUSTOMERS

Suppliers and customers influence management by creating a competitive environment. If the company is not effective and efficient, key suppliers may prioritise their resources to a better business partner, and customers will go elsewhere.

Customers and suppliers are also key sources of information about potential fraudulent or corrupt business practices by employees of the client company. They should be made aware of the code of conduct and whistle-blowing policy and encouraged to report any suspicion of potential fraud and corruption. An increasing number of organisations are including a right-to-audit clause in supplier contracts which enables internal audit to check that payments have been correctly accounted for.

External stakeholders who have a lesser influence on fraud prevention and detection include:

- controlling owners: in the United States and England, the shares of major listed companies are often widely dispersed, with no single shareholder owning enough shares to have influence. In the European model, companies are often controlled by a group of minority shareholders who have the votes necessary to determine who gets to sit on the board. Because the control owners decide the board composition and include their own people, the opportunity for the board to commit deception and fraud is much less;
- institutional owners, for example, pension funds, control enormous amounts of money, and are increasingly challenging boards and controlling owners, particularly over issues such as excessive executive remuneration packages ;
- other minority shareholders cannot themselves influence things very much;
- shareholder interest groups can take part in shareholders meetings, ask the pointed questions and organise lawsuits. They have the resources needed to study financial statements and board communications and the knowledge to ask the right questions. If there is abuse, they know how to bring it to the attention of the shareholders and the media;
- journalists and the media in general can play a role in exposing fraud and corruption. However, they are motivated to expose problems in order to sell newspapers or to bump up audience viewing figures. There is a risk that they create scandals out of nothing, or misrepresent the facts in order to make a more interesting story;
- lawmakers draw up the rules on company law that can be tested in court. Lawmakers are elected, and sensitive to public opinion. SOX is the perfect example of fraud affecting public opinion, leading to new laws;
- unions have a strong influence in many countries; and in some countries, appointees sit on the board. However, their role is primarily to protect the interests of their members;
- stock exchanges apply listing requirements according to the laws of their land. The rules can sometimes be far reaching. For example, foreign companies which require a listing on US stock exchanges must comply with SOX;
- lenders want to ensure repayment, not to protect shareholders. But by forcing management to avoid risky investments, they may help shareholders;
- law enforcement agencies: most have a keen interest in maintaining good relationships with commercial organisations. Reporting incidents sends a strong deterrent message to

employees and other third parties, and successful prosecutions of large-scale frauds are now widely reported.

Improving resistance to fraud and corruption

Implementing an effective fraud and corruption risk management strategy from the top down can dramatically improve an organisation's resistance to fraud and corruption and hence its competitive advantage. Organisations which have implemented no risk management strategy or only a partial strategy will have a much lower resistance to fraud and corruption. In these organisations it is likely that senior management neither understands how fraud and corruption affects them, nor how their strategic decisions affect the risk of fraud or corruption. Low fraud and corruption resistance arises because:

- a code of conduct may have been issued, but the board has not established a fraud and corruption risk appetite, there is no fraud policy and business decisions do not take account of fraud and corruption risks;
- the corporate message contained in the code of conduct does not reflect the actual tone at the top;
- outside known loss areas, employees have little understanding of the real risks of fraud and corruption;
- a control structure is in place, but employees believe that controls such as authorising signatures on documents, passwords to payment systems and segregation of duties provide strong protection from fraud;
- management has had some experience of investigations, for example, involving petty cash theft or expense fraud, but there is no systematic response plan and management has had no real training in how to deal with a major fraud;
- there is no fraud awareness training for employees, and managers have not been trained to interview in order to detect deception;
- there is no proactive fraud and corruption detection programme so symptoms are overlooked.

A high resistance to fraud and corruption should be one of the key indicators by which senior management performance is measured. This is discussed further in Chapter 7: Resistance the Ultimate Goal.

Summary of key points

- The board should set the anti-fraud and -corruption tone at the top and send a clear message throughout the organisation that the directors fully support the fraud and corruption risk management strategy.
- The board should be included in the fraud and corruption risk-management process, and determine the risk appetite.
- Don't get bogged down in creating lengthy policy documents which no one reads. Create short documents and concentrate on making sure that everyone reads, understands and applies them.

- Define clear roles and responsibilities for all internal stakeholders involved in fraud and corruption risk management.
- Sell the idea to top management that improving the organisation's resistance to fraud and corruption will bring positive benefits.
- Identify and engage external stakeholders, including suppliers and customers.

4 *Fraud and Corruption Risk Assessment*

Understanding where fraud and corruption strike

Taking the time to understand the fraud and corruption risks which an organisation faces is a fundamental element of an anti-fraud and -corruption programme. To defend against an attack, it is important to know the identity of would-be attackers, what they are after and what methods they are likely to use.

We find it surprising that many organisations pay so little attention to this aspect.

Managers will often respond to this observation with comments like 'that is not true, we have done a scorecard analysis of the risks', 'fraud is not possible because we have not had any incidents', or 'we have expended a great deal of effort in implementing controls to prevent fraud and both internal and external audit have checked the controls and are satisfied with them'. However, when the question is asked of senior management 'can you test what frauds your controls are trying to prevent', they often do not have an answer. Yet they firmly believe that they have good controls in place to prevent fraud. That is because they are focussed on controls, not on the fraudster.

There can also be a big difference between having what appears to be an effective risk management strategy on paper and really understanding the risks of fraud and corruption. The following examples from the banking world illustrate the potential for large losses.

The first involved Allfirst Financial in the US, at the time a part of Allied Irish Bank. Following the discovery of foreign exchange trading fraud by an employee, a subsequent investigation estimated the pre-tax loss at $691.2 million.

The investigation report (Promontary, 2002) was critical of the ease with which the trader was able to bully staff and bypass controls which had allowed the fraud to run for several years. This was in spite of the fact that a number of significant red flags should have raised concerns. It concluded that the size of the operation and style of trading had produced potential risks far exceeding potential rewards. The management of the parent company thought that they understood the risks of this type of business, when, with hindsight, there was a huge lack of understanding.

Obviously the lessons from this incident were not heeded because a similar example occurred a couple of years later on the other side of the globe in National Australia Bank when four traders concealed losses of $260 million by creating fictitious trades and using bogus transaction rates. The red flags displayed in this case bear a striking resemblance to the Allfirst case. The investigation report (PriceWaterhouseCoopers, 2004) made a similar observation in that the bank had placed too much emphasis on its processes and documentation and not enough effort in understanding the risks. In other words, National Australia Bank appeared to have been smitten by the beauty of its risk framework, but was blind to the actual risks. When combined with the culture of aggressive risk taking rather than risk management which was fostered by senior management, it meant that even when concerns were raised amongst employees and line managers, there was no effective way to initiate action to stop the losses accumulating. Management simply did not want to receive any bad news, as bad news would limit their careers.

The fundamental principle of the top management strategy to prevent fraud and corruption should be to first understand the risks, and then decide what measures need to be put in place to counter those risks.

Recognising the tools of fraud and corruption

The tools of fraud and corruption can be classified into two categories – psychological tools and hard tools. Psychological tools are those which are inherent in human nature (such as the ability to charm, persuade, coerce and deceive). Hard tools are those which you can buy to enhance your ability to commit fraud. Of course these categories are not definite in any form and easily overlap. For instance, persuasion, coercion, charm and even deception can all be purchased.

PSYCHOLOGICAL TOOLS

Multiculturalism has led to the global sharing of fraudulent and corrupt practices. Just as cuisine from one country is often adapted and even refined to suit the produce of another, corrupt methods originating in one country are now being refined in other countries to suit the local climate and conditions. For example, the psychology of the early 1990s crude, but successful style of Nigerian letter scams (commonly known as 419 schemes after the section of the Nigerian penal code which deals with fraud schemes) is used successfully today in false requests for payment around the world, so called 'bluff invoices' for example, for entry in non-existent trade directories. Also, sophisticated methods of illegal tax evasion, which sprung up in the face of one of the world's harshest tax regimes in Sweden are now taking root in a number of developing countries.

The ability to persuade lies at the heart of fraud and corruption. A willing victim is an easier victim. Persuasion can be brought about through natural charm, pretexts, social engineering and also coercion and violence. It can range from another employee simply asking to borrow a password to speed up processing, through to the chilling, precise and calculated machinations of corporate psychopaths who charm and manipulate all those around them. (The phrase 'I made him an offer he could not refuse' springs to mind here.) A number of fraudsters have succeeded because they acted in a friendly open manner so that honest employees thought nothing of answering their questions about how the controls worked.

In order to be able to persuade, a criminal will want to create the appropriate image and perceptions. In its simplest form image can be enhanced greatly by clothes and other trappings such as flash cars and jewellery.

Example

Clad in Armani and driving a shiny new Mercedes (rented for the day) a young Eastern European opportunist presented himself as the son of the founder and vice president of a construction mogul wishing to test drive a selection of luxury vehicles. Using a forged passport as collateral and buckets of charm, he and his friend persuaded the salesmen to hand over two sets of keys for test drives. The vehicles were never found again. Later on when asked how he could do something so stupid, the salesman argued that it had seemed insulting to question such a polite, credible man.

We are all gullible in some way. Fear of losing a deal, looking like a fool, or both, often acts against rational thought. This is something a fraudster knows all too well.

Clothes, luxury cars and identification, fancy Internet sites, hearsay and even notoriety all help promote a positive image and provide a stronger sense of security in the victim. Gentle persuasion is often much more successful than coercion and threats of violence although the latter are still used as psychological tools of fraud and corruption.

HARD TOOLS

Fraudsters can also make use of a wide range of tools which are available on the Internet and through advertisements in magazines and periodicals.

Example

A scan of the back pages of an airline's in-flight magazine revealed a total of 17 advertisements devoted to 'offshore companies', 'company registration agents' and other services where one can register an instant company, using a nominee name if required. Many of the suggested offshore companies were in exotic destinations such as the Cayman Islands, Bahamas and Cyprus, the less exotics Isle of Man and Guernsey, as well as Ireland, the UK and the USA. Similar advertisements can be found in leading weekly journals along with offers of second passports and genuine 'academic' degrees based on life experience (costing as little as $800). Sending off for the free information and browsing the advertiser's websites revealed that the services they offered existed and were apparently legal.

Judging by the nature of the target audience of these publications, the cost per square centimetre of these adverts must rank as among the highest media advertising costs on the market.

What is not so amusing is that bogus qualifications, fake identity documents, mail drop addresses and nominee corporations in tax havens are associated with alarming regularity with cases of fraud and corruption.

DEGREES FOR SALE

When an internal employee has been involved in fraud and corruption, a detailed review of the personnel file and curriculum vitae has often revealed exaggerated claims and qualifications. Sometimes the claims were wholly false or the certificates were forgeries.

False certificates are easy to obtain. One well-known forger has for years advertised genuine looking degree certificates from most major universities around the world. The certificate (at a cost of less than €100) is accompanied by a letter stating that it is not for official use.

Systems of accreditation are so nebulous today that the sale of qualifications is a major growth area. Some non-accredited universities are small enterprises, front-companies or just websites, which churn out certificates for qualifications based on life experience. Their advertising literature consists of impressive and convincing prospectuses praising the achievements of the university and its students. The benefits of a life-experience degree are stressed.

An Internet search using the right key words will identify many of these establishments. They churn out plenty of spam mail. They can also be found advertising in some leading periodicals and newspapers. The cost of one of these degrees is often in the region of $1000 for a bachelor degree and $1500–$2000 for a masters or doctorate. For a retainer, a reference service will ensure that any prospective employer will receive a full transcript of your studies and the relevant dates.

Even in the case of the more respectable qualifications given out by some established professional bodies, candidates are enticed by guaranteeing them a pass mark for the examination if they purchase the expensive interactive training study pack.

The truth today is that it is becoming increasingly difficult to distinguish educational qualifications from each other. Some non-accredited operations use names which sound very similar to existing, more solid, educational establishments. Their brochures and websites even display pictures of real buildings and people.

SECOND CITIZENSHIPS AND PASSPORTS

Second citizenships and diplomatic passports are available legally, for a price. Their use in fraudulent and corrupt schemes is extensive, ranging from the obtaining of loans to the movement of goods or establishment of a bogus company. In one instance a creative Italian fraudster was found not guilty of using a false passport as part of a scheme to obtain funds, because the passport belonged to Spanish Guinea – a country which does not exist.

ENHANCED IDENTITY

As with false qualifications, the Internet has spawned an industry of manufacturers of false identification cards ranging from simple photo-identity cards to the cloning of smart cards. It is even possible to acquire a title transforming yourself into a lord, baron, knight, squire or other member of the landed gentry of a number of countries in Europe.

The benefits of the title are less if used in the country of origin where people often understand its true nature. However, we have seen titles used to impress with much greater effect in other countries, especially those where the use of titles is uncommon.

ANONYMOUS AND PRIVATE MAILBOXES

It is easy to acquire a private and anonymous mailbox in most cities around the world. These can be used either for private mail or even to register a company, sometimes in a number of locations to give the impression of a large company. This simple technique is used very extensively in conjunction with front companies.

TAX HAVENS – THE SINGLE LARGEST RED FLAG

The single largest red flag of fraud and corruption is the use of tax havens to pay, receive or accumulate money anonymously.

We asked a professional offshore incorporation specialist about the legality of offshore companies, trust funds and shell corporations. His answer was simple: 'In principle they are perfectly legal in the jurisdiction in which they operate and we as a company would not attempt to break the law. However our clients can of course use them for illegal purposes, but that is their choice.' Later in the meeting he stated 'most of our clients prefer to remain anonymous'.

Many years ago it was recognised that in certain circumstances it was deemed necessary to have bank accounts which were managed by nominees. One infamous reason for doing so involved German citizens hiding assets in numbered Swiss bank accounts to escape confiscation by the Nazis. Since then offshore bank accounts, companies and trusts have traditionally been used to evade the clutches of punitive tax regimes.

During the past half century the use of offshore companies, shell corporations, offshore bank accounts and other fronts has mushroomed into a full-scale industry involving probably over a hundred countries or jurisdictions.

In its simplest form an offshore company is a limited liability company (LLC) which is registered in jurisdictions like Jersey, Guernsey, the Cayman Islands or the British Virgin Islands. The directors are nominees and the beneficiary owners do not need to be disclosed. The nominee directors are often residents of the jurisdiction or lawyers or accountants who lend their name to be used for a small fee. A professional intermediary, often an incorporation agent, typically a lawyer or accountant, takes care of the agreement between the nominee and the beneficiary. Normally neither the beneficiary owner nor the nominee know each other.

Similarly an incorporation agent or lawyer can also set up an anonymous bank account for a person or company. The bank account could be in the same jurisdiction but more commonly we are seeing bank accounts being set up in different jurisdictions where the banking laws also provide a degree of protection from intrusion.

Depending on how concerned you are about surveillance and how much money you wish to spend on protection, you can add as many levels of offshore companies and accounts to the scheme as you wish.

For example it is possible to register a branch office of an offshore company in a country where, for example, small companies have few disclosure requirements. In this way the company looks, at least at first sight, like a legitimate company.

If you wish you can also set up your own offshore bank and in some cases even issue your own charge cards.

A simple offshore company will cost about €2000 to set up and administer for a year. A company of this kind may be registered, for example, in the British Virgin Islands with the bank account in the Isle of Man.

This would not include the optional costs of having front offices registered at prestigious addresses, something that the agent would be all too happy to provide.

It is still a minor secret that onshore companies in one jurisdiction can be used as an offshore destination for someone who does not have any business there. Common examples are the non-resident LLCs in the USA. Let us say you do not do any business at all in the USA, then a non-resident corporation in New York will give you all the benefits and anonymity of an offshore company. You may even wish to keep your bank account in Switzerland. Examples have been seen in the UK, especially in London, and in Canada and other major countries where the legislation permits similar practices. A New York or London head office conveniently avoids the question as to why the head office is in a place like the Cayman Islands, Jersey or less known places like the Turks and Caicos Islands or Monrovia.

Sometimes trusts are used for asset and estate management as well as funding of enterprises. The rules and regulations are changing all the time and the offshore incorporation agents and their lawyers are often several steps ahead when it comes to exploiting new loopholes.

There are some legitimate uses for offshore operations, front companies and bank accounts but it is not always so easy to tell what is legitimate and what is not. Some of the largest Russian corporations use such schemes widely as a way of establishing control but avoiding anyone discovering the true nature of their vast corporate empires. As the Chinese economy opened up, it was reported that the second largest investing country was the British Virgin Islands with investments for the period January to July 2005 of $5.66 billion (US–China Business Council, 2006). It was also interesting to note that the USA was fifth with $1.66 billion, with the Cayman Islands and Western Samoa coming in seventh and tenth places respectively.

The problem is that the anonymity and secrecy also attract illegitimate uses. The following list, which is not exhaustive by any means, gives a flavour for the sort of fraudulent and corrupt purposes for which we have seen them used:

- bribes paid out through front and offshore companies. In some cases the payee has been responsible for the company and in some cases the payer has taken responsibility for the vehicle;
- embezzlement either by employees or even part owners using offshore companies, bank accounts and trusts;
- kickbacks paid to the management on the acquisition or disposal of a subsidiary via an offshore bank and company;
- the establishment of company-controlled off-book funds and the use of these funds to pay bribes, make political contributions and support other illegal or dubious activities. Sometimes these funds have been built up over years;
- the payment of secret bonuses and contributions to the pension funds of top managers and board members;
- false bribes – where a senior employee or director makes a case for paying bribes, but keeps the money;
- use of intermediary offshore companies to artificially inflate sales prices when goods are being shipped from one country to another such as from China or one of the former Soviet Union countries to the west;
- evading corporate tax by hiding assets and profits;
- using shell and offshore companies for fraudulent invoicing;
- concealment of a conflicting ownership interest in suppliers, customers and business partners;
- receipts of sales revenues from front companies which were eventually traced to sales orders for vehicles from the leaders of suspected drug cartels.

Of course, as has been seen in the USA recently with the major corporate fraud and corruption scandals, a combination of these methods can be used, involving numerous offshore companies and considerable legal and accounting expertise.

The use of front companies, numerous jurisdictions and bank accounts makes it extremely difficult for the investigators or law enforcement agencies to penetrate. In the end the cost of investigating or recovering lost money simply may not be worth it.

Occasionally ultimate beneficiary ownership of offshore companies can be proven, as the two examples below demonstrate. However these are usually the exceptions.

Example 1

A company paid out over €1 million in facilitation payments ostensibly intended to sway corrupt government officials towards the company's point of view. Several years later, it was discovered that the finance director who had proposed the payments in the first place, had actually made them to himself via a series of offshore companies and bank accounts. The reason that it came to light was because the finance director's third wife had declared the offshore companies and bank accounts as part of her divorce settlement and had produced the beneficiary owner documents from his desk at home to prove it in court.

Example 2

As one way of hiding money from the tax authorities and potential claimants, a consulting and services company that was paying bribes to obtain contracts and overcharging as a result, had invoices sent for 'patent and license fees' from an offshore company in the Bahamas which the management controlled. The total annual value of these invoices was more than 50 per cent of the company's turnover. After a tip-off, investigative work revealed that, in order to keep the formation fees for this sort of venture down, one of the company's junior lawyers had registered himself and one other senior manager as the founders of the offshore company. Because the two names were shown in the Bahamian corporate registry it was later possible to put together a case of embezzlement and a claim for repatriation of funds against the company based on this evidence. The end result was that the junior lawyer's cost-saving actions turned out very costly for himself and his colleagues in the management team.

In many cases of corporate fraud and corruption which we have investigated, we have noted that the company's legal advisors or accountants have assisted members of the management team to establish the offshore companies and vehicles used for paying the bribes or the perpetration of other frauds. In one example where over $70 million were paid out in bribes, some of which were paid direct to the finance director responsible for them, investigations revealed that the tax advisory arm of the global firm of auditors helped set up the offshore companies and bank accounts used.

Recently in what was described as 'the greatest tax evasion scheme in US history', it was revealed that a large accounting firm had been actively marketing tax shelters and other such instruments. The US Internal Revenue Service commissioner was quoted as saying 'accountants and attorneys should be the pillars of our system of taxation, not the architects of circumvention'.

Shortly after the attacks on the World Trade Centre on 11 September 2001, a number of articles appeared in the financial press describing the networks of offshore companies and bank accounts which terrorist organisations were using. As is the case with knee-jerk political reactions, there were widespread calls for the closure of these tax havens. International committees and task forces were established. So far it seems that little has been done although the official paper black list of jurisdictions which support terrorism seems to have been reduced. Even those financial papers which so vehemently called for closure back in 2001 are still carrying the same advertisements for offshore companies, trusts and bank accounts.

Whilst there may be many perfectly valid reasons for using tax havens and offshore entities, paying careful attention to anything that looks like a front company or tax-haven-based establishment when looking for the red flags of fraudulent or corrupt behaviour in, for example, payment and procurement systems, can be very productive. This is further discussed in Chapter 5: Prevention and Detection Up Front.

TECHNOLOGY, ITS USES AND MISUSES

Technology is a double-edged sword. Whilst it creates numerous possibilities for enhancing communication and administrative processes, it also opens up new worlds of possibilities for the criminals. Technology has changed from being a supporting tool in business to more a business enabler. In the same way we can say that twenty years ago computers played supporting roles in the perpetration of fraud and corruption, but today computers and technology are enabling fraud and corruption to take place. Corporate computer systems are requiring less and less human intervention in control processes, making it easier to insert and hide fraudulent transactions. Internet banking and money transfer systems are available to move money across the globe immediately. Criminals also misuse technology to steal information, create false documents and remove or bypass security mechanisms.

The impact of the Internet on business also has affected corporate fraud and the way fraudsters act. The speed at which transactions take place, and the increased information and computing power that is now available almost anywhere in the world has heightened such impact. As a result:

- there is increased greed and a desire to make money fast;
- the speed of transactions is so much faster than before – it is almost impossible to keep track of information;
- the anonymity of business on the Internet could result in an organisation doing business with some unsavoury characters and organisations;
- there may be misplaced trust – 'if it is on a computer, then it must be correct';
- the information and tools to commit fraud are freely available and easily located via Internet search engines.

As companies embrace new technologies and work practices, the number of physical documents in sale, purchase or other transactions, significantly reduces. Moreover, less people will be involved in processing each transaction, and there will be a reduced need for manual reconciliations.

As Figure 4.1 below illustrates, the leaner and less controlled companies become, the more the scales weigh in favour of the criminals.

Management should recognise that the controls which had been set up to prevent fraud and corruption and to catch errors may no longer apply. Certain segregations of duties, preventive controls, review procedures, and approval levels may not function effectively in the new environment.

Example

A multinational company implemented a new workflow system around purchase invoice approval. Invoices were scanned on arrival and e-mailed to the person who made the purchase. They were

Figure 4.1   Balance of risks

then automatically e-mailed to the manager who was responsible for the cost centre to which the invoice was charged. Many of these managers found they were faced with the tiring task of approving a large number of invoices which were e-mailed to them each day. To make life easier they delegated this task, and their approval passwords, to their secretaries.

Implementation of an integrated system can contribute to an atmosphere where the chances of fraud taking place are high. For example:

- Implementation can often take some time – roles and responsibilities will be changing and there may be long periods of uncertainty.
- Newly empowered employees are suddenly given more freedom and latitude than they were used to.
- Often internal control is not addressed during the design phase – as a result, many of the current internal controls become ineffective after the new system is implemented.
- Those who can understand and use the system gain the upper hand.
- Management often does not have a detailed enough understanding of the system to spot errors and irregularities before it is too late.

Integrated systems are replacing the former proliferation of systems, spreadsheets and scraps of paper, and are becoming the company's central repository of information and knowledge. Although this is highly efficient, companies have ended up with extremely well-organised sources of information which are much more vulnerable to industrial espionage and theft, especially in view of the proliferation of memory sticks, camera phones and other portable storage devices with capacities measured in gigabytes. For example, over the past couple of years, there has been a significant increase in cases involving theft of large quantities of credit card and customer information in both the USA and India.

The skill and technical knowledge of criminals has increased significantly and controls can be easily defeated by criminals using technology, for example, to steal passwords to payment systems. The situation is constantly improving for fraudsters because the technology needed to break security measures, which was once only available to government organisations, is now widely available over the Internet.

Figure 4.2 illustrates that, as the cost of equipment decreases (and conversely its power and portability increases), a point is reached where the reward for criminals exceeds the cost of purchasing the technology.

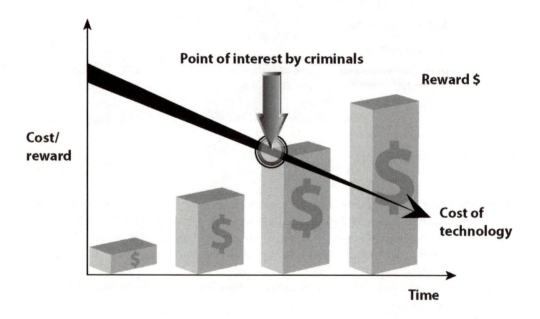

Figure 4.2   Misuse of technology

Fraudsters are now able to conduct a cost/benefit analysis of the advantages of moving away from traditional methods of fraud and corruption, and buying services such as reverse engineering, or insider knowledge or technology which enable them to remove whatever protection is built into organisational systems.

Major fraudsters are sophisticated businessmen and if they identify that a company has a valuable product which relies solely on technology for protection, then they will quickly find ways to break or bypass security measures. For example, 20 years ago, the theft of user ids and passwords to banking systems by the use of technology was rarely reported, despite the fact that software- and hardware-based techniques for stealing passwords were widely available. The risks were well recognised, but most financial institutions chose to ignore them because the techniques did not appear to be of interest to the professional criminal groups who target banks.

Now in the past few years, there has been a huge increase in cases using a technique called 'phishing'. This involves sending millions of bogus emails which pretend to be from genuine banks. The recipient is encouraged to open an attachment, which contains Trojan horse software that installs itself on the victim's computer. Once installed, it logs keystrokes, emails, and use of Internet banking and then mails the information to the perpetrator who can then extract and use the user id and password to milk the victim's Internet bank accounts. The process is highly organised, very profitable and hence has attracted the attention of professional criminal groups around the world.

The fraudsters have also realised that keystroke-logging technology can be used inside banks to gain access to high-value payment systems.

Example

It was reported in 2005 that a UK bank almost became the victim of a $423 million funds transfer theft in what may be the first significant case involving the use of keystroke-logging devices.

The attempt, which police have described as most carefully planned and coordinated, apparently involved an insider who let two co-conspirators into the bank after hours. Keystroke loggers were installed on computer workstations used to input and authorise funds transfers.

Two weeks later the perpetrators returned, collected the devices and extracted the user ids and passwords which were then used to send ten payments totalling nearly $423 million to bank accounts at overseas counterparties.

Fortunately, a discrepancy in one payment was queried by one of the counterparties which contacted the bank to check its authenticity.

Clearly, for an investment of a couple of thousand dollars in technology, a return of several hundred million dollars is a very attractive business proposition for a professional criminal group.

A similar pattern has emerged in the theft of credit card and cash machine information using a variety of well-engineered devices.

Profiling fraud and corruption risk

To understand the fraud and corruption risks to which your organisation is exposed, you need to ask what could be achieved by a dishonest, motivated person, or fraudster, whether internal or external. The most effective way to achieve this is for employees to look at control procedures and job functions from the fraudster's viewpoint and ask whether they can be bypassed by using a particular method of fraud. In other words they need to stop believing that fraud and corruption are not possible and 'think like thieves'. We use the term 'profiling' to describe the process.

Some senior executives have questioned the wisdom of this approach, suggesting that it might actually encourage honest employees to commit frauds. Our response is to ask the executive the question 'Which risk would you rather carry? The risk arising from allowing your honest employees, who have no motivation to steal, to lift taboos and talk about fraud and corruption so identifying loopholes which you can plug? Or that you remain ignorant, with the risk that a dishonest person may have already found a loophole and be exploiting it together with outsiders, having no intention of bringing it to the attention of management?' Everyone who has been asked this question has readily agreed that they would rather take the first risk. In fact in all the years we have worked with profiling we have only seen one occasion where an honest employee subsequently became motivated to commit fraud and this was probably down to his addiction to heroin.

The simple fact is that some job functions are so specialised or complicated that the particular employees are the only ones who can spot potential loopholes. Internal auditors, risk managers or other external parties will not usually have a chance.

Profiling exercises can also be very effective at uncovering fraud and unethical practices. On a number of occasions the imagination and creativity of participants in workshops has subconsciously taken them back to real incidents. The exercises have regularly led to the discovery of instances of fraud or unethical behaviour of which management had no prior suspicion.

In one profiling workshop, a senior purchasing director with more opportunity to commit fraud than anybody else leant back with arms crossed and said he was unable to think of a single fraud. A quick background check revealed that he owned three companies, two of which were invoicing his employer.

Another workshop identified that many people were running businesses on the side, something which was actually common knowledge. The company code of ethics and conflict of interest policy had been filed away gathering dust somewhere. Tackling the matter head on, the managing director insisted that an open declaration be made by all employees and the situation be reviewed immediately.

Obviously, there is a risk in every organisation that a dishonest person could be involved in a profiling exercise. This should be anticipated and, once each method of fraud has been identified and awareness transferred to line managers and supervisors, controls should be put in place to reduce the risk. Not everyone should be told which controls have been implemented in each particular area. This creates a deterrent for potentially dishonest employees.

The aim of a profiling exercise is to obtain an assessment which is as comprehensive as possible, and which both employees and management fully support. It is this buy-in by staff rather than the provision of an opinion by an external party that has proven to be the key factor when presenting the results to top management. The most effective way for you to obtain buy-in is to divide the profiling exercise into three stages:

- Profiling interviews
- Workshop 1
- Workshop 2.

PROFILING INTERVIEWS

Interviews are a very important part of a fraud and corruption profiling exercise, because by putting on a think-like-a-thief hat, employees can be guided to avoid concentrating on existing controls which they believe to be strong and instead to think about how they could be bypassed.

Choosing who to interview is an important part of the exercise. Not every employee needs to partake – just those who have hands-on knowledge of the operation. Usually these are team leaders, section heads, supervisors and line managers. The success or failure of the profiling exercise lies in transferring awareness to these employees who then identify the loopholes.

Loopholes in controls exist for various reasons: for example, because they are historically present in a process, because new systems have been installed, as a result of breakdowns in processing, or because no one has ever looked at the controls through the eyes of a fraudster.

If employees have worked in a function for some time, they may develop blind-spots which prevent them from seeing how dishonest persons or criminals can bypass the controls and systems.

It is vital to provide employees with the necessary stimulation to be able to see around the controls and identify the methods of fraud and corruption. For example, in-house fraud investigators (who do not believe that controls alone prevent fraud and corruption) are usually able to identify the most common methods which can affect a particular operation. Alternatively, external fraud specialists can be of assistance in providing that necessary stimulation and insight.

The important point is to open the eyes of employees to the methodology used by fraudsters. Once employees understand the method, they can by default readily evaluate whether or not the existing controls will prevent its use. There is therefore no need to produce detailed maps of the controls and processes which operational risk and audit teams may have already produced.

Quite often, employees will say that they are unable to see a way around the controls because they and their colleagues are all honest and would not attempt a fraud. In this instance, it is easier to ask them to imagine that they are on holiday and that a person has taken their job who is completely dishonest, and then ask what could that person do. Experience has shown once honest employees imagine that a fictitious dishonest person is in their seat or in the seat of their colleague, they can readily identify methods of fraud.

It should be stressed to employees that the intention of the exercise is not to look at their own honesty or that of their colleagues. The intention is to evaluate the potential for fraud and corruption in the job function assuming they were not there.

A useful method to assist employees to identify exactly what a fraudster sitting in their seat might be interested in is to draw a box and ask them to describe what crosses their desk, as shown in Figure 4.3.

They should consider the different assets relating to their own job function which they can access, for example:

- incoming and outgoing payments, cheques, cash
- saleable information – personal, operational, security
- physical assets
- company resources, such as computer and communications systems
- proprietary information: brand, patents, intellectual property
- inventory
- property, land

some of which provide ready cash, while others can be converted into a benefit.

Employees should also bear in mind that a number of different opponents may target the organisation, ranging from professional criminals to dishonest suppliers, customers, contractors, as well as dishonest employees.

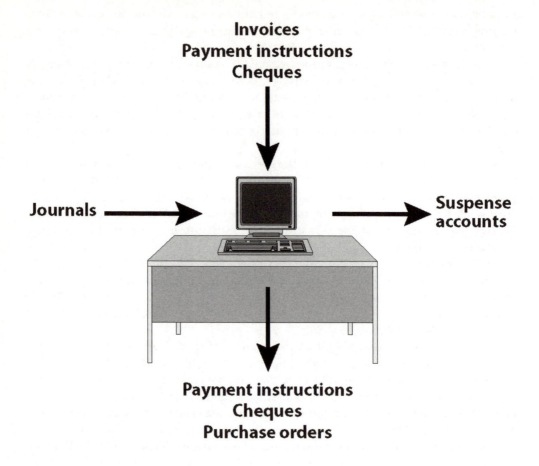

Invoices
Payment instructions
Cheques

Journals

Suspense accounts

Payment instructions
Cheques
Purchase orders

Figure 4.3   What crosses your desk?

In fact the easiest way to look at it is to assume that anyone could be a potential opponent.

In some cases some of the risks and opponents are well understood. For example, financial institutions know that professional criminal groups are continuously attacking their defences. As a result, they are well aware of the opponents and risk of fraud surrounding cheques, credits cards, Internet banking and loans. However, experience has shown that they are less aware of the risks arising internally from dishonest employees, contractors or other third parties. This is also the case with commercial organisations which have had little experience of fraud.

An important lesson is for employees to recognise how a seemingly secure control actually facilitates a fraud because honest employees do not suspect anything untoward is happening.

For example, one of the main anti-fraud controls for nearly every organisation is the reliance on a signature on a document or in many modern systems, an electronic signoff. However, a common method of fraud which has been successful for years is to create a false invoice or payment instruction with a forged signature and submit it for processing. In these cases, the signature provides a false sense of security. If a document looks genuine, it will be processed: honest employees do not suspect that the complete document and signature are forged. How could they? They are reliant on the authorised signatory having checked the document.

Example: So are ten names better or worse than one?

In the oil industry, a contract for the supply of materials (originally worth $10 million) had been grossly overspent. Changes in specifications, additional transport costs caused by nasty weather or a market shortage for large quantities of the materials, were all cited as genuine reasons for the overspend. Furthermore each incremental addition to the price of the contract had been signed off in a manner commensurate with the procedure manuals.

The documentation relating to the choice of supplier was examined and it was discovered that the supplier was chosen by way of a 'bid waiver'. The suppliers had fulfilled several earlier contracts and it was assumed that better prices could be obtained by negotiating directly with them rather than putting the contract out to tender.

We were told that the bid waiver document was properly completed and that all ten signatures from top to bottom were in order. Some months after the decision, each person who had signed the bid waiver was asked two simple questions:

- *why did you sign this document?*
- *why was this supplier chosen?*

In every case (except for a purchasing clerk) the managers said that they had signed the document because they had trusted the signatures of the person who signed before them. There was so much going on that they could not actually be sure why this supplier was chosen. The purchasing clerk was a temporary employee who said that he had been rung up by a senior board director and instructed to award the contract using a bid waiver just like the six previous contracts.

The senior director turned out to be a 'godfather' figure whose hand had been behind a number of contract awards in the past ten years. The ten people signing the document admitted that they were simply 'doing the paperwork' and felt no responsibility for the choice of supplier since that had already been made.

This is a common problem, particularly for fast-growing organisations, in that persons who are authorising invoices, cheques or payment instructions have little time to closely scrutinise the back-up documentation. In some instances they do not even understand the true nature of the transaction. Fraudsters are well aware of this and use this knowledge to their advantage

Another important realisation for employees is that a perceived control weakness does not necessarily translate into a fraud risk. For example, we have seen many audit reports where a control weakness has been identified, which auditors have said increased the risk of fraud. A common example is that 'users do not change passwords frequently enough'. However, when seen through the eyes of a potential fraudster, that fact that passwords are not changed is usually irrelevant. There are numerous methods using either software or hardware by which people could steal a password should they want to do so, however frequently an employee might change it.

Once a way to bypass controls has been identified, a criminal still has to obtain the benefit (such as receive money in a bank account or deliver stolen goods to a warehouse).

Employees should be encouraged to think about the objectives of the criminal, to determine how the opportunity or perceived control weakness could be used to gain a benefit, looking right across the organisation as illustrated in Figure 4.4.

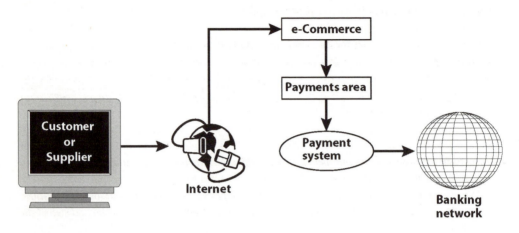

Which job would have the best opportunity?
Which method would work?

Figure 4.4   Look across the operation

Fraudsters, whether they are professional criminal groups, or dishonest employees, do not have a limitless number of methods of fraud from which to choose. Fraud and corruption have been present for centuries and allowing for novel twists enabled by new technology, the basic methods and motives remain the same year after year. Common examples include deception using false documents, theft of information, bribery and more recently the theft of passwords to payment systems.

There are usually no more than four or five methods which can affect any one job function. Interviewees should list as many of these as possible for their own job function. Examples are shown in Table 4.1.

The output from the interviews is a list of the methods by job function which are then collated by department or section ready for Workshop 1.

WORKSHOP 1

Workshop 1 should be attended by team leaders, supervisors and line managers who have hands-on knowledge of the procedures and transactions and who took part in the initial interviews.

Teams should be arranged by department or section and they should be provided with their own draft profile which has been compiled following individual interviews.

It should be stressed to the participants that the purpose of the workshop is to identify the worst-case losses, as otherwise senior managers will not be able to formulate a strategy. The other point to stress to participants is that the draft profile is going to become their working document on which the fraud and corruption risk management strategy will be

Table 4.1   Example methods of fraud by job function

IT manager	Payment officer
Collude with a supplier to inflate prices on purchase of IT infrastructure plant and equipment. Based on a $500 000 project, inflate prices by $50 000. Two projects per year	Steal passwords to online banking system and transmit a series of instructions to the bank for foreign currency payments
Over-specify equipment order and then re-sell to third party (for example, 5 hard drives at $1500 and 5 RAM memory at $500)	Create a false payment instruction and place in tray for processing, for example, fax from a client or a false email as if from another department to pay a supplier
Use superuser password to access payroll database and increase payroll amount	Download the vendor payment file onto diskette for transfer to the bank payment system. Access the text file on the diskette and change the account numbers to own bank details
Raise false electronic purchase order and approve using stolen passwords	Create false general ledger vouchers and send for processing to credit own account and debit general ledger suspense account
Once the accounts payable system has produced the monthly payment file on disk, access the text file and alter the bank account details prior to transfer to bank to divert the payments to own account	Remove blank cheques from back of cheque book and complete using forged signatures. Then cash through an account set up using bogus identity documents

based. It should not be distributed to internal audit, compliance or other outside parties until they have had a chance to review it. The reason for keeping senior managers out of this first workshop is that once they realise the scale of potential losses caused by fraud and corruption, some managers can become defensive and persuade their staff to water down the figures. This is completely self defeating.

The draft profiles should list each fraud method and contain two extra columns labelled 'Likelihood of success' and 'Worst-case loss $'. Each team should agree the likelihood of success (high, medium or low) if that method was used, and then potential worst-case direct financial loss. One method is illustrated in Table 4.2.

Table 4.2   Example Workshop 1 output

Method	Likelihood of success	Worst-case loss $
An employee can create false payment instructions with authentic-looking forged signatures. These would be input and authorised as normal by the payments team	High	$200 million

A full size example is provided in Appendix 2.

It is common during the discussions for participants to identify additional methods which are added to the profile. Nearly all participants to these exercises have reported that they have found the workshops have 'opened their eyes' to the risks.

There is often some confusion about the term 'likelihood' so it is important to clarify how we use the term.

Defining the likelihood

Those organisations which have implemented a risk management strategy have usually based it on a generic internal control framework such as the US-led COSO Enterprise Risk Management (ERM) framework, or risk management standards such as the UK's AIRMIC, ALARM, IRM: 2002 Risk Management Standard, or the Australia/New Zealand Standard for Risk Management, AS/NZ 4360-2004. These are powerful tools to ensure that risks are analysed in a consistent manner across an organisation, usually based on an assessment of likelihood and consequence. Generally, they lay down some fundamental steps which should be followed in a risk analysis process, but do not specify any hard and fast rules as to how the likelihood and consequence should be calculated. Assessment can be either quantitative (using a numerical value, for example 10, 50 or 90 per cent chance of occurrence) or qualitative (using a descriptive scale such as high, medium or low).

Unfortunately, some organisations require line managers to assess the 'likelihood' as the probability of a fraud occurring in a particular time frame, for example:

Table 4.3   Example definition of likelihood

Likelihood	Description
High	Likely to occur within one year
Medium	Likely to occur within ten years
Low	Not likely to occur within ten years

This works fine when the organisation has a lot of statistics to support the assessment. For example, a bank which issues credit cards knows that there is practically 100 per cent probability of fraud because credit card misuse occurs on a daily basis and losses can be quantified.

However, when it comes to corporate fraud and corruption, asking honest line managers to self-assess the probability of a fraud occurring in their area can result in wildly inaccurate assessments for a number of reasons:

- The probability of a fraud or corrupt behaviour occurring does not depend solely on the control framework; it depends on someone having the motivation to find or create an opportunity and exploit it. An honest person will not attempt fraud or accept bribes however weak the controls; a dishonest person may find ways to bypass even good controls.

- Some honest managers cannot see a way around the controls and cannot therefore identify potential fraud opportunities.
- Criminals on the other hand are unpredictable, devious and always looking for an opportunity, and they certainly don't tell anyone when they have found a way around the controls.
- Managers may be reluctant to admit that there is a high likelihood of fraud occurring in their work area.

Rather than assessing probability, the acid test for any organisation is to ask: 'what is the likelihood of this method of fraud succeeding today if attempted by a dishonest internal or external person?'

If a particular method will succeed, then it has a 'high' likelihood as shown below.

Table 4.4   Definition of likelihood of fraud and corruption

Likelihood	Description
High	The method will succeed given the current controls (we are sure there are no controls down the line which would prevent it)
Medium	The method may succeed (we are not sure about other controls down the line)
Low	We know the current controls would prevent the fraud succeeding

So instead of assessing the probability of a fraud occurring within a particular time frame, the organisation's ability to resist fraud attempts is assessed.

The benefit of this is that senior management is usually much more comfortable accepting this assessment rather than being presented with a profile which states that fraud has a high likelihood of occurring in their department.

WORKSHOP 2

The second workshop should be attended by senior managers and representatives from the first workshop. There are two reasons for you to invite senior managers: the first is so that they can provide a practical evaluation of the impact (or consequence) of risks to the organisation which more junior employees may not see. The second is that by participating, you get their buy-in to the resulting profile.

Before the risk assessment is carried out, they should agree the impacts which the organisation and other stakeholders are going to worry about. Typically these can include:

- direct financial loss
- damage to reputation and loss of market share
- erosion of the organisational culture
- risk of legal and regulatory actions
- effect on employee morale.

After considering the likelihood and worst-case monetary loss in the draft fraud and corruption profile, senior managers can evaluate the impact for example, to reputation, loss of market share, and the legal and regulatory impact according to a standard risk matrix as shown below in Figure 4.5.

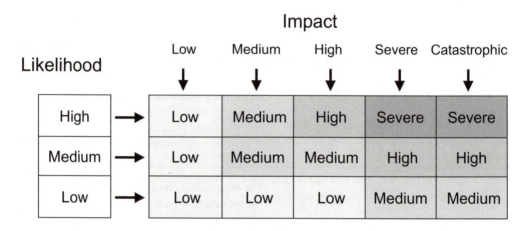

Figure 4.5   Risk matrix

Based on the likelihood and impact, an overall risk rating can then be assigned to each individual fraud and corruption risk and listed in the fraud and corruption profile as shown:

Table 4.5   Example Workshop 2 output

Risk level	Method	Likelihood of success	Worst-case loss $	Impact on reputation	Legal and regulatory impact
High	An employee can create false payment instructions with authentic looking forged signatures. These would be input and authorised as normal by the payments team	High	$200 million	High	High

A full size example is provided in Appendix 3.

It is worth reiterating to senior managers that the draft profile is going to become their working document on which the fraud and corruption risk management strategy will be based. Until they have had a chance to review the figures and reduce any high risks which have been identified it is not going to be distributed to outside parties.

If this not done, then senior managers may try to undermine the credibility of the profile, although once you have got the buy-in of employees and line managers in Workshop 1, it is difficult for them to argue the figures, particularly if representatives from Workshop 1 are in attendance and can answer any queries.

A sample fraud and corruption profile is provided in Appendix 4.

PROFILING THE EXECUTIVE DIRECTORS

There is often a big difference between what the chief executive and his senior executive directors are supposed to be able to do according to the audit committee and external auditors, as opposed to what these people can actually do through the force of their personality and position. One chief executive who took part in a profiling exercise quickly demonstrated that just by instructing subordinates, he could allocate a third-party company favourable trading terms and then instruct significant funds to be moved to its bank account. On another occasion, a chief financial officer realised the influence he had when it was pointed out to him that he had arranged for certain invoices to be paid by direct transfer from the bank account. He had inadvertently bypassed the whole procurement process including his own accounts payable function.

When looked at from this point of view, most organisations who think that they have low fraud risks usually find the opposite, particularly when the question is asked of the executive directors.

It is therefore important to include the executive directors in the assessment process by profiling the different methods which they could use. An example is shown in Table 4.6.

Table 4.6   Example executive director profile

Risk level	Method	Likelihood of success	Worst-case loss $	Reputation	Legal and regulatory impact
High	The CEO and CFO collude to acquire a 'strategic' company at an inflated price, in exchange for a kickback to an offshore bank account	High	$50 million	Severe	Severe

Performing an assessment based on methods which have in fact been used on many occasions by fraudsters provides a practical evaluation of fraud risks.

UNDERSTANDING PERCEPTIONS AND GETTING FEEDBACK

Through workshops and training it is possible to obtain valuable feedback about where the risks of fraud and corruption are, from a cross-section of employees. Perception surveys can be included in profiling workshops, or bolted on to fraud and corruption training courses and e-learning programs. Perception surveys and their value are covered in Chapter 5.

Taking immediate steps to reduce the risk

The anti-fraud and -corruption program works rather like a vaccination program as it increases resistance and reduces the chance of serious infection. Once the whole organisation is resistant, fraudsters and corrupt individuals will often walk away to find softer targets. However it is much more than a simple vaccination and involves several interrelated elements.

The fraud and corruption profile is used to identify and prioritise potential methods which have a high likelihood or impact or, most importantly, a combination of these two factors. While the assessment necessarily is subjective and qualitative, it provides management with the best possible radar plot of where and how fraud and corruption will strike. Once the most likely methods of attack are known, then it becomes much easier to:

- direct fraud and corruption awareness training to take account of these methods;
- identify what footprints each method is likely to leave behind and then tailor detection processes accordingly;
- ensure that any investigations carried out into suspected instances take into account related fraudulent and corrupt practices which could be occurring at the same time.

The value of a fraud and corruption profile is shown in Figure 4.6.

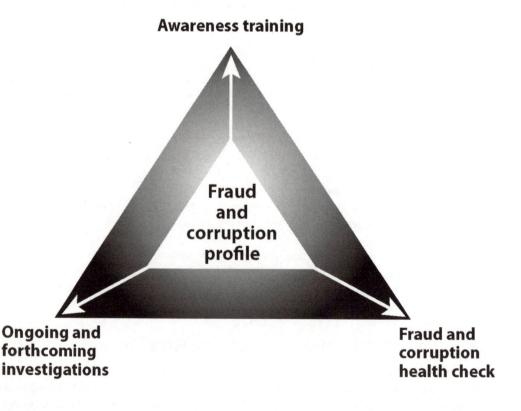

Awareness training

Fraud and corruption profile

Ongoing and forthcoming investigations

Fraud and corruption health check

Figure 4.6   Value triangle

Once a fraud and corruption profile has been developed the real risks of fraud and corruption will become more visible and quantifiable. It is then much easier to gain support for a number of short- and longer-term activities which help manage the risk of fraud and corruption, build consensus and hence drive down costs.

Example

A fraud and corruption profiling exercise and a very quick health check commissioned by Corporate Internal Audit and Security identified a number of payments and receipts of monies from shell companies and tax havens. Simple investigation showed that they had the potential to be used for fraud and corruption including deliberate schemes to avoid tax on remuneration to employees and consultants, facilitation payments and bribes, ownership of off-book companies, sales to customers with sinister criminal connections and several other categories.

The head of internal audit raised the matter at the next audit committee meeting using a single slide called 'Too Many Tax Havens' and after a short explanation of the risks involved was handed a firm mandate to monitor and review all such payments in the future. Actions were also taken within human resources to bolster up the code of conduct guidance on corruption and bribery as well as the payment of salaries.

Once a fraud and corruption profile has been agreed, managers can look at each method of fraud and examine why the current environment might not have prevented it occurring.

Starting with the highest impact risks in the fraud and corruption profile, additional controls can be identified to reduce those risks that the business does not want to carry. Some controls can be implemented quickly, but others may require board decisions on strategic policy changes or significant capital investment.

For example, a common quick fix can be identified in organisations which process payment instructions (or invoices) using a two-level check. The hard-copy document is input to the payment system by one person who checks the signatures, and is then approved by a second person. However, a common method of fraud bypasses this control: someone submits a completely false document with forged signatures, which both the inputter and authoriser take as genuine.

A quick fix to reduce the likelihood of this risk is to make it difficult for someone to insert a false document. The internal risk of an employee submitting false documents can be reduced by reconciling the documents coming in and going out of a department. The external risk can be reduced by telephoning customers or originators to verify that they despatched the documents.

A summary diagram of this document control strategy is shown in Figure 4.7.

We have found that each organisation usually has one or two unique fixes to reduce the risk of a specific method of fraud and corruption and these can be listed in a fraud and corruption fix report (see Table 4.7 below).

Sometimes quick fixes can be implemented immediately.

Example

During a workshop, some of the participants identified that the main bank used for payments and clearing would accept (in an emergency) a faxed instruction. The participants agreed that external fraudsters could easily obtain a transfer form and, if they knew which bank was used and were

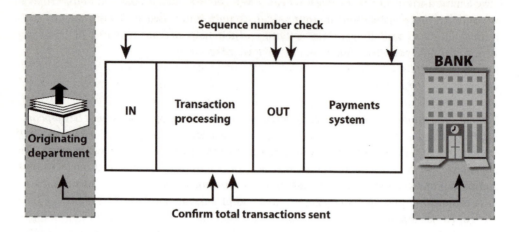

Figure 4.7 Document control strategy

Table 4.7 Sample fraud and corruption fix report

Risk level	Method	Quick fix
Severe	False payment documents input in the treasury area	• Mandatory call back to originator prior to processing • Reconciliation of documents despatched from originator to receiver
High	Manipulation of the tender and award process of major contracts by employee colluding with supplier	• Review of key employee conflicts of interest and background checks • Full post mortem review of bid evaluation (as deterrent) • Review of contract (after award and submission of invoices)
Medium	Submission of fraudulent supplier invoices where the excuse of an urgent payment is used to bypass the controls	• Training of accounts payable clerks in simple fraud detection techniques • Implementation of automated fraud detection tests embedded in accounts payable software • Regular capture/review of invoices which are submitted via direct payments system
Medium	Collusion with customers to reduce effective sales price	• Due diligence/vetting of customer • Automated monitoring of pricing and sales • Regular screening of employee conflicts of interest

able to obtain a director's signature, could easily forge and send an international transfer to any account. A review of bank mandates showed that accounts, which often had balances in excess of $100 million, had no limits on the size of transfers. The bank's call centre confirmed that this type of instruction would be paid, especially if someone called in advance.

The finance director magnanimously admitted that his signature was easy to copy and added that if the transfer was made before a public holiday in his country, it would probably go through. Everybody agreed there and then to adjourn the workshop and fix the problem. It took half an hour to do this and the atmosphere in the workshop was noticeably less tense.

Strategic measures are those which require consideration by senior management because they may need to be implemented across the organisation, or because implementation requires capital expenditure higher than that which business unit managers can authorise.

A number of strategic issues appear to be applicable to most organisations we have assisted. These are listed below.

FIDELITY INSURANCE

Some organisations reduce fraud risks by transferring the risk to insurers through employee fidelity or computer crime policies. They then sit back and believe that if a fraud occurs it will be a simple case of submitting a proof of loss to support a claim to recover the misappropriated amount. This can be an expensive misconception, for several reasons:

- Some policies contain specific requirements which exclude cover if they are not complied with, or specific exclusion clauses. Often, managers have not even seen the policy, let alone the requirements. This is particularly true for large multinational organisations which have organised cover on a group basis and distribute only summary policy statements.
- Policies may not been updated for many years and contain wordings which are based on obsolete technology (for example, computer tapes), but do not mention cover for electronic funds transfer systems.
- An insurer may be very reluctant to pay out on a large claim and will take a close look at whether the standards of control met those expected of a prudent organisation; in particular, whether the operations team had followed its own written standard procedures. If the company has not followed procedures or complied with policy conditions, the insurer could allege negligence and deny liability to settle the claim, leaving it to the company to launch civil proceedings to recover the loss. It would then become a war of attrition which insurers understand all too well: often the claim will be settled for far less than the original loss.

The directors of the company may feel secure in the knowledge that any major fraud will be covered by insurance, when in reality the company is virtually self-insuring itself through lack of cover.

The fraud and corruption profile should be used to determine whether cover does or could exist for each method of fraud, and whether the limits are sufficient for the level of potential loss.

Premiums for fidelity and computer crime seem to be increasing steeply. Some organisations choose to raise the excess or deductible amount to higher levels in exchange for reduced premiums. For example, rather than losses of $5 million being covered, losses under $10 million would not be covered. The fraud and corruption profile should enable directors to make strategic decisions as to whether or not to continue to pay the insurance premiums or whether to self-insure.

PRE-EMPLOYMENT SCREENING

Some organisations screen new recruits simply by taking up two references, either in writing or verbally. Contractors and temporary staff are not screened; the assumption being that the agency supplying the staff will take up references. This may not occur. This level of screening may not be sufficient to reduce the risk of a dishonest person gaining employment. Several frauds perpetrated in financial institutions recently have involved temporary staff.

Also, a number of financial institutions have found that when they have dismissed an employee for stealing and a prospective employer has telephoned seeking a reference, the legal advice has been to confirm only the dates of employment rather then provide adverse information. This has enabled dishonest persons to obtain employment in other financial institutions. Whilst there does not appear to be any legal obligation to provide adverse information, we believe that there will be increasing pressure for organisations to do so in the future. (One suggestion to try and overcome this problem would be to obtain legal advice as to whether a clause could be inserted into future employment contracts in which the employee gives an irrevocable consent that the employer can provide details of the reasons that they ceased employment.)

It is now accepted best practice in Europe and the USA to implement comprehensive screening programs, usually by out-sourcing to specialist suppliers. The implementation of such a screening program normally requires board authority and compliance with the law and with existing company policy. Strategic decisions need to be made about the capital expenditure to implement a screening program, and whether or not to apply it to existing employees across the organisation.

Considerations include:

- the extent of the program
- who will have responsibility
- levels of checking and vital factors
- whether to include retrospective screening for existing employees, or for internal promotions and transfers.

Having agreed to implement a screening program, a specially designed application form should be completed by all job applicants. Quite often, a dishonest candidate will not complete the form and will withdraw the application, seeking an easier target. The points to consider for the content of the form include:

- the questions should be legal, fair and unambiguous
- the questions should assess suitability, experience and qualifications
- the answers should be verifiable, with a consistent decision-making process as to how errors, omissions or discrepancies will affect employment.

Job descriptions then are categorised into different levels of sensitivity, with correspondingly different levels of screening. For example, a comprehensive screening program would include the following checks subject to relevant privacy and other legislation in each country:

- credit and bankruptcy checks
- electoral roll searches
- verification of the curriculum vitae, looking for gaps and inconsistencies
- confirmation of education
- checks with statutory bodies and associations to confirm professional qualifications
- verifying employment history with direct line managers and human resources
- directorship and media searches
- court record searches.

Follow-up interviews should be held with candidates to discuss any significant discrepancies.

CONFIDENTIAL REPORTING CHANNELS

Many preventable frauds occur because an employee who had a suspicion about a transaction or a concern about the behaviour of a manager did not have any mechanism to report the concern. An anonymous reporting route provided for employees, vendors or others who have suspicions of fraud or malpractice is a very effective method for detecting fraud.

For example, research in the USA by the Association of Certified Fraud Examiners (see reports on www.acfe.com) stated that tips were the single most effective means of detecting occupational fraud. An analysis of 508 frauds in 2004, totalling $761 million showed that 39.6 per cent were uncovered as a result of a tip either from an employee, customer, vendor, or law enforcement agent, or anonymously. In 2006, tip-offs accounted for 44 per cent of all multi-million-dollar fraud schemes

Confidential reporting channels or whistle-blowing lines now are legally required in several countries. Strategic decisions need to be made about whether to provide the reporting channel across the organisation, with capital expenditure for a central unit to provide awareness training and to provide follow up investigation services.

USER ID AND PASSWORD CONTROLS

A major area of concern in most organisations is the ease with which a dishonest employee can steal user identifications and passwords to computer systems by using simple hacking software or technical devices on local workstations. Despite the threat, many organisations (which have not had an incident) still rely on the employee's password as the sole control for systems access.

Fixing the problem usually requires major changes to the way systems are run (such as implementing smart card or biometric devices as well as a password), and this requires senior management approval for capital expenditure.

FILE MANAGEMENT

The increasing interconnectivity between companies, customers, suppliers and banks means that a large number of payment and invoice files are transferred electronically over networks for entry into payment systems. In some cases, these files are simple spreadsheet or text files which could be accessed to amend account or credit details in order to divert payments.

More and more firms are outsourcing their computer operations to third-party specialist companies. When an electronic payment is sent, it can sit in a batch file waiting to be processed – and accessible to third-party system support personnel who could amend it, without the knowledge of the sender. It is important to identify all areas where batch payment files are produced and stored, and to establish a fraud resistant process for managing batch files. In some cases, computer systems which are in use across the organisation can contain unacceptable fraud risks which local business unit managers are powerless to reduce. This requires senior management decisions about whether or not to carry the risk or to commit capital expenditure to reduce it.

RISK REDUCTION PROCESS

The risk reduction process should include the following steps:

- Management should reach a consensus on the definition of risks levels, likelihood and impact categories discussed in the draft fraud and corruption profile. For example, what would be considered a catastrophic impact as opposed to a severe impact.
- The methods and quick fixes applicable to each department should be extracted from the quick fix document and given to the relevant line managers, who should evaluate and decide which fixes can be implemented. They should report back to senior management within a specified time period.
- A workshop should be held where managers re-evaluate and adjust risk levels accordingly and revise the fraud and corruption profile.
- A decision should be made as to the management response to each risk level. An example is provided in Table 4.8.

Table 4.8   Management response

Risk level	Management response
Severe	To be managed by the chief financial officer with a detailed action plan and regular updates to the compliance and audit committee.
High	To be managed by the group financial controller with responsibility and ownership clearly specified and documented. Detailed action plan and mandatory reporting to the compliance and audit committee
Medium	Management responsibility and timescales must be clearly specified and documented with regular reports to the compliance and audit committee
Low	Managed by routine procedures and monitored within the business unit

This approach differs from the situation in most empowered organisations with autonomous business units where fraud is managed solely at the business unit level – because line managers have no effective means of identifying levels of risk or representing them to top management, while top management is not sufficiently aware of the potentially catastrophic consequences of certain fraud exposures.

Top management should also be proactively evaluating major exposures, and in a fraud-resistant organisation they will be aware of the risks and consider them in their decision-making process.

Following accepted principles for risk evaluation and treatment, they can first identify those risks which have a low impact and which can be accepted without further action. They can then identify options for treating the remaining risks, including:

- avoiding the risk (for example, by deciding not to do business in a particular country)
- reducing the likelihood or impact of the risk by implementing preventive and detective controls
- transferring the risk (for example, by taking out fidelity or computer crime insurance)
- retaining the risk as an acceptable part of doing business – typically this would apply to methods which have a low likelihood and impact.

Residual risks should be included in the overall operational risk register and reported at board level, for example, to the audit committee. Fraud and corruption risks should also be re-evaluated whenever major change initiatives are introduced; for example, new or re-engineered products or processes.

Once fraud and corruption have been properly recognised then senior managers at the level of head of operations, the chief financial officer or general manager, are usually eager to implement a strategy to reduce the risks because they have a desire to protect company assets or client funds (besides the concern that a significant fraud may adversely impact their own career prospects and remuneration).

Once the risks have been assessed, there is little problem getting line managers who report to these senior managers to implement fixes and re-evaluate the risks which they are willing to carry. The problem occurs when line managers are unable to reduce a risk because they require significant expenditure or increased headcount. They do not want to raise the issue at board level because it will look as if they are not capable of solving problems. So they may be tempted to sit on the issue and carry risks which could have severe impacts on the organisation.

This can create a situation where the board believes there are no severe risks, whereas line managers know there are such risks, but keep quiet in order to further their careers. To address these issues, the fraud and corruption risk management strategy should involve internal stakeholders such as operational risk management, which has a mandate to report on risks right across the organisation.

It is important that where line managers believe that a change initiative has created unacceptable fraud risks, that there is a mechanism for them to report their concerns.

An advantage of the resulting fraud and corruption profiles is that they can be used as a discussion document by operational risk managers in assessing, for example, how much capital to allocate to fraud risks. Line managers may 'undervalue' a risk, hoping for a lower capital allocation, and operational risk managers can revalue the risk to provide a more appropriate allocation.

This approach to addressing risk enables line managers to elevate issues so that directors need to make decisions about whether to commit expenditure and resources for fraud detection or prevention, or whether to carry the potential loss. Directors are given the responsibility for deciding on the organisation's appetite for fraud and corruption (that is, which risks they believe the organisation can carry as a cost of doing business efficiently).

Summary of key points

- Don't be blinded by the beauty of a theoretical risk management model: aim to obtain a practical understanding of the fraud and corruption risks.
- Make sure everyone involved in fraud and corruption risk management is aware of the tools which fraudsters use.
- Identify the areas in the organisation where technology could be misused.
- Obtain top management approval to first understand the fraud and corruption risks which the organisation faces before looking at countermeasures.
- Conduct fraud and corruption risk profiling exercises right across the organisation.
- Provide specialist resources to assist employees identify potential methods.
- Include the board in the profiling exercise.
- Implement a process to record fraud and corruption risks and follow up the treatment of them.
- Provide a route for line managers to report whenever a change initiative creates new fraud and corruption risks.

5 *Upfront Prevention and Detection*

Investing in prevention and monitoring

One of the saddest aspects of the investigations we have been involved in over the past 25 years is that we have seen at first hand the dramatic and damaging effect of fraud and corruption on innocent employees and third parties; loss of morale, and shattered confidence, and high stress from investigations and being under suspicion. Just as dramatic has been the reaction of employees who have confessed to partaking in fraudulent or corrupt activities, and who then suddenly discover that they are potentially facing a prison sentence. Just like management who wish that they had prevented the money going missing, they wish that they could turn the clock back. In most cases it is all too late.

Preventing fraud and corruption succeeding in the first place, especially as it is becoming increasingly difficult to recover stolen money, may sound like common sense, but monitoring of fraud and corruption risks is probably one of the least resourced areas in most organisations. Done correctly, it can be one of the most productive in terms of preventing losses.

There are some very good reasons to do this:

- Most incidents of fraud and corruption have cost far too much by the time they are discovered (by accident, by whistle-blowers or as a result of a corporate collapse).
- The longer a fraud is allowed to run undetected, the larger the losses which accumulate. For example, where managers have been addicted to gambling they start by stealing relatively small amounts each week; but if undetected, losses can easily build up over a number of years to millions of dollars.
- Stakeholders are now aggressively seeking answers from senior management as to why losses through fraud and corruption have been allowed to run unchecked for so long.
- Monitoring and detection is becoming a legal requirement for some major public corporations (for example, those which need to comply with SOX).
- Successful, active detection is one of the best forms of prevention.
- Actively looking for instances of fraud and corruption may expose potential loopholes which have been overlooked.

Detecting fraud and corruption can take two forms:

- *reactive* – employees recognising those behavioural, transactional, system and corporate red flags which provide early warning of a potential problem;
- *proactive* – applying detection tests as part of a regular corporate health check, which specialists such as security and audit personnel can design and run.

Most companies tend to be better at reacting to the signs of fraud and corruption than proactively looking for it. The benefit of a well-designed monitoring and detection programme is that it combines the best of reactive and proactive detection in the form of a systematic methodology. The model in Figure 5.1 shows the four components which are fundamental for the success of a monitoring and detection program, and the four main categories of red flags.

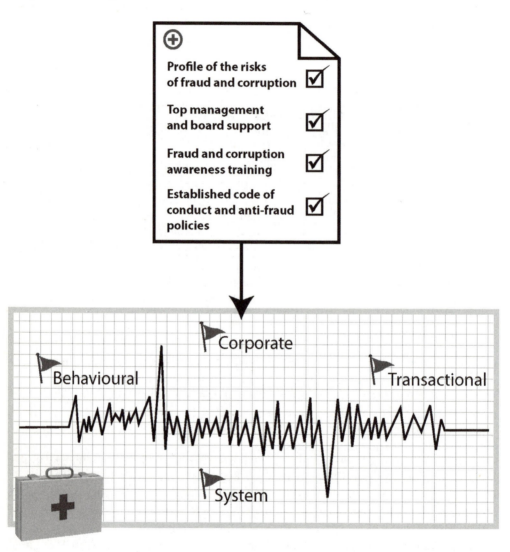

Figure 5.1   Four components

One of the most effective fraud prevention measures is the fear of being detected due to not knowing what controls have been put in place. Therefore, once the programme for monitoring and detection has been agreed and documented, access to it should be restricted so that only a limited number of people know the details of what is being done and where.

This chapter examines why upfront prevention and monitoring is a cost-effective investment and how it can be made possible by implementing:

- a comprehensive fraud and corruption awareness programme
- mechanisms whereby symptoms of fraud and corruption (called 'red flags') are recognised early
- a programme called the 'corporate health check' which is designed to identify the less obvious red flags on a regular basis.

Raising awareness

Practical awareness training increases the potential for all employees to recognise the red flags of fraud and corruption and know how to respond to them. Training sessions provide the ideal forum for communicating the essence of the code of conduct, and the anti-fraud and -corruption, and whistle-blowing policies.

It is common to find that very few employees have previously received any form of practical instruction. However, after training, all employees, whatever their position or level, have found the subject engaging and interesting and as a result have been much more prepared to do something about the problem of fraud and corruption.

It is clear that a well structured, interactive, company-wide awareness programme will serve to significantly drive down the costs of fraud and corruption inherent in the organisation. The objectives of an awareness programme should be to:

- raise the awareness of fraud and corruption in the organisation
- significantly improve prevention and timely detection
- stimulate interest and dialogue around the company's code of conduct and anti-fraud and -corruption policies, making these something that all employees are willing to adopt and support
- encourage all employees to feel that raising concerns is productive and in their and the organisation's best interests
- enable the organisation to better understand its own risks of fraud and corruption.

The most effective programmes are those which are realistic, enjoyable and interactive, and where feedback from the participants is an integral part of the programme. By realistic we mean that the message is one of common sense and is anchored in the practical field. Dry, one-way lecture programmes which rely on 'preaching' and 'you must do as I say' messages are not very effective.

In the past we have seen fraud, corruption or business ethics programmes which have been one-off events arranged on either an ad hoc basis or only for selected groups. For an awareness programme to have any lasting impact it should be a mandatory part of training for all employees. The content and examples used should be regularly reviewed and updated.

WHO SHOULD BE INVOLVED?

It is very important, before developing and launching a fraud and corruption awareness programme to identify a sponsor who will support it and ensure that it has received sufficient management attention. Sponsors can include corporate security, human resources, the CFO, legal and compliance, corporate responsibility and if possible, the CEO.

Not having a sponsor can lead to the programme not being taken seriously and people being too scared to report potential problems for fear of retribution. Often a joint sponsorship team involving one or more executive board members is the preferred and stronger solution.

Different departments in a company sometimes feel that they have overall responsibility for supporting one type of training. For example, financial controllers, internal auditors and corporate security officers may wish to be involved in the development of any fraud and corruption awareness training programmes. At the same time human resources, corporate legal and possibly corporate responsibility may wish to include anti-bribery and business ethics training in line with the code of conduct.

What is important is that that training is well coordinated and planned to avoid confusion and duplication of effort.

Sometimes, the start of awareness programmes and also other anti-fraud and -corruption activities can be delayed because the executive board and senior management wish to ensure that it has all the relevant policies and guidelines in place first. This is fine provided that it is done quickly. However, it is sometimes used as a delaying tactic by a senior manager who sees no value in the programme and who knows that the process of developing and approving detailed policies and guidelines can take several months, if not years. So, once some broad statements have been made at the top of the organisation regarding ethics and anti-fraud and -corruption, the awareness training programme should be launched and the feedback should be used to refine and clarify the corporate message. Once senior management takes the programme seriously and leads by example, then there is a good chance that the rest of the organisation will follow suit.

WHAT SORT OF TRAINING IS APPROPRIATE?

Fraud and corruption awareness training can be slotted into a variety of existing corporate training programmes such as management training, employee inductions or training in financial processes and procedures. However, independent stand-alone programmes are usually the most effective because they focus the participants' minds on what is usually virgin territory.

Specific training could also be provided to different groups such as senior management, middle management, project managers or people who work in higher-risk environments such as accounting, procurement or customer service. The training should incorporate core issues which are common to all, with the possibility of branching out into specific topics which are of interest to one or more groups.

Some companies also insist that key business partners and suppliers, too, undergo a minimum level of fraud and corruption awareness training.

Those persons who need to specialise in the investigation and detection of fraud and corruption should be provided with external training by experts in the field. Candidates for specialist training could include representatives of internal audit, legal, corporate security, risk management and human resources. The type of training is discussed later in this chapter in 'Corporate health check'.

We recommend a maximum of two related programmes for all employees along the following lines:

- *Programme 1: Code of conduct and anti-corruption training*

  The first programme covers the code of conduct, policies on prevention of bribery and corruption, and other related issues such as anti-bribery and corporate responsibility, human rights and environmental issues. The purpose is to reflect and communicate the corporate message and aspirations and the tone at the top. Posing ethical dilemmas and then discussing the correct choices is a useful mechanism to communicate the code of conduct.

- *Programme 2: Practical fraud and corruption awareness training*

  The second programme aims to demystify fraud and corruption for the participants, help their understanding of the methods used against the company by different opponents, and teach them how to defend against fraud and how to spot and deal with the red flags. Practical and engaging training scenarios and case examples should be used. In the next section we have provided some examples of the types of scenarios and cases which could be included. Participants should be encouraged to recognise the loopholes from the perspective of a potential criminal. This type of training is also an excellent precursor of the fraud and corruption profiling exercise which was covered in previous chapters.

Face-to-face group training is the most effective. However in recent years e-learning, interactive animation and video-based training has also proven very successful.

The programme should incorporate feedback mechanisms which:

- test the understanding of the participants
- capture their perceptions of the fraud and corruption risks which they believe exist in their areas
- allow them to raise any concerns over controls or possible frauds which they wish to discuss.

Appendix 5 shows excerpts from real code of conduct training programmes, fraud and corruption awareness training and also a knowledge and perception test.

PRACTICAL TRAINING EXAMPLES

The examples below are taken from typical code of conduct and fraud and corruption awareness training programmes. They demonstrate some of the most important issues which can be addressed by effective training when interpreting the company's anti-fraud and -corruption policies. Practical examples like the ones shown below are used to develop the participants' abilities to recognize loopholes in the current systems which allow fraud and corruption to occur.

Try them out for yourself by selecting the answer you think fits best and then turn to Appendix 6 for the guidance and a suggested answer.

Scenario 1: Marketing commissions

As part of your management duties you have recently visited one of the European marketing companies. At dinner one night with Mr Dominic Lestrange, the Chief Accountant, he tells you in confidence that a lot of strange marketing invoices are being bounced around between the head office and his department. He hints that the Marketing Director, Mr Edward Geiger, is trying to spread the cost of marketing commissions and other unusual costs across the businesses but he, Dominic, is not happy to book invoices such as the one he shows you below (Figure 5.2).

WWU HOLDING GROUP
Vaduz
Furstentum Liechtenstein

Zurich April, 200X

Attn: Messrs Geiger / Lestrange
YZW Corporation
135 Avenue Molière
1190 Bruxelles
Belgium

INVOICE 0010

In accordance with our contract,
we invoice you the initial marketing fee
for New Development #2
with the sum of   **USD 100 000**

Please transfer to the following bank account:

Soginvest Banca
6600 Locarno - Mursito
Via Statzione 9
Konto Nr: 55 000 71

Figure 5.2   Marketing invoice

What do you see as the red flags of fraud and corruption and what do you do now?

_____

_____

_____

_____

(Answers are shown in Appendix 6.)

Scenario 2: Inventory and logistics

It is reported to you that surplus stock from major refitting and maintenance projects is usually written down to zero value and kept in a separate area of the warehouse. This is used on later projects which have tight budgets. The fact that the stock is now free of charge means that its use does not impact on the budgets of the projects.

What are the fraud and corruption risks arising from such practices?

_____

_____

_____

_____

(Answers are shown in Appendix 6.)

Scenario 3: Spirit of the code of conduct

Your company has implemented a code of conduct which makes little mention of gifts other than that they should be kept to a reasonable level and in line with maintaining normal business relationships.

Your largest distributor recently concluded an internal incentive programme, whereby their best salespersons were awarded a choice of prizes: either a high quality wristwatch (which you believe would cost them around $1500), or a paid holiday for two at an island resort.

Three wristwatches are left over, and your customer offers one to you in recognition of your efforts on their behalf. Your colleague politely accepts.

a) *What should you do?*

☐ You accept the gift; you did make a special effort on this project and you don't want to offend the distributor.

☐ It is a valuable gift so you ask your manager's permission before accepting.

☐ You ask if you could have the holiday instead as you have several watches from before.

☐ You decline the gift, and consult your manager on this matter.

b) *How would you react to the fact that your colleague took the watch?*

_____

_____

_____

_____

(Answers are shown in Appendix 6.)

Scenario 4: Dealing with customers

You are meeting with a customer to finalize an important order. Just before the contract is to be signed, you are asked by one of the customer's senior representatives to increase the contract price by 1 per cent and pay the amount to a particular consultant company. You request a time-out and a member of your team tells you the company does exist on paper, and does provide consulting services. He has also heard a rumour that the company is controlled by members of the customer's management.

What do you do and why?

☐ You postpone signing the contract and contact your manager for guidance.

☐ You sign. The amount is immaterial, and you should help the customer by agreeing their request.

☐ You refuse to sign, walk out of the meeting, and tell the customer that you are shocked at having your arm twisted at the last minute.

_____

_____

_____

_____

(Answers are shown in Appendix 6.)

Recognising and looking for the red flags

There are occasions when the behaviour of an individual, the look of a document or transaction, or even unusual system activity, raises a question mark in the mind of a friend, work colleague or third party. Depending on how astute or alert the person is, the incident may either be followed up, sometimes to expose a potentially serious problem, or alternatively ignored and quickly forgotten. The following macabre story illustrates the fatal consequences when red flags are overlooked:

Example

In July 2002, an inquiry in England concluded that a doctor called Harold Shipman had murdered at least 215 of his elderly patients during routine home visits, by injecting them with lethal doses of drugs. He had carried out these activities over a number of years and, to the outside world, he appeared to be a nice, bearded, family man, and a respected doctor. The reality was that he was a killer and probably a psychopath. Today, even after his own suicide, the question continues to be asked why no one reacted to the telltale signs including:

- *abnormally high death rates on his call-outs*
- *exceptionally high order rates for certain drugs which were eventually used to murder his patients.*

The reason nobody acted was not apathy: Dr Shipman managed to get away with it for so long because the caring, honest people around him could never have imagined or believed that something so terrible was going on.

In the same way, one of the greatest hindrances to detection of fraud and corruption is that most relatively honest people cannot actually believe that a colleague, manager or third party is dishonest – that is the nature of people at work. When the working environment appears to be normal, safe and nurturing, people do not want to believe that something terrible is happening – whether it be fraud, corruption or some other shocking event.

Honest people do not suspect other apparently honest, nice people. This is especially true for junior employees who respect and like their managers. If the managers are nice to them and treat them with courtesy and respect, however tough their decisions are, the employees will rarely suspect them of being capable of being dishonest.

By training employees to be aware of the indicators of potential problems, or 'red flags', an organisation can make a huge leap forward in reducing fraud and corruption.

The skill is to balance the need for a harmonious, relaxed work environment with the need to spot and prevent the dishonest person or activities at an early stage.

A red flag is an indicator, and only an indicator, of a potential problem which may include fraud, corruption and other malpractice. We have chosen to categorise red flags as behavioural, transactional, system or corporate. Ultimately all four categories are indicative of abnormal behaviour.

Each category can be further classified into those which can be noticed by the trained eye, 'reactive red flags', or those which need the help of a detection or corporate health check process, 'proactive red flags'. Table 5.1 illustrates examples of both reactive and proactive red flags which are Behavioural, Transactional, System and Corporate.

Table 5.1   Examples of red flags

Examples of red flags	Reactive	Proactive
Behavioural	Noticing that some managers are reluctant to give proper explanations as to why certain budgetary decisions are made	Performing background checks to identify unsanctioned involvement in external companies
Transactional	Treasury and payments persons question payments of supplier invoices to tax havens, such as the British Virgin Islands, the Cayman Islands etc.	Looking for potentially collusive sales transactions where there are unusual patterns of low prices and credit notes
System	Repeated system failures and audit logs switched off	Monitoring and analysis of unsuccessful access attempts to sensitive systems and data
Corporate	Noticing that a sequence of acquisitions and joint ventures failed	Annual personal financial statement and conflict of interest statement completed by executive and verified by external party

This section describes those red flags which can be discovered by observation during the course of business activities (either by accident or by trained persons). The section at the end of this chapter describes a systematic programme called a corporate health check which can be used to regularly root out serious less obvious red flags.

The awareness training for each category of red flag should be provided to specific groups of employees as described below.

RECOGNISING BEHAVIOURAL RED FLAGS

All employees should receive training in behavioural red flags.

Red flags in behaviour and lifestyle indicate that an employee may have a problem. All line managers should be aware of these indicators and the actions to be taken to determine the nature of the problem. Behavioural red flags can be either objective (in that they can be measured or monitored) or subjective (in the sense of being reliant on the manager's knowledge of the employee). Typical objective behavioural red flags include:

- signs of excessive wealth or spending, increasing debts and lack of wealth, changes in personal circumstances
- long absences from work and poor timekeeping
- failure to take leave
- changes to work patterns, long hours after normal business hours
- the (repeated) override of normal controls and procedures.

Objective red flags give a reasonably good indication that something is wrong, and can usually be monitored in order to establish the cause of the behaviour change.

Subjective behavioural red flags include:

- abnormal social behaviour
- problems with gambling, drug or alcohol abuse
- excessive mood swings, aggression, marked changes in behaviour
- resistance to audit and questions, such as a confrontational, arrogant and aggressive approach to avoid answering questions and deflect attention
- misleading or ambiguous explanations to questions.

Subjective red flags are much more difficult to rely on and they should always be linked to other red flags in the systems to which an individual has access.

RECOGNISING TRANSACTIONAL RED FLAGS

Modern working practices generate more transactions than ever before. Because of the speed with which business is carried out today and a drive for leaner, more efficient administrations, transactions tend to be looked at only once, if at all. The mountain of processed transactions which is left behind can now, due to rapidly declining electronic storage costs, present new opportunities for effective transaction monitoring.

'Transactional red flags' is the name for indicators which are buried within transactions, held on computer systems, or on paper documents or reports. Employees in risk areas such as procurement or payroll should receive specific training in recognising transactional red flags.

Depending on the profile of the organisation, there are usually hundreds of transactional red flags. Some typical ones include:

- unusual supplier relationships
- business partners, intermediaries and so on, which are in effect front companies
- non-transparent counterparties where indications of criminal association exist
- payments for goods and services where the description is unduly vague
- preferential supplier treatment and/or a lack of competitive tendering
- payments to offshore or tax-haven-based companies or bank accounts
- preferential customer treatment in terms of service, prices and so on
- receipt of potentially 'dirty money' payments
- hidden salaries or other employee benefits
- private expenses processed through expense claims (which is also a key behavioural indicator)
- poorly monitored profit and loss and balance sheet accounts.

Arguably the single largest red flag of fraud and corruption is where a company or bank account located in a tax haven is involved as some sort of vehicle. While the misuses can range from terrorist and arms financing to tax evasion, the more common red flags include:

- kickbacks paid to the management on the acquisition or disposal of a subsidiary using a tax haven vehicle
- company-controlled 'slush funds' and the payments of bribes to and from offshore companies (bribes are often politely referred to as 'marketing commissions')
- secret bonuses to top managers and executives which are most commonly paid into such accounts
- money ostensibly for bribes paid instead into executive and employee-controlled accounts (this is much more common than one would expect)
- tax evasion in the form of split salaries (for employees, consultants and sometimes also the company)
- hiding a conflicting ownership interest in suppliers, customers and business partners using a cascade of offshore companies to disguise the ownership.

A number of attempted frauds have been prevented because an employee spotted something unusual about a transaction. By identifying red flags in a process, it is possible to put in place early warning systems about the use of a particular method of fraud. For example, a number of financial institutions, which have been the victims of unauthorised transfers from corporate accounts, now monitor all employee requests to view account details – in order to detect someone who may be identifying potential high value accounts for fraudsters to target.

Red flags in a process arise from anomalies on documents or transactions. For example, red flags on payment instructions being processed through a bank payment centre include:

- unusual delivery of instruction, for example through the mail or by courier with an urgent processing request
- photocopied document or attachment

- unnecessary words or explanations on the instruction to try to make it seem more plausible
- appearance or style not consistent with normal transactions
- beneficiary name spelt incorrectly, mismatching with account number
- payment not consistent with the normal business of the customer.

Even though accounting and payment clerks are performing a routine activity with hundreds of transactions per day, they can sometimes spot these anomalies very quickly.

RECOGNISING SYSTEM RED FLAGS

The information technology department of an organisation can play an important role in monitoring for red flags in systems. Nearly all large, multinational organisations will have an IT security function which should routinely monitor for unauthorised access or processes. This monitoring should be linked to the behavioural and transactional red flags.

Systems red flags arise from monitoring routines built into computer and communication systems. They are a powerful means of detecting illicit behaviour. For example:

- someone logs in to a system using the user identification and password of an employee who is on leave; or attempts to log in if the password is disabled whilst the employee is on leave
- a higher than average number of failed logins
- login from areas outside normal work area
- login at unusual times of the day
- unusual network traffic
- controls or audit logs turned off.

The knowledge about which specific transaction or activity is being monitored should be restricted to the systems team, but knowledge that some monitoring is taking place (without the specifics) is a valuable deterrent.

RECOGNISING CORPORATE RED FLAGS

As the corporate collapses around the world have shown, many red flags were flying – indicating that companies were in trouble well before the collapses took place. For example in the book *Collapse Incorporated* (White, 2001), one of the authors lists a number of warning signs in one of the companies, which were evident as far back as two years prior to its collapse, including:

- investment analysts blacklisted by the company for writing negative reports
- concerns raised by regulators up to nine months before the collapse
- downgrading of the company's credit rating
- solvency warnings by the company's actuaries.

Yet no one acted upon them. Why? Because it appears no one was in a position to act upon them. Senior management appeared to have had the opposite interest; to suppress information, rather than reveal the truth. Similarly, when frauds involve fraudulent financial reporting by executive directors, it is sometimes very difficult for anyone to act, because the only people who could (for example the internal auditors) possess neither the authority nor the independence to effectively follow up on their concerns.

Potential corporate red flags indicating fraud, which we have regularly seen in organisations where we have subsequently uncovered senior management frauds, include:

- over-zealous acquisition strategies (without proper screening and due diligence)
- autocratic management decisions around business relationships, such as a refusal to change a major supplier
- losses and declining margins on sales
- artificial barriers put up by directors to avoid answering questions
- excessive secrecy
- rumours and low morale
- complacent finance director
- overriding of budgetary controls
- discrepancies and deviations
- missing records or lack of detail
- unusual manual payments or adjustments
- consultants given a free rein.

Some red flags could be indicative of an impending corporate collapse; this should trigger concerns that there may be some fraud associated with the decline in business. However, a red flag is not firm evidence that a fraud is occurring. Once a series of red flags have been identified, specific detection tests will still need to be designed and implemented to gather enough evidence to warrant a full-scale investigation. This is relatively straightforward if the problem lies at the employee level and the internal audit department has the charter to add detection tests to its normal audits.

The problem is more difficult to solve when corporate red flags suggest that the CEO is perpetrating a fraud in an organisation which has neither a strong internal audit function nor a strong, independent audit committee.

Corporate red flags are arguably the most difficult group on which to build a detection programme because they are difficult to interpret, so specialist training may need to be provided. Corporate red flags are often closely related to other behavioural and transactional red flags as the following example illustrates:

Example

Mr Cassandra, a sales manager, got wind of the fact that certain marketing expenses in the region of a few thousand euros were being put through the company's accounts. These were paid into a company in Cyprus which was clearly an offshore company. However, it was rumoured that this business was under the direction of the regional general manager, who was considered to be one of the more successful regional heads. There had always been a reluctance to audit his area in too much detail for fear of upsetting the status quo. To pacify the CFO and the head of internal audit, the marketing director had had a quiet word with the manager about his lavish expense accounts and rumours about his private purchases.

After several attempts to find someone who would take him seriously, Mr Cassandra raised his concerns with the head of internal audit who, using available accounting data, tried to ascertain some of the red flags. A large number were identified including:

- *A large variety of payments made to one company for marketing, events, building works and printing; this company did not appear to be registered or even exist.*
- *The senior management's travel and other expenses included a number of apparent private purchases.*
- *Sales were made to one major wholesale customer at discounts much higher than any other customer. The wholesale customer was ultimately controlled by an offshore company which had nominee directors and secret owners.*
- *The primary service partner was also controlled by an offshore company, coincidentally at the same address as the offshore company which controlled the large wholesale customer.*

Discussions with corporate controllers revealed that on repeated trips to the region they had noticed the unusual behaviour of the regional general manager and his team including a reluctance to allow the controllers to ask questions directly to accounting and administrative staff. One of the controllers commented that he found it extremely hard to understand how the results were so good. He used the expression 'too good to be true'.

After a follow-up investigation which also included interviews with the key persons believed to be involved it was revealed that:

- *The regional general manager, as well as some members of his team, were actually controlling the key suppliers and the wholesale customer.*
- *Some bribes disguised as consultancy fees were paid to key customers in the public and private sector. Many of these bribes were paid via offshore companies.*
- *Results had been manipulated and sales figures inflated for years. Losses had been hidden or buried.*
- *Employees that had protested against the abuses were either moved or sacked, and on at least one occasion, threatened physically.*

Most of the management team confessed to some sort of involvement in the schemes saying that that they had believed the regional general manager. However, he refused to admit that he had put a foot wrong. On one occasion he staunchly defended his purchase of a €600 coat at an airport, saying that he had left his in the taxi and needed a new one. After all he was the general manager. When he was asked why he actually bought a women's coat he simply refused to answer!

Because of the swift action taken to discover and interpret the red flags, a turnaround replacement management team was able to redress most of the major problems within six months.

SPOT THE RED FLAGS – TEST YOURSELF

Given that red flags are usually there to be discovered, we have provided some scenarios below to test your ability to spot them. Scenarios like these should be used in training and awareness programmes.

Often red flags of possible fraud, corruption and abuse of the company's policy may not be immediately apparent. See if you can spot the possible red flags of fraud and corruption in the following four scenarios. Answers can be found in Appendix 6.

Test yourself: Scenario 1

Three years ago the newly appointed 43-year-old CEO had unveiled at a number of internal and external events the new corporate strategy, which included the statement as follows:

In order to maintain our competitive advantage we are required to invest and capitalise on opportunities in developing markets as well as consolidate our home market. If we apply our strategy of partnership, acquisition and of course internal innovation, I predict that in three years' time we will achieve our growth target of 170 per cent whilst 60 per cent of our business will be abroad compared to the 30 per cent today.

As of today very little mention is made of these statements and these targets have not been met by any means. Growth has been 150 per cent and the ratio of domestic to foreign business is 60:40. The CEO has stated that this is in fact a very creditable achievement considering that there was unpredictable downturn in the market. Less mention is made, however of the rising costs which can be attributed to higher entry costs to the developing markets, but also rising operating costs both domestically and abroad. There is very little discussion about this in the company. Press releases for the past six months have been in accordance with the CEO's upbeat statements like 'We need to look forward, not back.' However there is an ongoing tax audit into the nature of certain agency payments. Only one investment analyst wrote a negative report pointing out impending collapse and the rumoured resignation of the CEO, but this did not significantly affect the share price of the company.

The CEO himself has made a number of public appearances both at home and aboard and portrays a very positive picture of the growth and development of the company. Although he is not flamboyant, a well-acclaimed article about his newly built luxury home, complete with original artwork, was featured in a leading lifestyle magazine. In the interview, which appeared in the article, the CEO stated that aspects of his house and lifestyle demonstrated and reflected the positive spirit of the company.

The joint venture investment in one country has been divested at a very low price, only 17 months after its heralded opening. A lawsuit is ongoing with the local partners although it seems that there is little chance of recoveries.

The CEO has also assumed a number of non-executive posts on the boards of other public companies both at home and abroad. Some of these appointments have been well publicised in the press as has been his bonus package and also the terms of his golden handshake should his contract be prematurely terminated.

If you had a corporate crystal ball what red flags do you see which indicate risks further down the road?

_____

_____

_____

_____

(Answers are shown in Appendix 6.)

Test yourself: Scenario 2

Your company is the market leader in a particular segment in Region X and works closely with local partners.

Recently there has been a special focus on a joint campaign to boost customer loyalty in the face of mounting competition. The loyalty campaign is aimed at ensuring that the majority of re-sellers and partners push your company's product as the prime brand.

You have joined a marketing brainstorming round table. Representatives from the partners and resellers, the local company, legal advisors and your corporate public relations and marketing agency are present.

One idea which gains popularity involves the use of a competition for resellers, whereby those that reach certain sales targets will be awarded prizes. Prizes will consist of premium brand watches, and at the top end, free holidays. This competition is to be funded by your company in the name of marketing support. The local representative chips in that he has a healthy relationship with the travel agency and that 'maybe they are able to contribute the free holidays since we put a lot of business their way?' Apparently this scheme has been very successful in a couple of other regions.

It is pointed out by legal advisors to you that the competition would still technically have to be called a lottery, otherwise the prizes would be seen as a personal taxable benefit. Also, even though this was a technicality, each reseller would only be eligible for a prize in a lottery so that there could be no insinuations of bribery of customers at a later stage.

The local representative, although on the face of it is enthusiastic about the idea, asks for a separate meeting with you to discuss it.

What red flags do you see which indicate that the whole proposal should be examined more closely?

_____

_____

_____

_____

(Answers are shown in Appendix 6.)

Test yourself: Scenario 3

The internal network is protected by a firewall which was set up at considerable expense. Two systems in particular are considered highly sensitive, for different reasons, namely the central payments and treasury system and the technical development master data.

In recent weeks logging into the network has taken longer and longer which led ultimately to a system crash. Although no critical data appear to have been lost and the situation has been rectified, the network was down for a total of three days, two of which luckily were the weekend.

The IT specialists who were called in to help resolve the situation produced a close-out report which included the remarks extracted below:

Extract from report of the IT specialists

- *3 Internet connections which circumvented the firewall were discovered. One of these was in the human resources department and two in the technical development areas. These have been temporarily disconnected.*
- *There have been repeated attempts, some unsuccessful, to send large file attachments containing technical data. It appears that Hotmail and Yahoo addresses have been used to send the data which, due to the restrictions on the size of attachments, may have been the reason for the lack of success.*
- *It was noticed that user IDs in the payments department were left logged in all day. Sometimes the same user ID was logged in up to 4 times concurrently.*
- *The 30-day forced change of password feature has been turned off. According to the IT Manager he received too many complaints that persons, especially in sensitive and critical functions, could not remember their passwords.*

To what extent some of these anomalies contributed towards the system crash is yet to be determined.

What system red flags do you spot here?

_____

_____

_____

_____

(Answers are shown in Appendix 6.)

Test yourself: Scenario 4

For the past 10 years all repair and maintenance work has been carried out by a local building contractor. The argument for this is that the company needs to be local and since they have always done a good job then there was no reason to change supplier.

Recently, however this supplier was a lead entrepreneur in a new construction project. There were some delays and the project costs were 27 per cent over the original budget. At the outset, putting it out to tender was considered, but the facilities manager had been strongly in favour of a bid waiver because of the preferred supplier's local knowledge of the site. Afterwards when asked by internal audit whether with hindsight he felt the job could have been done cheaper if there had been a competitive tender, he replied that 'Budget overruns are not uncommon and there is no cause for concern. The end product is better than expected.'

Two of the many project invoices are shown in Figures 5.3 and 5.4.

It has been rumoured that the step-daughter of the facilities manager helps out in the administration department on Saturday and the nephew of the supplier's project manager has had summer jobs at the company.

XIX CONSTRUCTION CONSULTANTS
Riverside House, Brookdale, Rutland RX4 7HY

To:
YZW Corporation
28 Queens Road
London
W1 3QZ

Date: 27/01/0X	Terms of payment: Immediate	Invoice no: N⁰ **A200X0045**

Eagle Landing Project – Site works – prepayment in in accordance with contract # 200X9876374	£50.000
Please instruct your bank to pay directly without any intermediary bank, by SWIFT to Findlays Bank, Douglas, Isle of Man	
Total	£ 50.000

For payments in GBP

XIX Service Ltd   Findlays Bank (Douglas)
                         ACC. NO 70001324
                         SWIFT: FBCCEH

Figure 5.3   Project invoice #1

XIX CONSTRUCTION SERVICES
Riverside House, Brookdale, Rutland RX4 7HY

To:
YZW Corporation
28 Queens Road
London
W1 3QZ

Date:	02/03/0X	Terms of payment:	14 days	Invoice no:

N⍛ A200X0054

Eagle Landing Project – Site works (contract # 200X9876374)

120 hours @ £80	£9600
43 hours @ £56	£2408
Materials:	£2169
Ancillary charges	£1200

Please instruct your bank to pay directly without any
intermediary bank, by SWIFT to Findlays Bank, Douglas,
Isle of Man

Total	£ 15376

For payments in GBP

XIX Construction Ltd   Findlays Bank (Douglas)
                             ACC. NO 70221583
                             SWIFT: FBCCEH

Figure 5.4   Project invoice #2

What red flags of potential fraud and corruption do you see?

_____

_____

_____

_____

(Answers are shown in Appendix 6.)

FOLLOW-UP ACTIONS

It is important that once employees have been trained to look for red flags they then need to be made aware of the follow-up action should they have a concern. It is vital that concerns are reported upwards because the last thing the organisation needs is for employees to leap to a conclusion about a colleague which turns out to be completely the wrong answer.

Historically, line managers have been given the responsibility to make their own decisions about how they respond to a concern about the behaviour of a particular employee. A position often taken by senior management has been that managers are paid to manage, and therefore they must make decisions. This is fine if the employee has a personal or work-related problem, but not so good if the employee is involved in, or is planning a fraud, because:

- Managers may mistakenly believe that they understand the problem (for example, if they know that the employee is having trouble at home), and so they do not dig any deeper to uncover a more serious problem.
- Few managers have any training in interview techniques which would identify deception: when the fraudster is questioned, providing he or she acts in a friendly, affable manner, a plausible explanation will usually be accepted without further follow up.
- A senior manager may treat an employee who is making lots of money for the company completely differently from a junior clerk who is seen as dispensable. In some cases this has extended to ignoring minor cases of fraud.

We have found that a useful way to illustrate the issue is to ask employees to complete the following exercise.

Changes in behaviour
Please indicate how you would view the following changes in behaviour in another employee whom you know very well both at work and socially. You know he earns $30 000 per year. Over the past few months:

- *he has changed his office routine – regularly accesses the network on a different workstation to his normal one;*
- *he has started working long hours – even volunteers for overtime;*
- *he frequently goes outside to use a mobile;*
- *he has bought a new top-of-the-range BMW and has had an expensive extension added to his house. You have heard that he has three children in private schools;*

- when you asked him about the car, he said that a rich aunt had died and left him a lot of money;
- you heard him borrowing the passwords of colleagues because he wanted to process things in a hurry.

Remember, you like and trust the employee. Select the option in Table 5.2 below which most closely matches what you would think.

Table 5.2   Options

Please select the option closest to what you would think	Circle your option below
I believe the story about the aunt dying – I know and like the employee and he would not do anything dishonest	A
He must be stealing money from the organisation or somewhere else to fund an expensive lifestyle	B
He must be dealing in drugs	C
The red flags would cause me concern but I would not assume I knew what the cause was	D

In most workshops we have run, it is common to find there is an even split between Options A and D. However, some cynical senior managers choose Option B, and one call centre workshop we ran, which comprised mainly employees under 25, over 50 per cent immediately chose Option C.

The important point to impart to employees is that with the information provided, Option D is the only real choice. He may be borrowing the money, or be a shrewd investor or has indeed had a rich aunt die, or he could be dealing in drugs or stealing. The occurrence of behavioural red flags may be for one of many different underlying reasons: stress at work, personal or medical conditions, family problems, drug or alcohol abuse as well as potential criminal activity; all can cause changes in someone's behaviour or lifestyle. A number of frauds have occurred whereby employees, who were depressed, developed gambling addictions which eventually led to them feeding their habit using company funds.

Having identified that there are some red flags, employees should not rely solely on intuition, gut feel or personal liking for a colleague when assessing the nature of the problem. Follow-up actions to resolve a concern about someone's mental health are totally different to actions taken about someone who is about to commit a major fraud. Premature actions could alert fraudsters, or they could cause a severe adverse reaction in a person who is mentally unwell. In these situations, employees must report concerns, usually through their line manager or, if it involves their line manager, must use a whistle-blowing procedure.

Fraud-awareness sessions should be run alongside sessions which cover the symptoms of depression and other mental illnesses and how they should be followed up.

It is also important that there is close cooperation between support functions such as human resources, and enforcement or control functions such as security or internal audit to ensure that follow up and resolution of red flags is consistent across the organisation in order to protect innocent employees from unnecessary suspicion, as well as protecting the organisation from a potential fraudster or corrupt individual.

Managers should also have some guidance as to:

- what they can do themselves to obtain further information, such as sources and restrictions
- who to contact to obtain further information – human resources, security, audit or external providers such as investigating companies
- escalation procedures – as defined in an incident response plan
- rules for gathering evidence, particularly from computers.

Corporate health check

NOTION OF A HEALTH CHECK

Fraud detection programmes have been used in companies, over the past few years, with varying degrees of success. This may be because some of the tests used were unnecessarily technical or complex, or because the results were never understood, or simply because the programme itself was not properly supported at the top of the organisation. Without the full support and understanding of senior management any programme aimed at detecting fraud and corruption will usually fail.

In the eyes of the average employee or manager the word detection can conjure up notions of spying on the employees behind their backs and delving into their private affairs. Names like 'fraud detection programme', 'continuous monitoring, or 'penetration audit' can trigger negative associations of intrusion and a culture of fear, which can harm the credibility of the programme.

Modern attitudes call for a more proactive, open and all-inclusive programme, hence the name 'corporate health check'.

Rather like a medical health check, the principle objective of a corporate health check is to test for those indicators which are hidden below the surface in order to proactively identify and root out the red flags of fraud and corruption. This contrasts with and complements awareness programmes, which train people to react once they spot red flags during the course of their normal work. Red flags identified in awareness sessions comprise only the visible signs of fraud and corruption at any particular moment in time. The corporate health check probes much deeper looking at transactions and patterns, that is, the actual footprint of fraud and corruption. It provides intelligence for further investigation to uncover hard evidence. The emphasis is on prevention and early detection.

A corporate health check complements any internal audit programme and can become a routine part of corporate life. It can be applied to an entire organisation or company, a division, a single department or subsidiary, or even to just one process within the organisation.

A properly performed corporate health check will provide extremely valuable information to financial controllers, internal auditors, risk managers, corporate security, human resources and not least the executive management. However, it is important to recognise that a corporate health check can only work within a climate of transparency and integrity.

Therefore, before a corporate health check programme is launched, it is crucial to obtain as broad a base of support as possible at the top of the company. This will help avoid resistance later on and in itself will help to contribute towards a more honest and open culture.

The sponsors of a corporate health check should be the executive management, endorsed by the non-executive board, and supported by business units such as procurement, sales support, accounting, legal and human resources.

The executors of the corporate health check could be corporate security, corporate internal audit, risk management, corporate financial controllers, or best of all, a team which combines representatives from each of these functions. The greater the buy-in to the concept of a corporate health check, the greater the chance of success.

When a corporate health check is carried out, expectations will vary considerably. At all stages the expected nature of the findings should be communicated clearly to all persons involved. The importance of a broad base of management support is demonstrated by the following experiences:

Experience 1
During a corporate health check, it was discovered that very substantial payments had been made to an intermediary run by a person with links to organised crime, operating from the cover of a tax haven. When the findings were raised, people from the division concerned displayed outrage, stating that the person concerned was a legitimate businessman with whom they 'had eaten dinner several times'. The division also tried to discredit the corporate health check, saying that the findings were misleading; and the programme was put on hold for two years until the true facts emerged.

Experience 2
A corporate health check which examined the behaviour of fifty senior managers was quietly discontinued when it was discovered that over 25 per cent of the managers had benefits from outside undisclosed business interests. This was on top of the fact that a number of managers were often submitting wholly inappropriate or private business expense claims.

Experience 3
When indications of price fixing and cartels were discovered with the help of a corporate health check of sales and marketing, management decided that the internal auditors had probably 'gone too far'.

Experience 4
Three round-sum million-dollar payments to a front company and numbered account should have been enough to indicate that systematic bribes (incidentally contravening the company code of conduct) were being paid. The marketing department furiously defended these payments as legitimate agency fees and dismissed the corporate health check findings as 'trivial'.

Although these reactions may seem a little unusual, they are typical of managers when confronted with a problem in their own territory. In other words, when the problem is ours, we often become defensive.

It is a fact that people simply don't like being watched or monitored. Therefore the corporate health check has to be introduced and performed with sensitivity and care.

Sometimes a corporate health check is not politically acceptable to senior management. The reasons for this can include a fear of the unknown, a dislike of intrusive testing or even a reluctance to lay their past transactions and behaviours open to scrutiny. It is the fear or chance that inappropriate transactions and behaviours will be discovered which can lead to a corporate health check being delayed or even put off indefinitely.

The ability of persons trying to undermine the programme should not be underestimated. Typical counter-arguments to performing a corporate health check include:

- 'The corporate health check infringes on human rights and data protection legislation. We want our people to believe that they can be trusted so we don't want to spy on them.'
- 'Fraud and corruption is a next generation issue, not something we have to deal with now.'
- 'We have an awareness programme so why do we need to do more.'
- 'We already have auditors so why do we need a corporate health check?'

It is important to anticipate these objections and the reasons for them. The fear factor and the perceived intrusiveness can be addressed fairly easily. A corporate health check should always be a non-intrusive and non-disruptive process where the subject is involved throughout the process. In addition the corporate health check should comply with data protection or human rights legislation, as well as be in full compliance with company policies and employee relations agreements. Furthermore, legislation will vary considerably from jurisdiction to jurisdiction. Therefore it is advisable either to begin the corporate health check in areas which clearly have no relation to individuals or to take appropriate legal advice at the start.

SETTING AIMS AND OBJECTIVES

The aim of a corporate health check is to identify symptoms of fraud and corruption as early as possible. The objectives also need to be clearly defined. The following are typical objectives of a corporate health check:

- It should target those fraud and corruption risks which have the highest impact on the business and provide warnings of ongoing fraud and corruption as early as possible.
- Tests should be repeatable across the organisation and provide results which are consistent, comparable and easy to classify and act upon.
- Specially trained persons within the company should perform the corporate health check.
- It should be integrated with the work of the internal audit, corporate security or risk management functions.
- It should not lead to, or raise, any false alarms.
- It should avoid contentious data protection issues by focussing on data which cannot be classified as personal data.
- It should be equally applicable to the whole organisation, a division, a single department or subsidiary, or to one process within the organisation.

HOW A CORPORATE HEALTH CHECK WORKS

The five steps below summarize how a corporate health check is done:

- Understand the risks of fraud and corruption, document them in a fraud and corruption profile and then identify what sort of footprint would be left behind if each method was used.
- Decide where to collect data and information and build a model.
- Select which tests to apply, run the tests and summarise the results in the form of a diagnostic report.
- Interpret and understand the diagnostics report and run further tests if deemed necessary.
- Perform preliminary research into the findings, evaluate them and decide on the next steps.

Just as with any form of health check, a wide range of equipment, tools and techniques can be used. However it is wise to be selective, as the more tools used the greater the volume of information generated, not to mention the cost. If you have a good idea what you are looking for, the scope and extent of the corporate health check can be much narrower. A well developed fraud and corruption profile is the key to knowing what to test for.

A corporate health check provides the insider's view of the extent of fraud and corruption in the company. It is true to say that raised awareness together with the health check will still probably not uncover every instance of actual fraud and corruption. However, interpretation of the results combined with the use of a well developed fraud and corruption profile makes it much easier to target those areas where the company is most exposed. Fraud and corruption is often a function of the culture of an organisation. If it is in one area it is likely to be in others. Therefore it is not necessary to look absolutely everywhere. Unethical behaviour in one area of the business often leaves its footprint in another area.

WHERE TO USE THE CORPORATE HEALTH CHECK

The corporate health check can be used for example to identify:

- signs of procurement fraud and relationships with potentially unsuitable business partners
- unusual payments to front companies and offshore destinations
- symptoms of overspending
- signs of repeat fraud
- collective customer arrangements and other unhealthy customer relationships and potential employee conflicts of interests
- deliberate misstatements.

Because many of the tests used are in fact a way of testing the culture within the business, a well-designed corporate health check will often also identify problems related to management's investment and divestments strategy and other inappropriate business behaviours.

A typical template is provided in Appendix 7 showing how a corporate health check can be designed and constructed, by focussing on the major risks and developing key tests. For illustration purposes we have also provided some examples of the findings.

A number of international companies have already used corporate health checks as a way of improving their testing for the symptoms of fraud and corruption. One of the lessons learnt has been that rather than using too many tests, more time should be spent in interpreting and classifying the results. Also, it is important to hold back from investigating red flags as they are uncovered. Often a health check will throw up a large number of symptoms which can, if not properly analysed and understood, be easily misinterpreted. It is only by clearly defining, then grouping and analysing the symptoms that the problems can be properly diagnosed. Those companies which have been doing this are now becoming more and more self-sufficient and are able to perform several health checks a year with very impressive results.

When a company-wide corporate health check is carried out we usually see one of the two following diagnoses:

- There are just a few isolated symptoms of fraud and corruption.
- There are numerous incidents of fraud and corruption, often at many levels in the company or division, touching the upper echelons.

Once the symptoms have been analysed they can then be grouped, analysed again and various treatments proposed. Treatments will include emergency fixes, longer-term changes to procedures and in some cases more in-depth investigation of certain potential problems. An extract from a typical diagnostic report from a corporate health check is provided in Appendix 8. This was performed on external payments across over 1 million transactions over a 14-month period.

Specialist training should be provided so that internal departments can carry out health checks. Asking one simple question could uncover a major fraud, but only if the question is asked correctly. We believe that for external or internal audits to be more effective, auditors should receive training in how to detect specific methods of fraud.

Example

Using some of the simplest fraud detection tests, we discovered several paid invoices. One invoice was for work done in the USA, but the company's bank account was in the Cayman Islands (and also the amount of $49 799 seemed unusual for unspecified work). There also were strong indications that the US-based supplier was in fraudulent collusion with a locally based project manager, but was skilful at hiding it from the head office.

The head office of the company paying the invoice was in Scandinavia. Internal rules stipulated that the project manager had to fax the invoice for approval. The cost centre manager at head office was asked why he had approved these invoices for payment. He responded:

'I have so many of these invoices to look at that to be totally honest I don't get the time to really look at them. I remember this one however because I thought it a bit odd that we were paying money for an American supplier into a Cayman bank. I even called an accountant that I knew in the shared service and asked him if we could actually pay these invoices to the Cayman Islands. He answered that there was no problem whatsoever and they had done it many times before. On reflection, I think he misunderstood my question...'

Statistical and trend analyses may provide an indication of where fraud and corruption are hidden. However, in order to actually find them, someone has to look at the details. Complex tests require extensive interpretation of results, while thorough application of simple tests tends to consistently deliver useful results.

However, as the powerful example below demonstrates, a corporate health check will only work when management ceases to ignore the symptoms:

Example

The marketing department of an international company X had for the past ten years been using a single supplier for all marketing and corporate events. This supply company had been incorporated by two people round about the same time as the contract commenced. On average the company had doubled its turnover every year and was now about 40 persons strong. Approximately 70–90 per cent of this supplier's turnover each year had originated from X. One year's spend alone was around €10 million.

The marketing department resented any intrusion in its affairs by what they called 'outsiders' (which included the corporate procurement team and corporate internal audit) and for ten years managed to carry on their affairs as they liked. They were supported throughout by an executive director who agreed with them that marketing was such a specialised area that corporate procurement could not possibly understand the intricacies of choosing a supplier. Their involvement would only add to the costs.

Corporate internal audit noticed these indicators and conducted a corporate health check on paid invoices and supporting documentation in the accounts payable department. It was quickly discovered that:

- *The supplier had been awarded work without any competitive tendering for over 10 years.*
- *There were no contracts for what should have been provided, who should provide it and what sort of mark-up the supplier should have made on their bought-in services.*
- *Pro forma purchase orders were created based on old invoices as a way of giving the impression that a procurement process had taken place. These purchase orders were usually dated some days or weeks after the supplier's invoices.*
- *The supplier submitted a large number of very vaguely specified invoices which in fact hid mark-ups of subcontractor costs (which were in excess of 200 per cent) or in some cases, were wholly fictitious.*

This was in addition to red flags such as:

- *The marketing department staunchly resisted involving the procurement department (procurement department personnel were too scared to act and felt they had no channel to communicate their concerns).*
- *No projects in marketing were put out to competitive tender.*
- *A senior member of the management team supported the marketing department's practices.*
- *The supplier had doubled its turnover each year but still was reliant on the company for approximately 90 per cent of its business.*

However, as is often the case, people in X, including the auditors, assumed that a logical explanation for all these symptoms had to exist. The fact that the situation had been ongoing for so long supported the theory that 'if something was wrong then something would have been done already'.

Five years later, another corporate health check of the accounts payable area was performed. Once more, major red flags and a number of other ones cropped up. However, this time the new CFO set about trying to understand why the situation had endured so out of control and why his policies and procedures were being ignored. Probably most importantly, before taking action he managed to quantify what cost-savings could be made by doing things the way he had expected things to be done.

Six months after the second corporate health check was performed the end result could be summarised as follows:

- *A substantial refund was obtained from the supplier.*
- *New procurement experts were brought into to work alongside the marketing department and after a competitive tendering process new suppliers were identified.*
- *It was estimated that cost savings in the future were in the region of 30–50 per cent.*
- *Several organisational changes were made.*
- *The case caused a number of waves in the organisation and the example was taken up repeatedly in training and awareness workshops as an illustration as to how bad things can get if the organisation does not recognise the risks of fraud and corruption.*

The above case example illustrates how important it is to recognise the importance of not just identifying the symptoms but also understanding what they are telling us and acting upon them.

GETTING STARTED

Before getting started on corporate health checks we should provide a word of caution. The person doing the tests should be able to think creatively as well as be able to use analysis software, otherwise the output may be so huge as to be useless. Many financial institutions, for example, have successfully implemented automated fraud detection software using artificial intelligence and neural network technology to detect suspicious credit card transactions. Some organisations have attempted to mirror this for detection of corporate fraud in procurement systems, by installing specialist data-mining software. The software alone has then produced many hundreds of red flags which cannot possibly be followed up in the time available to the auditor.

The flaw lies not in the software itself, but in the approach that is applied. Experience has shown that only up to 20 per cent of fraud detection time should be spent using the computer and doing data-analysis. The rest of the time requires:

- the person implementing the detection programme first thinking like a fraudster in order to understand what frauds are most likely, and then developing a fraud profile which is endorsed by senior management – a healthy suspicious mind is needed
- the person thinking before using a computer – automated fraud detection software is generally a poor substitute for thinking
- looking for the simple tests – then the results usually are understandable
- understanding what 'footprints' would be left behind
- dedication to following things through and attention to the sort of details which management usually does not have time to deal with
- spending time evaluating and researching existing findings – much more important than producing hundreds of new findings.

When something looks like a fraud – evidence should be obtained by examining the details.

No assumptions or gut-feel decisions should be made. Pitfalls which can and should be avoided include:

- relying too much on the computer to do the work and not using enough intelligence and judgement in interpreting the results; the degree of automation can be gradually increased as time goes by and experience is gained
- creating a wall of opposition by delving at an early stage into sensitive areas, such as senior manager's lifestyles and personal interests in companies; this can be dealt with later if and when it becomes a problem
- over-reacting to individual symptoms raised by the corporate health check and then going out into the organisation and demanding explanations (or worse still making accusations) before reviewing all symptoms first
- when looking at symptoms, assuming that there must be a logical explanation without actually looking for that explanation (humans have a natural tendency to believe or hope for the best).

We suggest that you approach getting started with corporate health checks along the following lines:

- Use the initial time to go through the methodology, review your objectives and then develop a framework for how the corporate health check programme will be piloted and rolled out.
- Decide which internal people will become your corporate health check experts and what basic skills they should acquire. Broadly speaking the following skills are necessary:

  - understanding the methodology itself
  - knowing how to define and collect the required data
  - knowing how to conduct data analysis, using fast international desktop research such as metasearching and various online databases, to quickly sift through and prioritise the findings.

- Begin by looking at payments and purchasing, moving into receipts and sales. This targets the money flows from and to the company and opens up many potential areas of abuse. In this way you can also steer clear of any contentious personal data issues.
- Prototype the corporate health check system on one region, department or country and then refine and improve it and move to the next target.
- Review, refine and roll out the system. Parts of the computerised testing of transactions can now be automated.

Summary of key points

- Investing in monitoring and detection can lead to a significant reduction in losses from fraud and corruption.
- All employees should receive fraud awareness training.
- The fraud and corruption awareness programme should have the backing of the CEO and board.

- Training should be interactive, interesting, and based on real-life case studies.
- Employees should be trained to spot red flags, including changes in behaviour, transactions, systems and corporate activities. This training should link into human resource awareness sessions on the symptoms of depression and other mental illness, and on follow up actions.
- A programme to carry out corporate health checks should be approved by the board and audit committee.
- Corporate health checks should be carried out by trained company employees and overseen by a senior manager who is sensitive to the political, ethical and legal issues which may arise, but possesses enough determination not to be put off by resistance from the top.

6 *Managing Incidents*

Navigating the minefields of investigations

Although we have placed great emphasis on prevention in the previous chapters, an organisation cannot totally eliminate the risks of fraud and corruption. Even with a strong fraud risk management strategy, a determined individual may still find a way to perpetrate a fraud.

The anti-fraud and -corruption programme would not be complete without the ability to report, control and manage incidents. Whether investigations are outsourced or undertaken in house, it is important that the guiding principles and rules for conducting them are properly documented and agreed at the top of the organisation.

Here we set out some of the fundamental issues which need to be considered when conducting an investigation into suspected fraud and corruption as well as some of the mistakes to avoid.

It is vital that the response is planned because every investigation is a minefield of potential problems for the inexperienced or over-eager investigator. When a potential fraud is first discovered, the immediate hours or days following can be very confusing and stressful if the organisation is unprepared. Experience has shown that managers handle the same problem in different ways – sometimes with disastrous consequences. Also some incidents, such as detecting an attempted smash-and-grab type, high-value fraud, may leave little time to prevent the money clearing.

If the fraud is ongoing, premature actions could alert the perpetrators, allowing them to destroy evidence. Uncoordinated investigations by untrained personnel could taint evidence, prejudice witnesses and upset honest employees. The result can be legal actions, inability to recover stolen funds, and damage to reputation.

It is relatively straightforward to formulate a contingency plan to ensure that incidents are escalated and investigated in a consistent and uniform manner across an organisation. Most large organisations have formed crisis management teams to respond to major incidents (such as a fire or a flood), so it is not uncommon for the fraud and corruption response plan to link directly into the business continuity plan.

We discussed in Chapter 3, how responsibilities for reporting incidents of suspected fraud and corruption are usually laid down in a fraud and corruption policy. This should result in all reports being directed to a central location so that they can be handled in a consistent manner. The fraud and corruption response plan should then include:

- a policy statement containing names of persons who will initially evaluate the reports and grade incidents
- the criteria for the plan's activation, which typically include the size of the potential loss, the complexity and nature of the fraud and the potential impact on an organisation's reputation

- the composition of the response team, for example CFO, head of the affected business unit, head of legal and audit committee member
- escalation procedures and reporting lines to all stakeholders
- co-opted members such as IT, security, HR, legal, audit and communications
- contact numbers for external service providers such as investigators, external lawyers, police, telecommunications agencies and forensic services.

Some larger organisations require that where an employee discovers a potential fraud, it must be reported to internal audit, legal and compliance, or increasingly these days, to an ethics committee, which in turn hands the matter to an internal department to investigate. However, as a number of organisations have found out, some incidents of fraud and corruption have impacts far beyond the remit of an audit or security manager to deal with (for example when a company's reputation is threatened, or the fraud is being committed by the CEO and CFO).

It is increasingly common, even for large organisations, that once an initial evaluation has been made which suggests a potential large fraud has been perpetrated, the management of the investigation is handed over to a professional firm of investigators working with external litigation lawyers. This is an effective and sound approach because the laws and evidential requirements surrounding a major investigation, particularly one that is multi-jurisdictional, are complex and constantly changing. Consequently, opinions as to the legality of investigation techniques and presentation of evidence need to be regularly updated.

The other strong reason for using experienced professionals is that investigations are usually difficult, time consuming and stressful. By using their experience, investigators will often follow up leads which an in-house auditor or manager will ignore or not recognise. Also, they will always look for different routes to obtain evidence, whereas an untrained person will commonly only use one route and if that fails, the investigation grinds to a halt.

Many experienced investigators are cynical and suspicious by nature. These can be useful traits when it comes to dealing with people who are lying. Good investigators are also tenacious and determined. When engaging investigators, as with using any consultant, the golden rule is that individuals should be retained for their proven investigation skills and reputation, rather than just because the firm is well known. Having already developed a relationship with a high degree of trust and respect rather than one where there is continual suspicion about the size of the invoices or investigative techniques used will mean that a difficult, protracted investigation is more likely to succeed. This is especially important should the investigation uncover fraud or corruption at the highest level of the organisation, when intense pressure may be brought to bear to close the investigation down or to discredit the evidence or investigators.

In these instances, internal staff responsible for the investigation would have to display a high degree of personal strength and determination to see it through to a satisfactory conclusion, knowing also that their own careers are potentially on the line. Using reputable and experienced investigators should ease some of the unnecessary stress.

Ground rules for investigations

A typical reaction of an executive when faced with the symptoms of fraud and corruption is to tackle the problem head-on and try to solve it immediately by confronting the suspect and demanding explanations for the allegations which have been made. This is perfectly understandable, particularly if the suspect is a senior manager who has been known for a long time. However, it is usually a futile exercise because, in the absence of overwhelming evidence, the suspect will simply deny the allegations. This is especially true if the fraudster has any elements of a psychopathic personality and so will not display any hint of stress or emotion, but will present an entirely convincing explanation. The executive will then have tipped off the suspect, allowing time to alter or destroy evidence or even try to point the blame at somebody else.

The most important rule of any investigation is that you should not make any overt move if you only have intelligence suggesting that a fraud has occurred, but have no evidence.

Example

Following the receipt of anonymous letters alleging that a senior purchasing manager had been taking kickbacks from a supplier in exchange for awarding large contracts, the CEO of an organisation authorised an investigation into the manager's activities. The investigators recommended that a range of covert techniques be used. However, when the director to whom the manager reported heard about the letters, he demanded that he be given the opportunity to discuss them with the manager whom he had known for 14 years and whom he trusted implicitly. Against the strong advice of the investigators, he did confront the manager who emphatically denied everything and suggested that the letters were malicious. The director was satisfied with his explanations.

*   What the CEO did not tell the director was that after consulting the company's legal advisers, he had authorised that a tape recorder be placed on the manager's office telephone. The first thing that the manager did when he had finished his interview with the director was to go to his office and telephone a supplier to discuss the allegations and how they would need to cover up and get rid of any evidence.*

Evidence should be gathered covertly before any overt move is made, and the two stages should not be mixed. The following simple strategy, as shown in Figure 6.1, illustrates the approach.

Each potential incident of fraud and corruption, whatever its size, should be reviewed as if it could be a piece of a more complex puzzle.

A vertical line representing time should be drawn on a blank piece of paper. Halfway down the page, a horizontal line should be drawn. This is the line of discretion separating the overt and covert phases of an investigation. Informants and witnesses only should be spoken to during the covert phase. No suspects, internal or external should be confronted or otherwise alerted until the company is ready to cross the line. To the left-hand side of the vertical line, sources of relevant information inside the company (invoices, contracts, key persons and so on) should be listed. To the right-hand side, external sources of evidence and intelligence should be listed. Once the covert stage has produced sufficient evidence, then legal advice should be obtained prior to moving to the overt stage.

There are a large number of internal and external sources of evidence and intelligence which can be legally obtained and used in an investigation (Comer, 2003). An experienced, professional investigator would always consider all potential sources of information, giving special consideration as to whether they should be used covertly or overtly.

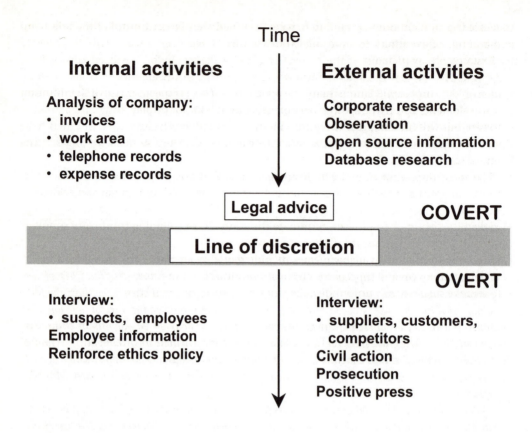

Figure 6.1   Investigation strategy

There must be no jumping back and forth between the overt and covert stage. The important point to remember is that all the techniques used in the investigation should have been approved by both top management and the company's lawyers.

Once the first overt move is made, experience has shown that if the fraudster is an ordinary employee with no psychopathic tendencies, then a carefully structured and well-planned interview will normally result in a confession. If the fraudster is tipped off or interviewed too early in the investigation, then typically the perpetrator's lawyer will attend the interview and advise the client not to say anything. The investigator in reality gets one chance at obtaining a confession.

Timing the overt move also means that simultaneous interviews can be carried out, including employees, suppliers and other relevant parties, which reduces the risk that suspects can get together to work out their stories or to hide or destroy evidence.

Setting objectives and realistic expectations

An unplanned investigation with no clear objectives can quickly waste considerable resources and money on fruitless enquiries, so objectives should be agreed beforehand. By setting objectives and having a clear plan of action, senior management can demonstrate to stakeholders that although a fraud may have occurred, they are in control of the follow-up and that full recovery actions are going to be taken.

Objectives may include:

- to control the immediate situation, continue business operations with minimum disruption and restore the business to normality as quickly as possible
- to minimise loss or damage and maintain business confidence
- to maintain effective communications internally, and with customers, the media and other stakeholders
- to uncover the full extent of the fraud and corruption and all the persons involved
- to determine why existing controls did not prevent the fraud and enhance them where necessary
- to dismiss dishonest employees, terminate the contracts of colluding third-party suppliers or contractors, and prosecute all the perpetrators
- to recover losses by all available means, including fidelity insurance and civil litigation;
- to deter employees and third parties from attempting frauds in future
- to remove suspicions or unfounded allegations aimed at innocent parties.

The last point is particularly important because when suspicions are raised about the behaviour of an individual, the actions taken should be planned to protect the welfare of innocent employees as well as to protect the organisation from a successful fraud.

Example

A director became suspicious when he noticed that a manager was displaying signs of excessive wealth and spending grossly in excess of what he appeared to be earning. There was a suspicion that he could have been involved in a collusive relationship with a broker. A covert investigation established that, instead of obtaining money corruptly, he was borrowing huge sums, with no hope of repayment, because he had had a mental breakdown due to the pressure of work. The company arranged for urgent counselling and subsequent treatment.

Once objectives have been agreed, a budget for the investigation should be allocated and then tightly controlled.

A major investigation can quickly become a drain on management time and enthusiasm, something which clever fraudsters exploit with great skill and ruthlessness. Management should be made aware at the commencement of an investigation what may result. After the initial shock of learning that a major incident of fraud or corruption may have occurred, management usually enthusiastically supports an investigation until interviews have taken place and follow-up action has been initiated. Many managers assume that after this point, fraudsters, when confronted with proof of their wrongdoing, will admit liability and accept their punishment – allowing the case to be swiftly closed and business operations to carry on as normal. This rarely happens when the perpetrators are seasoned in hostile business tactics with access to their own sophisticated legal and media resources. An increasingly common reaction is that the perpetrators counter-attack, using tactics such as:

- leaking adverse media stories about the way in which the investigation was conducted or the techniques which were used to gather evidence

- releasing compromising information about the victim's business dealings in order to discredit management in the eyes of stakeholders
- spreading malicious rumours within the victim organisation in order to demoralise employees
- launching their own civil, libel or defamation actions
- threats of violence against persons involved in the investigation, although thankfully this is rare.

When the subject of an investigation is a wealthy corporate psychopath, senior management can expect a whole range of dirty tricks as well as legitimate law suits led by the most talented lawyers – this is not a war that the psychopath expects to lose.

As a civil or criminal case drags on, senior management starts to lose heart and begins to complain about the amount of time, money and resources that is being taken up. Internal politics and point scoring begin to take their toll, as managers look for scapegoats on which to lay the blame for all the disruption. The perpetrators counter-attack through malicious claims and civil suits, adding to the pressure on management. It then becomes a war of attrition, and management enthusiasm waxes and wanes accordingly. This is illustrated in Figure 6.2.

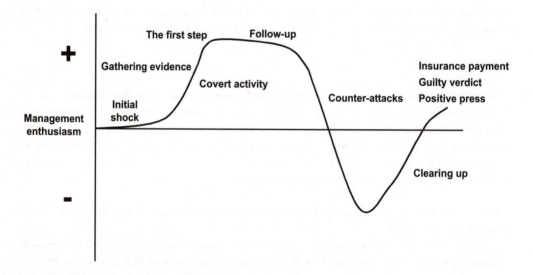

Figure 6.2 Stages in management enthusiasm

Before launching an investigation, the organisation should anticipate that malicious counter-claims may be made. Responses about the organisation's ethical stance should be prepared, reiterating that all interview methods and investigation techniques are legal and have been reviewed by legal advisers.

One of the most disturbing factors upon discovering that a trusted employee or manager is a criminal is the effect on the perpetrator's colleagues and management. Normally, it is shattering for work colleagues to realise that the person that they have befriended and trusted has been using and lying to them. The effect is equally pronounced on managers who may have promoted the individual. We have often found in workshops that delegates who had had a fraud in their workplace had seen a marked bad effect on employee morale. Not least important is the constant worry of innocent employees who may have been under suspicion.

Removing the cloud of suspicion or unfounded allegation from innocent employees requires that, once a case has been finalised, all the people who were interviewed and assisted in the investigation to be notified that the case is closed and that their help was appreciated. It can be a valuable boost to employee morale at a time when rumour and uncertainty have been rife.

Managing the investigation and following through

Information must be gathered in a controlled and legal manner. If this is not done, the organisation could lose all its options to prosecute or litigate and end up with financial penalties and damage to its reputation. The initial stages of gathering evidence should be as discreet as possible to avoid alerting potential suspects. The need for secrecy is vital, as leaks of information can ruin an investigation.

Example

A senior board director told his secretary that there were suspicions about fraud involving employees. The secretary shared this information on a confidential basis with another secretary, who in turn informed her manager. The problem was that her manager was one of the main suspects, and he promptly confronted the director.

Professional investigators can use a range of covert investigative techniques, including:

- audio and video recording
- searching through the discarded rubbish bags placed on the public pavement outside a suspect's home address
- undercover operations or pretext, test purchases.

Some of these computer and other forensic techniques are legal in some countries and jurisdictions and not in others. Some, such as searching through discarded rubbish, could potentially have a severely adverse effect on the organisation's image should their use become publicly known. Different techniques should be carefully evaluated to determine whether they are legal in the relevant country or jurisdiction, and then weighed against corporate culture and ethics before deciding on their use; their use should be approved by executive directors and cleared with the organisation's legal advisers.

Care must be taken at all times, because mistakes in the handling of critical evidence cannot be corrected at a later stage. The most difficult area to control is well-meaning, enthusiastic managers pushing to conclude matters quickly. For example, by calling in an IT support person to examine a suspect's desktop computer using generally available utility programs and loading a utility program, the resultant evidence becomes inadmissible in legal proceedings because the original data on the computer have been altered.

There should be a clear demarcation between evidence which can be gathered using in-house resources and that which requires outside experts. Some of the more common sources of information used in fraud investigations are shown in Table 6.1.

Table 6.1   Collection of information in fraud investigations

Source of information	Collected/analysed by
Personal computers	External forensic computer specialist
Servers and mainframes	External forensic computer specialist, internal IT support
Audit logs	System security administrator, system supervisor
System logs	System security administrator, system supervisor
Diskettes, tape and back-ups	External forensic computer specialist
E-mail messages including deleted messages	IT support, IS security manager, investigator
Relevant documents	Legal advisor, company secretary, investigator, external forensic document specialist for handwriting, ink and paper analysis including fingerprints
Contents of disk	Investigator, HR
Telephone call log	IT support, investigator
Contents of waste bin	Investigator, external forensic document specialist
CCTV recordings	Investigator, head of security, equipment supplier, external forensic video specialist
Datafiles of transactions held on computer	Investigator, forensic accountant
Access control records	Investigator, head of security, system manager, system supplier, engineer
Any tape recorded evidence	Investigator, external forensic audio specialist, systems manager
Interviews with informants/witnesses	Investigator

The initial actions to collect evidence are crucial. When evidence is subsequently presented in court or as part of civil or criminal proceedings, the way it was collected and handled will come under intense scrutiny; judges are increasingly taking the view that persons charged with conducting investigations must follow established rules exactly and the slightest deviation may cause the evidence to be ruled inadmissible.

Interviewing a suspect to obtain a confession requires specialist skills, and we recommend that all crucial interviews should be conducted by an experienced professional. (For a detailed description of the required preparation and techniques, see Comer and Stephens, 2004.)

From time to time this may not be feasible, so we will mention the two most important categories of interviews related to investigation into fraud and corruption:

• sources of information (informants), internal or external to the organisation
• persons, internal or external, who are suspected of being involved in fraud.

Reliable informants usually take some time to find and it is vital to weed out persons who only wish to spread malicious gossip or gain revenge on a disliked colleague or manager. The investigator must, over time, identify an informant's motive; an honest desire to help is the best. As in interviews with suspects, described below, one of the golden rules is to listen and take the time which the interview needs. Once found, genuine informants can be very valuable. Informants need time and support, and mutual trust is required between informants and the person interviewing them. The first hesitant contact, if rebuffed, is probably going to be the last.

The people committing a fraud usually are the ones who know most about it, and getting them to talk is an art form which takes practice. A well-structured interview can be ruined by an inexperienced interviewer. Some basic ground rules of interviewing informants or suspects are:

- Material should be prepared and understood before the interview, in order to learn as much about the subject as possible.
- The last 10–20 per cent of preparation will happen when the interviewer meets the subject.
- The interview should take place in a neutral location.
- The interviewer should not become aggressive during an interview – it is the weight of the interviewer's questions which will eventually achieve results.
- Preferably the interviewer should document the interview, as tape recording or having a third person present can destroy rapport with the suspect.
- Appropriate legal advice should be taken before interviewing suspects.

In our experience most well-planned interviews have resulted in suspects feeling relieved after unburdening themselves about their involvement and after providing significant new information on the extent of fraud.

Example:

After two hours spent reviewing the company ethics policy and discussing the relevance of the employee's position as manager, and the suppliers he used, the employee was asked the following question: 'Have you at any time received money from a supplier, gifts over $50 or have you asked a supplier to make a payment on your behalf.' The immediate answer was a sharp 'No'. The interviewer then asked the subject to consider for a few minutes why he may have been asked that question. After a silence of 45 minutes, when the subject looked everywhere but in the interviewer's eyes, he changed his answer to 'Yes', and after seven hours (including lunch and coffee), he had admitted accepting bribes totalling $300 000.

An interview which is part of an investigation into suspected fraud or corruption is not an interrogation. It is a structured and planned conversation designed to uncover a series of events.

Some organisations have a policy of always reporting cases of suspected fraud to the police. In others there is sometimes much soul searching about whether to call in the police, because the victim does not want to publicise the fact that a fraud has occurred; arguments both for and against are shown in Table 6.2.

We believe that it is beneficial to discuss a case with the police as soon as practicable, even if no complaint is subsequently filed: the police may already be investigating similar frauds

Table 6.2   Bringing in the police

For

- Prompt disclosure of information to financial markets and stakeholders may produce a positive reaction and reduce the risk of future legal liabilities
- Management is seen to be determined to protect the organisation's assets
- The organisation does not have to pay the expensive costs of civil litigation
- Calling in the police may deter other employees and third parties from commencing frauds
- Successful prosecution may assist in other actions, such as fidelity insurance claims

Against

- Financial markets and other stakeholders may suffer an adverse reaction, particularly if it appears that there has been a fundamental breakdown in controls
- Police may have insufficient resources to complete the investigation quickly and efficiently
- Management may have to allocate considerable time to assisting the police
- Police may concentrate only on one aspect for prosecution and not uncover the full extent of the frauds
- Victim loses control over the disclosure of documents and other evidence

which have occurred in other organisations, particularly where these involve organised criminal groups.

The police can also advise whether potential courses of action taken by the organisation could prejudice any subsequent investigation conducted by them.

However, most police forces around the world have found that their resources are becoming very stretched as far as taking on fraud investigations is concerned. Some now set a lower limit of several million dollars, below which they will not take on a case. Others make it clear that they regard the investigation of fraud in large organisations as the responsibility of the victims because they have the resources and funds to pay for it.

There is a greater chance of the police taking on a case if the organisation has prepared a professional case file with documented exhibits and transcripts. However, sometimes even this is not enough:

Example

A multinational client had uncovered a major fraud in a subsidiary located in a tough, run-down inner city district where the local police did not have the resources to investigate. The case was rejected by several different police squads who had other priorities, but eventually the superintendent of a regional crime squad decided that it would make an interesting change to the normal day-to-day routine of tackling armed criminals who were holding up security vans. His problem was how to sell it to his officers, all of whom had an intense dislike for fraud investigation because of the associated paperwork.

He solved the problem by announcing, at the initial briefing which was being held to plan a raid on the premises, that the suspected ringleader was a heavily built man with a known violent temper, so it was likely that at least two officers would be needed to arrest him and that there could be a punch-up. Some of the other suspects, who were mostly drivers, could also turn nasty.

At this point, the roomful of rather disinterested and bored looking officers perked up, and several hands immediately went up to volunteer to make the arrests. The raid and follow-on investigation was a great success. Twelve people were subsequently convicted, with the ringleaders receiving lengthy jail sentences.

An internal investigation into major fraud and corruption is a complex project which leaves little room for error. Nevertheless, with enough care and attention, meticulous planning and follow-through, you can achieve successful prosecutions and recovery of misappropriated funds.

Summary of key points

- If you do not already have a fraud response plan, prepare one today.
- Never leap into an investigation or interview someone by fishing for evidence or a confession.
- Obtain intelligence or information first, then collect evidence, and only then make overt moves against the suspects.
- If you want your evidence to stand up in court, make sure it is collected by someone who understands the legal rules for collecting it.
- Expect that suspects will counter-attack so plan accordingly; and be prepared for a bare-knuckle fight.
- If your company does not have in-house investigation skills, use a proven, professional investigator.
- You may only get one shot at obtaining a confession from a suspect; use the best available interviewer for the job.
- Most police fraud squads are under-resourced; presenting a professionally prepared case will help them considerably.

7 *Resistance – the Ultimate Goal*

Recognising the cost

Given that fraud and corruption are possibly two of the greatest unmanaged risks faced by organisations today, it is an interesting question that if companies and organisations were completely untainted by fraud and corruption, how much more profitable would they then be?

It is a difficult question to answer because although academic research and empirical work indicates that the total direct and indirect cost of fraud and corruption is in the region of two to five per cent of turnover for 'normal' organisations, the truth is that nobody really knows the actual cost.

Furthermore, when organisations have not had a major loss and are making profits, there can be a strong degree of complacency by executives who believe that because they cannot see any losses, then there are none. This can be a dangerous assumption. The diagram below (Figure 7.1) was originally drawn by the head of internal audit of one of Europe's largest corporations.

We believe it is applicable to most profitable organisations, prior to the hidden costs of fraud and corruption becoming visible. The x-axis represents time, and the y-axis represents

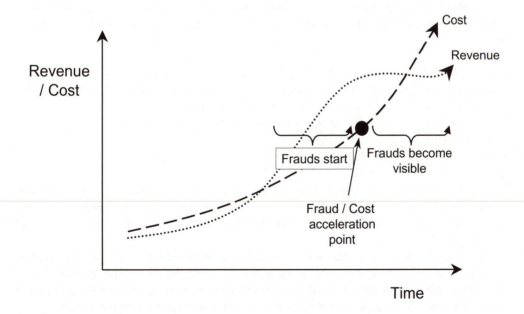

Figure 7.1 Invest in prevention now

the increasing (or decreasing) costs and revenues of a company. When a company first commences operations, costs may exceed revenues and budgets are tight. When the business plan eventually succeeds and the profits begin rolling in, the company tends to focus on revenue growth and further increasing market share. Cost control and also fraud prevention are often neglected at this time. Simultaneously, spending habits and managers become less disciplined and diligent, so fraud and corruption opportunities increase. Then, when the revenue growth slows, as it almost always does, costs do not decline at the same rate. Spending momentum is supported by fraudsters who are reluctant to stop their profitable schemes.

When revenues level off suddenly and costs continue to accelerate, the previously hidden frauds are likely to be exposed as attention turns to cost management and reduction, often in circumstances of panic, uncertainty and redundancies. Usually it is too late to invest in fraud and corruption risk management, but the cost of fraud becomes very visible.

The ability to significantly increase profit margins is one compelling reason to systematically manage fraud and corruption risk. If the cost of fraud and corruption in a company was say 3 per cent of sales and the current operating profit margin was 5 per cent, then a fraud- and corruption-free company would have profits which were a massive 60 per cent higher.

Phrases like 'one way of making money is to stop losing it', 'it's not a problem, it's an opportunity' and 'prevention is better than cure' have all been overused in business. However, in the context of fraud and corruption, they are indisputably true.

External influences on fraud and corruption

In addition to the internal pressure to improve profits, and hence avoid unnecessary costs such as those caused by fraud and corruption, there is increasing focus by organisations on complying with principles and legislation. Some of the most important external influences are:

- the United Nations Global Compact Principle 10 'Businesses should work against corruption in all its forms, including extortion and bribery.' (UN Global Compact, 2004)
- the OECD Business Approaches to Combating Corrupt Practices
- Transparency International's Business Principles for Countering Bribery
- the COSO Internal Control Framework
- the Sarbanes-Oxley Act of 2002.

In response to public outrage over corporate collapses, the courts seem to be taking a much harder line against corporate fraudsters than in the past, with long prison sentences being handed down in well-known cases such as WorldCom, Tyco and Adelphia Communications (White, 2005).

New laws should make it easier for prosecutors to do deals with suspects who are small fry in an investigation, but who may be facing prison time and significant fines if found guilty. In exchange for lesser penalties, they may agree to give evidence against the main targets of an investigation, for example, members of the executive board or senior management.

Considering the track record of legislation, it would be naïve to believe that new laws alone will prevent corporate fraud and corruption in the future. However, they may well have an impact on the behaviour of some executives who in the past indulged in sharp practice and unethical or fraudulent behaviour. But these are the types of individuals who could have been stopped just by implementing a good fraud- and corruption-prevention strategy.

Laws will not stop a small minority of executives. People defraud because they believe they can get away with it and this is especially true for those executives who can be classed as corporate psychopaths. Laws have as little relevance for these dishonest individuals as they do for professional fraudsters or criminal groups and in this context do not prevent fraud and corruption.

The essence of successfully managing fraud and corruption risk is active prevention. What has become obvious is that organisations which are serious about prevention should treat fraud and corruption as a single problem, at least from a corporate or organisational point of view. They should clarify the often blurred boundaries between fraud and corruption and simplify the many definitions of fraud, which already include the words corruption and bribery, and the numerous other vague and varied definitions of corruption.

An increased focus on prevention, recognising the risks and early detection of red flags will contribute to a greater resistance to fraud and corruption.

Developing resistance to fraud and corruption

The notion of developing resistance to a problem is not altogether unfamiliar. On a personal note we would all like to develop resistance to illnesses like cancer, malaria, flu and even the common cold. Similarly in companies and organisations, internal systems to develop resistance to errors and omissions and to improve efficiency and quality have been in place for many years. From an external perspective, ratings aimed at improving resistance to corporate greed and mismanagement by measuring, benchmarking and enhancing corporate governance, corporate responsibility and environmental performance are coming into vogue. External ratings, such as FTSE4Good, are excellent motivators. However, an internal assessment such as the one described in the following sections goes much deeper in enabling an organisation to measure its resistance to fraud and corruption.

By evaluating the external and internal pressures and influences, an assessment can be used to satisfy the external requirements for a well governed and more transparent, corruption-free organisation, as well as the internal goal of significantly improved profitability. The fraud and corruption 'resistance assessment' is a measure, or snapshot, of the resilience of an organisation, corporation or entity to the effects and impact (on profitability, long-term value, reputation and internal culture) of fraud and corruption. When this assessment is performed against a baseline standard, it is possible to identify and prioritise the improvements which need to be made.

The assessment is based on the six-point cyclical strategy, shown in Figure 7.2, for managing the risk of fraud and corruption which can be applied to virtually any organisation.

The executive board and senior management should set a clear message, often called the 'tone at the top', be fully aware of and then treat the risks to which they are most vulnerable, ensure that all warning signs of fraud and corruption are detected early, establish a system for the investigation and management of incidents and finally use all experiences gained to enhance resistance.

Figure 7.2   Fraud and corruption risk management strategy

How a fraud and corruption resistance assessment works

Having implemented a risk management strategy based as described in Figure 7.2, the elements can be expanded in order to measure resistance to fraud and corruption in a consistent manner across the organisation.

The Fraud and Corruption Resistance Assessment System[1] which is described here has been developed based on the definitions of fraud and corruption contained in Chapter 1 and embodies the most important principles developed by the organisations described earlier in this chapter. It comprises 12 main elements as shown in Figure 7.3.

The amoeba in the centre is a unique fraud and corruption resistance profile of the particular organisation being reviewed and the gaps represent where there is room for improvement.

The *tone at the top (1)* evaluates the degree and effectiveness of senior management's commitment to preventing fraud and corruption. The tone set at the top of an organization regarding fraud and corruption prevention has a crucial effect throughout the rest of the organization. Senior management should send a message that fraud and corruption will not be

1. Reproduced by kind permission of Det Norske Veritas (DNV), an international certification and assessment agency. In 2005, the authors were external participants in a DNV project initiated to design, develop and pilot a Fraud and Corruption Resistance Assessment System.

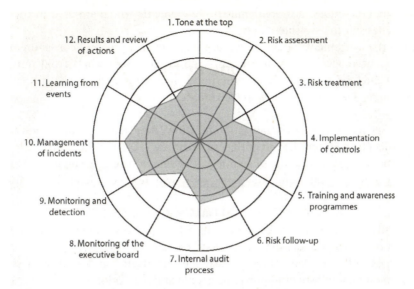

Figure 7.3   Fraud and Corruption Resistance Assessment System (DNV)

tolerated anywhere in the organization. This commitment should be visible to all employees, credible, embedded in the organizational culture and also apparent to external parties.

A thorough *understanding of fraud and corruption risk (2)* across the organization is a prerequisite for effective prevention. The assessment would involve systematic identification and ranking of those fraud and corruption risks which can and do affect the organization at all levels. Fraud and corruption risk assessment also involves looking at how resistant the controls are to specific methods of fraud and corruption.

Once fraud and corruption risks have been understood plans can be made for their *treatment (3)* in a top down manner, the *implementation of effective control measures (4)* and the development and launch of across-the-board *training programmes (5)*.

Monitoring and the detection of red flags is one of the most difficult processes to implement and is split into four elements, namely:

- how the *fraud and corruption risks already identified are continuously followed up (6)* and kept up to date taking into account changes in the business and its personnel
- the *effectiveness of the internal audit process (7)*
- how *monitoring of the executive board (8)* and other senior management takes place, its effectiveness and independence
- the nature, extent and quality of *proactive monitoring and detection (9)* taking place within the organisation.

Investigations are often expensive and uncomfortable, and when incidents occur it may be tempting to negotiate a settlement, such as voluntary resignation or early retirement, without investigation. It is, however, through successful *management of incidents (10)* of suspected fraud and corruption that management gain credibility.

Finally, all incidents present a wealth of learning opportunities. It is how they are used to *learn from events (11)* and how management are able to *measure results and review actions (12)* accordingly which provide the impetus to continuously improved performance.

Appendix 9 describes in more detail the 12 elements which are used in the Fraud and Corruption Resistance Assessment System.

Behind the assessment model shown above, a detailed protocol consisting of over 500 questions has been developed in an attempt to ensure consistency and avoid ambiguity. Also a weighting and scoring system for each of the 12 elements is applied.

For example, Element 1, the *tone at the top* is defined as:

- The tone set at the top of an organisation regarding fraud and corruption prevention has a crucial effect throughout the rest of the organisation.
- This element explores the role of senior management in setting the tone at the top and how the message that fraud and corruption will not be tolerated is communicated throughout the organisation.
- Demonstrating commitment to fraud and corruption prevention is a management responsibility that needs to be visible to all employees, credible, embedded in the organisational culture and also visible to external parties.
- The purpose of this element is to evaluate the degree and effectiveness of senior management's commitment to preventing fraud and corruption.
- The tone at the top is measured by the combination of the following two factors: 1) the message sent from management through its code of conduct and anti-fraud and -corruption policies and, equally important, 2) how managers are seen to apply their own rules.

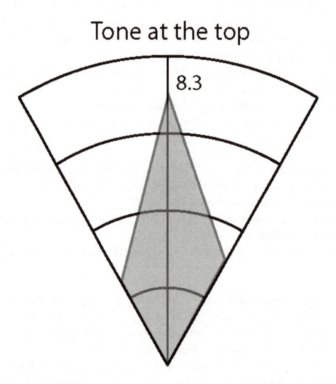

Figure 7.4   Element 1 – Tone at the top

This is then further divided into eight sub-elements:

1.1. Policy
1.2. Quality of policy
1.3. Fraud and corruption resistance management strategy
1.4. Stakeholder engagement
1.5. Management representative
1.6. Operational risk management
1.7. Existence of relevant standards and procedure
1.8. Senior management participation

with a total of 46 key questions which carry a weighting equivalent to 12.5 per cent of the total. The end result is an assessment as shown in Figure 7.4.

It is essential that auditors who conduct assessments fully understand and recognise the real risks of fraud and corruption in the organisation they are evaluating; otherwise the exercise may turn into a pro forma checklist exercise providing little or no value whatsoever.

The essence of the assessment is that assessors should be able to put themselves in the mind of a fraudster or corrupt person and compare how successful the organisation would be at preventing particular methods from succeeding. Assessors can reference a list of the main generic methods in order to familiarise themselves with those most likely to apply to a particular organisation. An example library of typical fraud and corruption methods across a variety of generic business processes is provided in Appendix 10.

Achieving a high resistance

The concept described above is an internal assessment measured against a benchmark standard. External ratings such as the well-known credit ratings may implicitly take into account fraud and corruption when attempting to identify the risk as to why a company may be a poor bet or go bankrupt. However they appear to do little to measure the true resistance of an organization to fraud and corruption.

Achieving a high resistance to fraud and corruption presents some tough challenges. For example:

• The tone at the top is often reflected in a code of conduct, something which is becoming a legal requirement for more and more organisations. However, management often struggle with issues such as actually living up to their own code in the face of harsh realities and choices. Vigilantly looking for violations of any part of the code can get downplayed. Many codes of conduct necessarily include sentences such as 'conducting business in an open, honest and transparent manner'. Management teams which recognise and state that this is something to aspire to are in a much better position to improve resistance to fraud and corruption than those which blindly and falsely claim that they have already achieved transparency in every part of the organisation.

• The whole area of monitoring, from defining and looking for the red flags of fraud and corruption, to monitoring the activities and behaviour of the executive board, can be a political minefield. Senior management should first recognise that whilst they are not usually the owners of the organisation, they have so much power and ability to override the controls that nobody within the organisation is able to monitor their behaviour without both a mandate and also very strong external support. Secondly, although the tools and techniques to look for the signs of fraud and corruption in an organisation are available, actually finding the people willing to devote time and attention to using and applying them thoroughly is not always so easy. Finding and reporting internal fraud and corruption has historically tended to be a poor career move.

- The need to learn from events is obvious, but in practice this requires that incidents of fraud and corruption which are discovered need to be discussed openly and not be swept under the carpet. Perceptions need changing in those organisations where any discovery of fraud and corruption is still too often seen as an indicator of management failure rather than the successful result of strong management controls.

A regular fraud and corruption resistance assessment would typically be requested by either a non-executive board member or the audit committee, but it could equally well be initiated from within the company, provided that there was some degree of independent assessment. While the specific questions asked and the weightings applied may differ somewhat depending on the type of organisation being assessed, a fraud and corruption resistance assessment such as the one described above would be equally applicable to financial institutions, global corporations, small- and medium-sized business, public sector bodies, in fact to any organisation which is exposed to fraud or corruption.

Future

In the future, we envisage that assessment and measurement systems will capture an organisation's resistance to fraud and corruption as a way of helping investors and other stakeholders (such as insurers, officers and employees) make more informed decisions. As the concept develops, fraud and corruption resistance indices could be created for different industry types.

Measuring resistance to fraud and corruption is all about measuring how good an organisation is at doing things in practice, not just fulfilling legal and other requirements on paper. We believe that as soon as some organisations start applying fraud and corruption risk management techniques with the objective of eliminating these hidden costs from their business, the effects may so dramatic that other organisations will have to follow suit in order to stay in business.

Throughout this book, we have attempted to illustrate how a focus solely on a structured control framework and legislation has led to the creation of blind spots in the defence against fraud and corruption. Nowhere has this been more apparent than in organisations where frauds have been committed by top management. Therefore it is time to put in place some practical measures, which recognise and prevent fraud and corruption.

In the coming years we see the emergence of:

- enhanced frameworks for preventing and detecting fraud and corruption
- organisation-wide training and awareness programs
- the engagement of shareholders and stakeholders alike in the prevention of fraud and corruption.

We do not believe that any organisation is ever going to be 100 per cent fraud- and corruption-proof. Just being in business carries an inherent risk of fraud and corruption, and fraudsters are very adept at identifying and exploiting new opportunities. However, executives who can build an organisation with a high resistance to fraud and corruption will be able to bridge some of the most significant gaps between theory and practice which still exist today, thereby adding significant value for shareholders and stakeholders alike.

Increased shareholder and stakeholder pressure, improved legislation and greater awareness all round are elevating the management of fraud and corruption to the boardroom. Those senior executives who dismiss fraud and corruption as an issue that they don't need to deal with, or who are resigned to carry a problem they feel they can do nothing about or, worse still, who themselves are involved in fraud and corruption, will hopefully soon find that they have no place at the table.

Summary of key points

- If you want to increase profits, then reduce the hidden costs of fraud and corruption.
- Don't expect new laws to stop corporate psychopaths and determined criminals from committing fraud and indulging in corrupt behaviour.
- Invest in prevention and detection and then measure how resistant your organisation is to the methods of fraud and corruption.

Appendices

1 *Sample Fraud and Corruption Policy*

1. Purpose

YZW Corporation (YZW) is committed to conducting its business with honesty and integrity and as a result, promotes an organisational culture from the top down that will not tolerate any act of fraud or corrupt conduct, whilst still maintaining an open and stimulating work environment.

This policy is designed to mitigate YZW's exposure to fraud and criminal acts committed by employees, customers, vendors or other third parties. It is also designed to protect YZW's reputation and that of its clients and other stakeholders. This policy should be read in conjunction with the YZW Code of Conduct.

The policy applies to all divisions, business units and subsidiaries of YZW. It also applies to all persons employed or engaged by YZW. All staff are required to read and understand the policy. Compliance is mandatory.

2. Definitions

For the purpose of this policy, YZW defines fraud[1] as:

an intentional act by one or more individuals among management, those charged with governance, employees, or third parties, involving the use of deception to obtain an unjust or illegal advantage.

Corruption[2] is defined as:

the abuse of public or private office for personal gain.

Examples of fraud and corruption include:

- using false payment instructions, invoices or cheques in order to receive a payment to ones own account, or to a third party account in exchange for a benefit

---

1. International Auditing and Assurance Standards Board, (2004), International Standard on Auditing 240, 'The Auditor's Responsibility To Consider Fraud In An Audit Of Financial Statements', International Federation of Accountants.
2. Adaptation of a World Bank definition in 'Anti-corruption Policies and Programs: a Framework for Evaluation', Policy Research Working Paper 2501.

- the manipulation of accounts in order to unlawfully obtain customer funds
- using inside knowledge to obtain a financial advantage for oneself or an associate
- stealing passwords to payment systems and using them to make unauthorised funds transfers
- false accounting, including material and deliberate misstatement of financial information
- accepting or providing bribes or kickbacks in exchange for business with an adviser, contractor or supplier, whether or not it is to the benefit of YZW.

The above list is not exhaustive: if you have a concern about a transaction or someone's behaviour, please discuss it with your line manager, or follow the procedures in the Whistle-blower Policy.

3. Responsibility

Overall responsibility for the management of fraud and corruption risk within YZW rests with the Chief Executive Officer.

All employees have a responsibility to act honestly and to diligently follow the procedures and controls that have been implemented to mitigate fraud and corruption. They must not bypass or avoid using those procedures or controls. They must immediately report identified weaknesses or loopholes in controls that could facilitate a fraud. They must also report immediately any incident of fraud or corruption, whether it is suspected or actual, either to their line manager or by following the procedures laid down in the Whistle-blower Policy.

4. Risk management

The Audit Committee is responsible for arranging and reviewing an annual fraud and corruption risk assessment covering the Board of Directors, and Senior Managers.

All business units must conduct a fraud and corruption risk assessment as part of their ongoing assessment of their risk profile, or whenever there are major change initiatives (including new and re-engineered products, processes or third-party initiatives). The risk assessment must include:

- a description of the risk, its likelihood given the current controls, the financial, legal and regulatory impact, and the impact on reputation and market share
- for unacceptable risks, the controls which have been or will be implemented to reduce the risks to an acceptable level
- identification of the residual risk level which management opts to carry.

Following the fraud and corruption risk assessment, senior management must decide on the risk management strategy, that is whether to accept, transfer or manage the risk, in a manner consistent with other types of business risk; and on the strategic issues which need to be raised at Board level which may require significant expenditure or policy decisions.

Business units should regularly monitor their fraud risk profiles and material exposures to fraud losses, taking proactive steps to mitigate risks.

5. Reporting fraud incidents

If YZW employees suspect an incident involving fraud or corruption has occurred, you must immediately report your suspicions to your line manager who in turn will raise it with the Head of Risk and Compliance. If you are not comfortable reporting directly, suspicions of fraud or corruption may also be reported by following the procedures in the Whistle-blowing Policy. All reports will be treated with the utmost confidence.

A YZW employee who makes a report of suspected fraudulent or corrupt behaviour will be protected from any adverse reaction to the report, providing that this report is not malicious and that the employee has not been involved in any fraudulent or corrupt activity. Reports will be used for internal investigations and will only be released externally if required to comply with legal requirements.

The Head of Risk and Compliance will coordinate any further investigation.

6. Investigation

The Head of Risk and Compliance is responsible for leading any investigations conducted, in a professional manner, and in a way which is consistent across YZW and which complies with relevant legislation and statutory requirements.

Under no circumstances are staff and management to conduct an investigation on their own or confront a suspect in relation to an allegation of fraudulent or corrupt conduct. On discovery of potential fraud or corruption, they must not take any actions that could prejudice the subsequent collection of evidence or influence potential witnesses.

7. Post investigation

Where an investigation shows that fraud or corruption has occurred, YZW in consultation with legal counsel will take appropriate action which may include disciplinary action under the Code of Conduct, referral to the police and civil action.

Each incident provides an opportunity to strengthen controls which are already in place. As a consequence, the Head of Risk and Compliance, together with Internal Audit, will work with the relevant business unit manager to ensure that any recommendations for improvement are properly implemented.

PROFILE: YZW CORPORATION – EXAMPLE BUSINESS UNIT

	Method	Likelihood of success	Worst-case direct loss $
1	A manager colludes with a supplier to create false quotations purporting to be from different suppliers in response to a number of tenders. The supplier is awarded several contracts and the employee receives a series of kickbacks	High	$25 million
2	Create false faxes as if from other subsidiaries or business units requesting foreign exchange payments to suppliers and place in the wire basket for processing in the treasury back office	High	$5 million
3	A manager colludes with customers to reduce effective sales price. $5000 per month would be feasible	Medium	$60 000
4	A batch payment file is created on the general ledger system and transferred to a server prior to input to the bank payment system. A person accesses the file and changes the bank details for suppliers. This would be a one-off smash-and-grab type fraud	High	$500 000
5	Financial controller creates false invoices for a major project, and asks the authorisers to set up a new bank account on the payment system. Then instructs staff to process payments. Similar frauds would be feasible if perpetrated by the CIO, CFO or other senior managers. $20 000 per month would be feasible	High	$240 000 p.a.
6	Steal relevant input and authoriser passwords to the bank payment system, create a new bank account, then input and transmit a series of payment instructions to clear out the bank accounts. This would be a one-off high-value fraud and the money would have cleared before the bank reconciliation picked up the discrepancy	High	$50 million
7	Submit false expense claims. $200 per month would be feasible	High	$2400 p.a.
8	An accounts person steals incoming cheques and pays them into own account	Low	$20 000

© Hibis Consulting Pty Ltd

3 *Example Workshop 2 Output*

YZW Corporation

1. Introduction

The draft profile on the next page contains output from interviews and workshops with supervisors, team leaders and line managers. The methods, likelihood of success and worst-case loss ($) have been agreed by each department.

Please complete the remaining columns. Firstly, assess the two impact columns on the right and then the overall risk level on the left using the matrix. Where different impacts are identified for a specific risk, for example, a severe impact on reputation and medium regulatory impact, the higher impact should be used to evaluate the overall risk level.

Risk level	Method	Likelihood of success	Worst-case loss ($)	Impacts	
				Reputation/ market share	Legal/ regulatory
Severe High Medium Low		High Medium Low	$	Catastrophic Severe High Medium Low	Catastrophic Severe High Medium Low

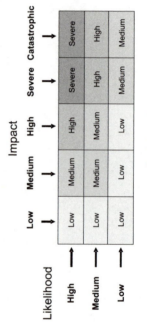

Risk Levels

© Hibis Consulting Pty Ltd

YZW Corporation
2. Profile: Example business unit

Risk level	Method	Likelihood of success	Impacts		
			Worst-case loss ($)	Reputation/ market share	Legal/ regulatory
	Steal relevant input and authoriser passwords to the bank payment system, create a new bank account, then input and transmit a series of payment instructions to clear out the bank accounts. This would be a one-off high-value fraud and the money would have cleared before the bank reconciliation picked up the discrepancy.	High	$50 million		
	A manager colludes with a supplier to create false quotations purporting to be from different suppliers in response to a number of tenders. The supplier is awarded several contracts and the employee receives a series of kickbacks.	High	$25 million		
	Create false faxes as if from other subsidiaries, or business units, requesting foreign exchange payments to suppliers and place in the wire basket for processing in the treasury back office.	High	$5 million		
	A batch payment file is created on the general ledger system and transferred to a server prior to input to the bank payment system. A person accesses the file and changes the bank details for suppliers. This would be a one-off smash-and-grab type fraud.	High	$5 million		
	Financial controller creates false invoices for a major project, and asks the authorisers to set up a new bank account on the payment system. Then instructs staff to process payments. Similar frauds would be feasible if perpetrated by the CIO, CFO or other senior managers. $20 000 per month would be feasible.	High	$240 000 p.a.		
	A manager colludes with customers to reduce effective sales price. $5000 per month would be feasible.	Medium	$60 000		
	An accounts person steals incoming cheques and pays them into own account.	Low	$20 000		
	Submit false expense claims. $200 per month would be feasible.	High	$2400 p.a.		

© Hibis Consulting Pty Ltd

4 Sample Fraud and Corruption Profile

Sample fraud and corruption profile

YZW Corporation

Introduction

A fraud and corruption profiling exercise was carried out in YZW Corporation (YZW). The key objectives were to:

develop a fraud and corruption profile of YZW by analysing resistance to specific methods

assess the severity of individual risks, including where possible the maximum loss which could occur

transfer specialist fraud awareness to key staff.

This was achieved using a combination of interviews and workshops.

This *sample fraud and corruption profile* lists potential frauds which could affect YZW.

© *Hibis Consulting Pty Ltd*

YZW Corporation

Sample fraud and corruption profile

Fraud and corruption profiling

The fraud and corruption profiling exercise involved interviews with managers and employees to assist them to understand specific methods which might apply to their area. Each method identified was analysed according to the *likelihood* (high, medium or low) and potential worst-case monetary loss ($).

It is important to note that *likelihood* is not an indication of how likely a fraud is to occur. It is the likelihood of a fraud succeeding if a dishonest person, either internal or external to YZW, used that method. For example, a high rating by participants meant that they believed that a particular method of fraud would succeed given the current controls. It should be borne in mind that a number of the methods identified by participants have in fact been used on many occasions by fraudsters in other financial institutions.

Senior managers then evaluated the impacts based on the effect on reputation and loss of market share, and the legal and regulatory impact (catastrophic, severe, high, medium, low).

Based on the likelihood and impact, an overall risk rating was then assigned to each individual fraud risk according to the matrix below, and also taking into account the size of the worst-case monetary loss.

YZW Corporation

Sample fraud and corruption profile

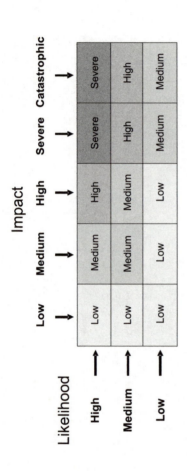

Where different impacts were identified for a specific risk, for example, high impact on reputation and medium regulatory impact, the higher impact was used to evaluate the overall risk level.

Each profile has been sorted according to the risk level to enable senior managers to prioritise their mitigation strategies.

YZW Corporation

Sample fraud and corruption profile

Profile: Example business unit

Risk Level	Method	Likelihood of success	Worst-case loss ($)	Reputation/ market share	Legal/ regulatory
				Impacts	
Severe	Steal relevant input and authoriser passwords to the bank payment system, create a new bank account, then input and transmit a series of payment instructions to clear out the bank accounts. This would be a one-off high-value fraud and the money would have cleared before the bank reconciliation picked up the discrepancy.	High	$50 million	Severe	Severe
Severe	A manager colludes with a supplier to create false quotations purporting to be from different suppliers in response to a number of tenders. The supplier is awarded several contracts and the employee receives a series of kickbacks.	High	$25 million	Severe	High
High	Create false faxes as if from other subsidiaries, or business units, requesting foreign exchange payments to suppliers and place in the wire basket for processing in the treasury back office.	High	$5 million	High	Low
High	A batch payment file is created on the general ledger system and transferred to a server prior to input to the bank payment system. A person accesses the file and changes the bank details for suppliers. This would be a one-off smash-and-grab type fraud.	High	$5 million	High	Low
Low	Financial controller creates false invoices for a major project, and asks the authorisers to set up a new bank account on the payment system. Then instructs staff to process payments. Similar frauds would be feasible if perpetrated by the CIO, CFO or other senior managers. $20 000 per month would be feasible.	High	$240 000 p.a.	Low	Low
Low	A manager colludes with customers to reduce effective sales price. $5000 per month would be feasible.	Medium	$60 000	Low	Low
Low	An accounts person steals incoming cheques and pays them into own account.	Low	$20 000	Low	Low
Low	Submit false expense claims. $200 per month would be feasible.	High	$2400 p.a.	Low	Low

© *Hibis Consulting Pty Ltd*

5 *Example Training Programmes*

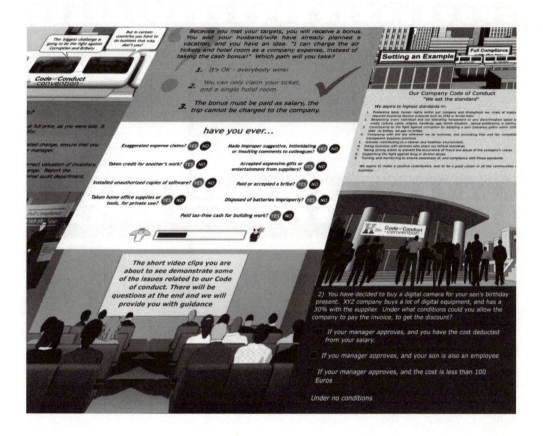

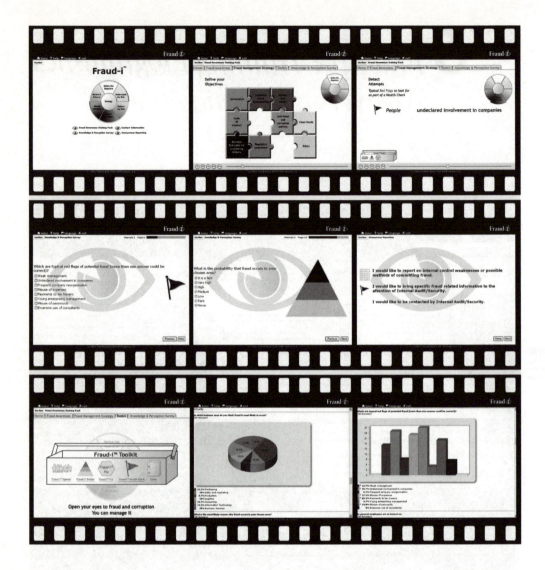

6 *Practical Training Examples – Answers and Guidelines*

This appendix provides answers and guidance to the Case Scenarios and 'Spot the Red Flag' exercises in Chapter 5.

CASE SCENARIOS

Scenario 1: Marketing commissions

The invoice exhibits the following red flags:

* low number invoice
* tax haven (Liechtenstein)
* round amount payment
* insufficient detail, for example 'marketing fee'.

In other words the invoices could be cover for a bribe or Mr Geiger could be perpetrating a fraud by raising his own bogus invoices.

Mr Lestrange's story appears credible so far and it is important to gain his trust as well as maintain strict discretion as far as this information goes. Maybe Mr Lestrange does not wish himself to be identified with the allegations because he fears retribution. Before raising this matter in the appropriate forum, you could do more work to identify further transactions which support or refute the allegations.

Scenario 2: Inventory and logistics

If the report is true, then there is a serious reporting fraud taking place in relation to the management of refitting and maintenance projects. In addition the establishment of a zero-value stock warehouse could increase the temptation for theft, the argument being that if the stock has a zero book value then it should not be missed.

Scenario 3: Spirit of the code of conduct

You should decline the gift, and inform your manager. When interpreting the code of conduct, it is necessary not just to consider the specific guidance printed there, but also the spirit intended. Excessive gifts are not appropriate, even if offered in good faith.

You should discuss the company code of conduct with your colleague who took the watch and if the gift is not returned, you should consider reporting the matter. Finally if you are a manager, and one of your direct reports requests permission to accept a valuable gift from a third party, you should refuse permission, and also ensure that the third party is informed about the code of conduct.

Scenario 4: Dealing with customers

The last minute demand for payment to a third party looks like you are being asked to pay a bribe, especially if the rumour that the beneficiary company for the payment is controlled by some of your customer's managers. In such a serious matter, you should take the time necessary to consult with a manager, who should then take whatever steps necessary.

SPOT THE RED FLAGS – TEST YOURSELF

Test Yourself: Scenario 1

The key red flags and questions are:

- There are signs of an overzealous acquisition strategy which may lead to the use of shortcuts, such as bribes, or even to collapse of the organisation.
- The CEO is clearly on the board of a number of other companies. If he does this work in company time (which appears to be the case) are the directorship emoluments going to him personally? Has anybody ever dared to question this and if it is paid personally, what sort of signal would this send down the organisation?
- The CEO's lifestyle raises questions as to his real motives in making acquisitions: are they in order to boost the company's performance so he can get his bonus, live flamboyantly and so on?
- There is possibly very poor control over investments once they are made. Are they left to go downhill?

It is a fact that good news motivates and bad news often demotivates. However, taking note of negative investment reports is often a good way of pre-empting future problems.

Test Yourself: Scenario 2

Some of the most obvious red flags are:

- It is suggested that, in effect, bribes should be paid to resellers who are customers and be concealed as a 'competition'.
- The message in the code of conduct may not be applicable to (or have reached) the local representative and legal advisors.
- The relationship with the travel agency could indicate that free holidays may have been provided to employees.
- There may be poor control over marketing support funds at head office.
- That similar competitions have been successful elsewhere in the world suggests a culture of turning a blind eye in order to get the results.

Test Yourself: Scenario 3

The red flags are as follows:

- The circumvention of the internet firewall is unusual: this is possibly where the attachments to emails are originating.
- The fact that people were using Yahoo and Hotmail for attachments instead of the company email is unusual: it suggests that someone may have been trying to steal data.
- Is the expensive firewall really an ineffective control which just provides a false sense of security?
- Personnel in the payments department appear to be sharing user IDs and passwords and may be leaving their computers logged on.
- The IT manager is becoming too service oriented rather than control oriented.

Test Yourself: Scenario 4

Some of the more obvious red flags are:

- The facilities manager is strongly resistant to change.
- This supplier has been awarded lots of work for a long time which could conceal a hidden relationship.
- The immediate payment terms on invoice #1 suggests that the company may have cash-flow problems and need the money fast, or that the participants in a collusive relationship want their cut of the cash as soon as possible.
- Invoice #1 indicates that it is from a possible front company, with payment to XIX services, a tax-haven front company.
- Invoice #2 indicates that some changes may have taken place in the ownership structure of the company as a new tax haven company has been set up, with 14-day payment terms.
- There is no supporting documentation with invoice #2 so there is no way to check whether or not the hours on the invoice are inflated.

The placing of the step-daughter and nephew in each other's respective companies suggests a close relationship between the facilities manager and project manager, which may make it difficult for him to consider putting work out to tender.

Sample Design for a Corporate Health Check

YZW Corporation

Example fraud and corruption health check

This appendix demonstrates how a fictitious company, called the YZW Corporation, has developed a typical corporate health check based on the major methods of fraud and corruption identified and documented in its fraud and corruption profile. As this is an example only, the reader should note that the tests suggested are by no means comprehensive. Each and every organisation is unique.

It should be assumed that the YZW Corporation has taken legal advice to ensure that the tests proposed and performed comply with current data-protection and labour laws.

Some of the tests can be done with the assistance of a computer (using programs like Microsoft Excel or audit software such as ACL or WinIDEA). However some tests are best performed manually. It is unlikely that one single test will prove or disprove the existence of fraud or malpractice. It is a combination (or portfolio) of tests which in the end will provide the basis for a credible diagnosis.

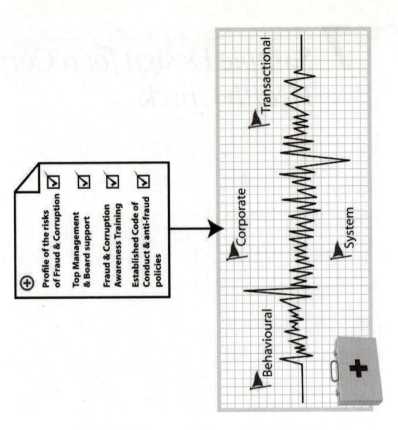

The document checklist shows:
- Profile of the risks of Fraud & Corruption
- Top Management & Board support
- Fraud & Corruption Awareness Training
- Established Code of Conduct & anti-fraud policies

Categories: Corporate, Transactional, Behavioural, System

YZW Corporation

Health check pilot #1

1. Unethical behaviour by management and employees

Red flags	Examples of what to test for	Case examples
Misuse of corporate expense accounts	• Unusual or private expenses	A senior director clearly had an overdeveloped sense of entitlement as he had repeatedly submitted expense claims containing expensive private gifts for himself and his girlfriends. In addition he had four company mobile telephones in his name which, when the call specifications were analysed, showed that they were repeatedly calling each other. They turned out to be for his family. These open abuses of company policy were just the indicator of a much wider selection of frauds and bribery in which he was involved.
Undisclosed conflicts of interest	• Misuse or circumvention of budgets	
Deliberate override or abuse of corporate procedures	• Large round-sum transactions	
	• Gross misuse of mobile and company phones	
Other inappropriate behaviour	• Unusual lifestyle characteristics	
Unusual corporate transactions		The fact that a trader had established his own trading company some years after he joined turned out to be the red flags which lead to the discovery of complex trading and supplier frauds and money-laundering schemes involving the trader and a number of suppliers and brokers.

© *Hibis Scandinavia A/S*

YZW Corporation   Health check pilot #1

2. Payment of bribes to third parties to facilitate business and secure contracts

Red flags	Examples of what to test for	Case examples
Payments to offshore companies through the accounts payable system	Suppliers (in the supplier file, or one-off payments file) which either have a bank account or address in an offshore destination	Millions of dollars of bribes were discovered as round-sum amounts to a front company. These 'agency payments' to the Far East never produced a result – just a promise of a result. During the project post-mortem it was discovered that it was likely that most of the money had been spent by the agent on the import of beer and other provisions intended for the agent's wholesale company.
Manual payment requests which appear urgent and override the controls	Large cash withdrawals or payments to personal accounts	One review unearthed numerous invoices showing that goods were purchased from the former Soviet Union, the invoices were from a Cypriot shell-company and the money was paid into a Swiss bank account. However, senior management had approved the arrangement. During a discussion on the morality of this practice (in light of the corporate code of conduct) the head of audit commented, somewhat ironically, 'We like morality here – double morality is even better.'
A culture of 'getting the business at all costs'	Large round-sum, one-off payments	When some rather unusual British Virgin Islands invoices were detected, the initial reaction of the company was to tell the audit team that this was an old problem which had been fully investigated and that no more deals were being done with this company (believed to be the commercial arm of an organised crime syndicate). However, further analysis of the customer database revealed a telephone number of a related company, which turned out to be an unassigned number in the company's St Petersburg offices, indicating that the criminals had already infiltrated.
	Ask the question (for example in a workshop of senior marketing and finance people) 'What is the best way of making facilitation payments so that we do not get caught out?'	

© Hibis Scandinavia A/S

YZW Corporation

Health check pilot #1

3. Corruption within supplier relationships

Red flags	Examples of what to test for	Case examples
Overcharging by suppliers	• Totals of the supplier's invoice amounts (net of tax) greatly exceed what is registered in the purchasing system (or covered by contracts)	Comparison of several purchase orders estimated against invoices showed that they matched exactly, every time with amounts such as $17 654.34 and $21 320.00. Closer examination showed that the purchase orders were completed weeks after the invoices were created. The construction company turned out to be a fifth floor apartment in a salubrious suburb of a small Italian town. The invoice numbers from the supplier were in no particular order and appeared to have been made up spontaneously. The use of a suspicious tax number '1234...' on the invoices (which subsequently proved the company was also committing tax fraud) gave the impression that the people behind this fraud had, over time, become careless (or even arrogant). Templates for the invoices were subsequently discovered on the plant manager's computer and the supplier made a full confession that he would never have got the contract had he not paid 10–20 per cent of the invoice sum to the plant manager.
Irregularities in the tender and award process		
Employee–supplier conflicts of interest	• Sequential supplier invoice numbers	
Price fixing/cartels	• Employee is a director or owner in a private company	
	• The major supplier's head office address is an accommodation address, a multiple accommodation address or even an offshore shell company	By analysing orders and invoices it was discovered that supplier A, which invoiced around $10 million per annum, had order coverage for around 60 per cent of this value. The remaining invoices related to ad hoc work. The invoices were sequential and deeper analysis showed that the supplier had been set up a number of years ago to act as an intermediary to handle a large number of small subcontractors and one-man bands. Supplier A, which was still only a two-man operation, had turned into a conduit through which services were sourced. Complaints were now pouring in from the subcontractors that supplier A had been artificially inflating its prices whilst only allowing those who paid exorbitant entry fees and commissions to supply services to the ultimate client.
	• Supplier invoices show scant details of the supplier and/or what services have been provided	

© Hibis Scandinavia A/S

YZW Corporation

4. Unethical customer behaviour and preferential customer treatment

Red flags	Examples of what to test for	Case examples
Customers receive goods free of charge or other special treatment in collusion with employees	• Sales transactions which show consistent net underpricing to particular customers when taking all credit notes, low prices, free deliveries, returns (which may be fictitious) and delivery costs into account	Detailed analysis of customer sales revealed that one particular customer was receiving many deliveries of small quantities of product. What was especially unusual was that the prices were in most cases lower than those which the high volume customers were paying. Further analysis revealed that the supplier was funding the full cost of delivery (sometimes even at two-minutes notice and a three-hour taxi journey). Investigation uncovered a collusive relationship between certain managers and the customer.
Credit notes are suppressed	• Customer addresses showing several customers sharing the same address or even bank accounts	On first impressions, the star salesman, Mr S, seemed to be achieving high volume sales at good prices with a small customer with whom he had a very good relationship. Management questions about why the company was selling such high volumes to such a small company were met with plausible if not slightly protective answers from his manager Mr B.
Customer orders and receives large amounts of goods and services and does not pay (subsequently declaring bankruptcy)	• Unusual patterns of visits entertaining on expense claims	However after performing some fraud detection tests it was found that the prices that had been shown to management did not include all the credit notes, returns, free 'samples' (several truckloads on some occasions), and an early payment discount which was granted even though the customer paid usually after 60 days. When the annual customer 'bonus' was taken into account, it was calculated that Mr S was selling the product at a loss of
Sales at very low prices to customers which are in fact 'grey market' resellers	• Customer address is in fact a front company or 'drop address'	around 10% per sale. Further investigation showed that Mr S was actually behind all the sales orders and was also administering the company's financial affairs and bank accounts. It was also shown that the customer was, in fact, a trading house which sold the product on, in competition with the company's main customers and destroying its market share.
	• Large, unusual credit notes	
	• Complete absence of credit notes (can indicate suppression and diversion of funds to other accounts)	
	• Scant documentation to support sales orders	

YZW Corporation

Health check pilot #1

5. Deliberate incorrect reporting or concealment of losses

Red flags	Examples of what to test for	Case examples
Unusual and irregular accounting entries	• Unusual, loosely controlled balance sheet accounts (such as '999' accounts) or cost accounts which are not examined	When looking at the actual cost of construction and maintenance projects it was noticed that the maximum variance was plus or minus 0.6 per cent against the original budget. Closer examination showed that project costs were being 'smoothed' by the chief accountant using a zero value materials store which was created when surplus materials arose.
Unrealistic or 'too good to be true' figures	• Reported figures which are always in line with budgets	An invoice for $500 from a Panamanian offshore registration agent was examined more closely. This was found to be a company which had been registered by the local finance director and over time had been used by the local management as a secret off-book fund and company to pay commissions, submit orders, and even pay management tax-free bonuses.
	• Large unusual movements and accounting entries or journals	
	• Use of offshore companies	

© Hibis Scandinavia A/S

YZW Corporation

Health check pilot #1

6. Unethical or inappropriate behaviour by third parties such as consultants

Red flags	Examples of what to test for	Case examples
Consultants (third parties) steal sensitive information	• Consultants who hold directorships in other companies (including suppliers), whether they have court judgements against them or a history of bankrupt companies behind them	A consultant had for several years been the key to the development and maintenance of a company's customer management system. During a fraud profiling workshop the system was identified as a key asset and consultants (in general) were identified as potential fraudsters. As part of the remedial action following the workshop, background screening revealed that the consultant had been convicted on at least one occasion for misusing the intellectual property of his clients.
Consultants (third parties) initiate purchases from own companies	• A network of consultants and third parties controlling key positions	
Consultants (third parties) overcharge their clients	• Common characteristics and hidden relationships between suppliers, customers and consultants	A consultant who held the position of Stock Accountant, wrote off surplus stock and sold it in the Far East through his secret materials management company.
	• Round-sum invoices for services provided	A consultant acting as deputy project manager on a construction project, steered millions of dollars of purchasing to his affiliated company.
	• Unusual expenditure patterns including expenses and travel	A sequential test on invoices submitted by a consultant, who also occupied a senior management position, showed that he also added a sum for three mugs of tea on each invoice. A healthy suspicion as to why anyone invoicing $20 000 per month would include such trivial expenses on his invoice led to the company discovering that 'Mr 3 Mugs of Tea' was also a paid director of one of his employer's key service suppliers.

© *Hibis Scandinavia A/S*

YZW Corporation

Health check pilot #1

7. Misappropriation and manipulation of inventories

Red flags	Examples of what to test for	Case examples
Missing goods (presumed stolen)	• In-depth analysis of major projects	Analysis of warehouse records showed large numbers of stock write-offs for a particular warehouse. This had initially not been seen as significant, as warehouse stock write-offs were generally high. However, when reviewed in more detail it could be shown that delivery notes were raised and then cancelled within the system, and goods had been leaving the premises anyway.
Deliberate write-downs of stock to scrap or zero value and sale on market	• Scrutiny of materials certificates	
Misuse of inventory and logistics process for the purposes of a concealed 'business within a business'	• Analysis of inventory movement codes • Analysis of warehouse records	Examination of materials certificates showed that a large number had been faxed in and no original had followed. Careful scrutiny of these faxes and certain dates indicated that they may have been altered. Further analysis and investigation identified the companies which had sent in the materials to be front companies.
		Analysis of stock movement codes identified a code with the prefix 'XX'. Further enquiry identified these as returns of consumer goods (such as fridges, TVs and microwave ovens) which had been ordered by staff working on an offshore oil platform. The goods were sent to the platform by helicopter and then returned by supply boat as 'not required'. The employees actually did pay for the goods but had invented this scheme as a way of avoiding sales tax. (The XX code was not reported in any system). The logistics costs of this 'harmless operation' were exorbitant.

© *Hibis Scandinavia A/S*

8 *Example Diagnostic Reports from a Corporate Health Check*

YZW Corporation

Example diagnostic reports from a corporate health check

These two diagnostic reports illustrate the nature and extent of the results of a corporate health check. When trying to identify the red flags of fraud and corruption, maintain confidentiality and discretion, minimise disruption, and work with limited resources, it is essential that tests are used selectively. The phrase 'follow the money' (which gained recognition during the Watergate Scandal in the USA in the 1970s) should be borne in mind when examining suspicious transactions.

By closely examining money which comes in and goes out of YZW Corporation, and the patterns inherent within these transactions, it is possible to apply a select number of tests to detect the possible footprint of fraud and corruption. The tests performed are shown in the vertical columns to the right of Diagnostic Report #1 (Payments) and Diagnostic Report #2 (Receipts). Results are then analysed, correlated and interpreted.

The examples described are based on cases which were discovered by real health checks. All names and references to persons are fictitious. The reports are samples only and in reality can be several pages long.

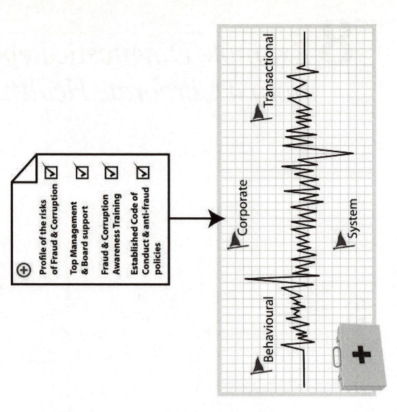

© *Hibis Scandinavia A/S*

YZW Corporation - Health Check 200Y

Sample Diagnostic Report #1

Payments and accounts payable transactions

(August 200X - September 200Y)

Transactions

Supplier invoices, credit notes and manual payments

Number	1,100,245
Value	270,130,532

Suppliers in use (in period)   14739

Evaluation Criteria

No further action required

Should review and possibly follow up

Should review in detail

Discuss, review findings, review and follow up

Primary Selection Criteria

Secondary Selection Criteria

© Hibis Scandinavia A/S

No	Evaluation	Supplier no.	Supplier name	Date of sample invoice	Sample invoice no.	Curr.	Amount	Total amount invoiced from this supplier (1 Aug 200X - 30 Sept 200Y)	No of invoices and credit notes period	Main indicators or issues
1	⚑⚑	0000239321	CREMONA ELECTRONICS GMBH	23.01.200Y	76	GBP	2,291.00	264,833.00	109	Very little information was available about this supplier. It appears to operate from a terraced house in the city of XXXXXXXXX. Company searches indicate that the company has not filed accounts for 19 months and is due to be struck off for non-compliance in five months time.
2	⚑	0003813074	A AND Z INTERNATIONAL LTD	N/A	N/A	N/A	N/A	1,200,272.96	1,123	In spite of being a major supplier to YZW, this company appears to be registered as having 3 employees. In addition the company was set up on 01.05.200X and in a short time appears to have become a major supplier. So far no formal contracts with A and Z have been found.
3	⚑	000030634	TONY NEWMAN LTD	08.03.200X	1285	GBP	4,465.00	540,252.00	119	The invoice reviewed is poorly specified, no order number or address information is included. However, an order number appears to have been added at YZW. It appears that the supplier is not registered in the UK Companies House. There is no listed website or email address on Google.com or 192.co.uk. The home address of Mr Andrew JONES is identical to the supplier address. According to the telephone catalogue of YZW, a Mr Andrew Jones works in Dept 200380 as Manager Logistics and Transportation.

Indicator columns (diagonal headers):

1 - Large suppliers (> 500,000 in year)
2 - Round invoice amounts
3 - Low or unusual supplier invoice no
4 - Potential duplicate supplier details
5 - Potentially duplicate invoices
6 - Potentially sequential supplier invoice no's
7 - Low purchase order coverage
8 - Many large year-end transactions
9 - Early (or advance) payment
10 - Invalid or missing company registration number
11 - Unusual supplier (little footprint)

© *Hibis Scandinavia A/S*

Evaluation	Supplier no.	Supplier name	Date of sample invoice	Sample invoice no.	Curr.	Amount	Total amount invoiced from this supplier (1 Aug 200X - 30 Sept 200Y)	No of invoices and credit notes period
4	000030099	K&J WALTHAMSTOW AND PARTNERS	04.03.200Y	247A	GBP	2,856.90	3,010,911.00	1,153

Indicators:

1 - Large supplies (> 500.000 in year)
2 - Round invoice amounts
3 - Low or unusual supplier invoice no
4 - Potential duplicate supplier details
5 - Potential duplicate invoices
6 - Potentially sequential supplier invoice no's
7 - Low purchase order coverage
8 - Many large year-end transactions
9 - Early (or advance) payment
10 - Invalid or missing company registration number
11 - Unusual supplier (little footprint)

Main indicators or issues

The invoice reviewed makes no references to a purchase order or contract. A number of potential duplicate invoices were identified. Company research indicates the company was established in 1991 and has been a long term supplier to YZW.

© *Hibis Scandinavia A/S*

Evaluation	Supplier no.	Supplier name	Date of sample invoice	Sample invoice no.	Curr.	Amount	Total amount invoiced from this supplier (1 Aug 200X - 30 Sept 200Y)	No of invoices and credit notes period	Indicators (1–11)	Main indicators or issues
5	000030845	ABC CARTELOMA LTD	27.05.200Y	A-74-3265	GBP	10,000.00	1,220,300.00	35		There appears to be very little available information on ABC Carteloma Ltd. The company appears to be some form of consultancy or trading company operating from a host of "office hotels" in the UK, the Channel Islands, Monaco, Cyprus, the Bahamas and Moscow. The web page referred to on the invoice, www.cartelomainternational.net was under construction at the time the Health Check was performed. It is not clear from the sample invoice(s) examined what services have been provided. The invoice refers to an email address cartelomainternational@rambler.ru.
6	000012532	ARLINGTON CONSULTANTS INC	29.04.200Y	09389-77734	USD	120,000.00	?	2		The payment has been booked directly into the General Ledger, bypassing the Accounts Payable System. The supporting documentation is an e-mail with a reference to the company. Initial research indicates that Arlington Consultants is registered in Panama with a New York correspondance address and the money was paid into a bank account in Switzerland. One other similar manual payment to this account has been found so far.

Indicator legend:

1 - Large supplies (> 500,000 in year)
2 - Round invoice amounts
3 - Low or unusual supplier invoice no
4 - Potential duplicate supplier details
5 - Potential duplicate invoices
6 - Potentially sequential supplier invoice no's
7 - Low purchase order coverage
8 - Many large year-end transactions
9 - Early (or advance) payment
10 - Invalid or missing company registration number
11 - Unusual supplier (little footprint)

© Hibis Scandinavia A/S

Evaluation	Supplier no.	Supplier name	Date of sample invoice	Sample invoice no.	Curr.	Amount	Total amount invoiced from this supplier (1 Aug 200X - 30 Sept 200Y)	No of invoices and credit notes period	Main indicators or issues
7	0000302454	BILL SMITH	28.07.200Y	261	GBP	5,000.00	173,225.00	52	The invoice reviewed appears to cover 5 purchase orders (written on the invoice). Information about the supplier only includes what appears to be a private name and address. The company is not listed in the companies register and the address on the invoice coincides with a Ms Alyson Burge, a Sales Assistant currently employed in YZW's NNNNNN office.
8	0000132663	FVB MANAGED SERVICES LIMITED	04.12.200X	499	GBP	259,957.53	3,091,215.49	53	According to Companies House, FVB Managed Services is a Business and Management Consultancy but research indicates that the company may be in financial trouble. Press articles allude to impending civil and criminal charges against the former Chairman and founder Mr Frenton van Boler for misleading the shareholders, false reporting and embezzlement.

Indicator columns:

1 - Large suppliers (> 500,000 in year)
2 - Round invoice amounts
3 - Low or unusual amounts
4 - Potential duplicate supplier invoice no
5 - Potential duplicate supplier details
6 - Potentially sequential supplier invoice no's
7 - Low purchase order coverage
8 - Many large year-end transactions
9 - Early (or advance) payment
10 - Invalid or missing company registration number
11 - Unusual supplier (little footprint)

The diagonal column indicators are:

1 - Large suppliers (> 500,000 in year)
2 - Round invoice amounts
3 - Low or unusual invoice amounts
4 - Low or unusual supplier invoice no
5 - Potential duplicate supplier details
6 - Potential duplicate invoices
7 - Potentially sequential supplier invoice no's
8 - Low purchase order coverage
9 - Many large year-end transactions
10 - Early (or advance) payment
11 - Invalid or missing payment
12 - Unusual supplier (little footprint)
13 - Unusual company registration number

Evaluation	Supplier no.	Supplier name	Date of sample invoice	Sample invoice no.	Curr.	Amount	Total amount invoiced from this supplier (1 Aug 200X - 30 Sept 200Y)	No of invoices and credit notes period	Main indicators or issues
9	0000301069	FIDEL AB	24.12.200X	PK162/FT	EUR	22,190.76	2,278,608.00	317	The supplier appears to be significantly dependent on YZW. Although the head office is in Stockholm, Sweden the contact address and telephone number on file matches exactly the address of the consultancy company Swedecraft Ltd (reference case #25). Many of the payments to Fidel are made up to 20 days before the due date and up to three bank accounts (in Sweden, the UK and Jersey) have been used. Cursory research indicates that the company is part of the CASCO group.
10	0000305052	GLOBAL SERVICE GROUP LTD	05.01.200Y	5001965	EUR	21,823.00	127,402.00	8	The invoice itself is poorly specified and provides very little additional information about the Global Service Group Ltd or what it does. However it appears that reference is made to a contract with the Molvanian Sea and Rail Freight Co. made by YZW Corporation in 200W. Initial research (ref: Molvania: Calauro, Gleisner and Sitch) indicate that the country is landlocked and has a limited rail network.

Evaluation	Supplier no.	Supplier name	Date of sample invoice	Sample invoice no.	Curr.	Amount	Total amount invoiced from this supplier (1 Aug 200X - 30 Sept 200Y)	No of invoices and credit notes period	Main indicators or issues
?	0000304035	NEW MASTER AND SLAVE LTD	09.05.200Y	4553	GBP	5,980.28	123,250.00	681	Very little information was available about this supplier. The invoice appears to be very poorly specified. It appears to be related to the construction of premises.
	0000308351	BRIAN JONES MERCHANTS LTD	24.05.200Y	764	GBP	10,868.75	2,080,542.28	683	Company details indicate that the the company Brian Jones Merchants went into voluntary liquidation on 21.03.200Y

Indicator columns:

1 - Large supplies (> 500,000 in year)
2 - Round invoice amounts
3 - Low or unusual invoice amounts
4 - Potential sequential supplier invoice no
5 - Potential duplicate supplier details
6 - Potential duplicate supplier invoices
7 - Potentially sequential supplier invoice no's
8 - Many large order coverage
9 - Early (or advance) payment
10 - Invalid or missing company registration number
11 - Unusual supplier (little footprint)

Row references: 11, 12

© Hibis Scandinavia A/S

YZW Corporation - Health Check 200Y

Sample Diagnostic Report # 2

Receipts and accounts recievable transactions

(August 200X - September 200Y)

Transactions

Customer invoices, credit notes and miscellaneous receipts

Number	1,100,245
Value	303,986,839

Active customers (in period)   5751

Evaluation Criteria

No further action required

Review before closing out

Need to review

Review and discuss next steps

Primary Selection Criteria

Secondary Selection Criteria

© *Hibis Scandinavia A/S*

Evaluation	Customer / Recipient no.	Customer name (s)	Date of sample transaction	Curr.	Amount	Total sold to / recieved from this customer / party (1 Aug 200X - 30 Sept 200Y)	No of invoices and credit notes period	1 - Large customers (> 500,000 in year)	2 - Potential Tax Haven Company or Bank Account	3 - Multiple customers with common address detail	4 - Pricing significantly below average for market	5 - Possible front company	6 - Large, unusual year end transactions	7 - Significant credit notes issued	8 - Also a supplier	9 - Possible agent / trader	10 - Mismatch company details	11 - Lack of supporting documentation	Summary
1	C-2008654-1	WEISS HANDELL AG	07.02.200Y	EUR	75,012.00	26,483,301.00	1,300			■	■								Large volumes of a multitude of products have been sold to Weiss Handell AG. It appears that Weiss has been sold to at prices equivalent to those reserved for manufacturing and development partners. Information collected on Weiss Handell indicates that they are a trading company employing 10 people and are selling at lower prices to customers of YZW Corporation in the open market.
2	C-6008348-0	MOLTON COMMERCIALS INTERNATIONAL	23.12.200X	GBP	N/A	1,200,272.96	1,123				■					■			The invoice samples show that YZW is selling equipment and providing services at rates up to 50% below normal market rates to Molton Commericals. Some used equipment is being provided Free of Charge. Molton Commercials appears to exhibit all the characteristics of an authorised reseller of YZW Corporation. However, enquiries to date show that no such reseller agreement exists.
3	C-2004356-0	NAVONA ILLIAS PTY, BERNT ANKER AS, WHYCLIFFE LTD, ANDERSEN TOOLS INC	various	EUR	N/A	97,183.00	460							■					It appears that invoices to these customers are regularly being sent out with incorrect prices, hence the unusually large number of credit notes. Approximately 70% of the errors are for pricing which is too high. All customers appear to pertain to the salesman Mr Ronald Navarro, based in XXXXXX.

Evaluation	Customer / Recipient no.	Customer name (s)	Date of sample transaction	Curr.	Amount	Total sold to / recieved from this customer / party (1 Aug 200X - 30 Sept 200Y)	No of invoices and credit notes period	1 - Large customers (> 500,000 in year)	2 - Potential Tax Haven Company or Bank Account	3 - Multiple customers with common address detail	4 - Pricing significantly below average for market	5 - Possible front company or small company	6 - Large, unusual year end transactions	7 - Significant credit notes issued	8 - Also a supplier	9 - Possible agent / trader	10 - Mismatch - company details	11 - Lack of supporting documentation	Summary
4	C-4007392-1 C-4007345-0 C-9990000-0 C-4006539-1	VARIOUS CUSTOMERS (Pertaining to salesman Harry L)	various	USD	N/A	120,321.00	119				■								Analysis of sales to certain customers pertaining to salesman number 824 in the XXXXX region shows that low volumes of product are being sold to these particular customers at wholesale prices. Freight costs are also denoted as "Free of Charge". Many of the customers are located within a 5 mile radius of Mr Harry L's home address.
5	C-9006434-0	MEENATAR TRADING LTD	01.08.200Y	GBP	65,291.00	3,010,911.00	754	■	■										A number of companies appear to be operating from this address. Sales patterns indicate shipments have increased significantly in the last 3 months but payments from this customer have virtually ceased. According to correspondence files reviewed and information found on the internet it appears that the main company at this address, Meenatar Trading Ltd is experiencing serious financial difficulties and is in danger of going bankrupt.

© Hibis Scandinavia A/S

Evaluation	Customer / Recipient no.	Customer name (s)	Date of sample transaction	Curr.	Amount	Total sold to / recieved from this customer / party (1 Aug 200X - 30 Sept 200Y)	No of invoices and credit notes period	1- Large customers (> 500,000 in year)	2 - Potential Tax Haven Company or Bank Account	3 - Multiple customers with common address detail	4 - Pricing significantly below average for market	5 - Possible front company or small company	6 - Large, unusual year end company or transactions	7 - Significant credit notes issued	8 - Also a supplier	9 - Possible agent / trader	10 - Mismatch - company details	11 - Lack of supporting documentation	Summary
6	C-6004826-0	ACTON MERIT (BVI) LTD	14.07.200Y	USD	400,100.00	5,002,200.00	14		■										The receipt in question is from a company, ostensibly based in the British Virgin Islands. The money has been paid out of a Swiss Bank Account pertaining to this company. There are no indications on the other payments which were examined, or in the customers master files as to who the actual customer (and recipient of the goods) were, and in which country they were located.
7		MODENA COMMERCIALE SPA	12.02.200Y	EUR	120,000.00	3,720,632.00	135	■											Although there is a large volume of low-priced goods being delivered it appears that these are "seconds" or "off-spec". Modena Commerciale SPA is a small company which trades product and has an associated finance company "Modena International Finance SPA". The product is marked as originating from the XXXX plant. What is unusual is that the recorded volume of off-spec produced by the plant in the period is less than half of the volume sale to Modena Commerciale SPA. All transactions are controlled by the salesman Mr Francis Goodname.

© Hibis Scandinavia A/S

Evaluation	Customer / Recipient no.	Customer name (s)	Date of sample transaction	Curr.	Amount	Total sold to / recieved from this customer / party (1 Aug 200X - 30 Sept 200Y)	No of invoices and credit notes period	1 - Large customers (> 500,000 in year)	2 - Potential Tax Haven Company or Bank Account	3 - Multiple customers with common address detail	4 - Pricing significantly below average for market	5 - Possible front company or small company	6 - Large, unusual year end transactions	7 - Significant credit notes issued	8 - Also a supplier	9 - Possible agent / trader	10 - Mismatch - company details	11 - Lack of supporting documentation	Summary
8	C-300-6478-1	HAIDER AND HAIDER MANUFACTURING	N/A	N/A,USD	N/A	50,000,000.00	310												There appear to be virtually no credit notes booked against this customer's account. At the accounting centre we were informed that when the customer makes a genuine complaint the credit notes are produced but not sent and are booked to an account called the Rosebud account. Payments are made out against this account. Furthermore we are informed that when revenues are booked against this customer, 1.5% of these revenues are re-booked to the Rosebud account. Apparently this practice has been taking place for many years.
9	C-300-6360-1	FAR EAST CABLE SUPPLY	08.09.200Y	USD	5,000.00	173,225.00	123												The large number of credit notes appear to indicate that this has been a very unprofitable supply contract. Enquiries indicate that when faults are discovered, goods are not returned due to the high freight costs.

© *Hibis Scandinavia A/S*

9 *Elements of a Fraud and Corruption Resistance Assessment System*[1]

Element	Name and description

1   **The tone at the top**

This element evaluates the degree and effectiveness of senior management's commitment to preventing fraud and corruption. The tone set at the top of an organization regarding fraud and corruption prevention has a crucial effect throughout the rest of the organization. This element explores the role of senior management in setting the 'tone at the top', and how the message that fraud and corruption will not be tolerated is communicated throughout the organization. Demonstrating commitment to fraud and corruption prevention is management's responsibility. It needs to be visible to all employees, credible, embedded in the organizational culture and also visible to external parties.

2   **Fraud and corruption risk assessment**

A thorough understanding of fraud and corruption risk across the organization is a pre-requisite for effective prevention. The assessment involves the systematic identification and ranking of those fraud and corruption risks which can and do affect the organization at all levels. Fraud and corruption risk assessment involves looking at how resistant the controls are to specific methods of fraud and corruption. The purpose of this element is to evaluate the extent to which the organization's ability to resist fraud and corruption has been assessed.

3   **Fraud and corruption risk treatment**

Once fraud and corruption opportunities have been assessed, effective and mitigating measures have to be put in place by all levels of management, from the top down. Treatment in the form of a strategic plan and management responses will lead to a reduced risk of fraud and corruption as well as a significantly increased chance of early detection. The purpose of this element is to measure the degree and effectiveness of mitigating measures.

---

1. Reproduced by kind permission of Det Norske Veritas (DNV), an international certification and assessment agency. In 2005, the authors were external participants in a DNV project initiated to design, develop and pilot a Fraud and Corruption Resistance Assessment System.

© Det Norske Veritas

Element	Name and description

4   **Implementation of controls**

The implementation of internal control measures should correspond to the specific fraud and corruption risks which have been identified and documented. In addition certain fundamental controls such as screening of employees, channels for reporting of malpractice and protection of assets need to be working effectively. Unnecessary or redundant controls should be identified and eliminated. The nature and purpose behind corporate governance regulations needs to be recognized by management and properly embedded within the organization. The purpose of this element is to measure the degree and evaluate the effectiveness of how the anti-fraud and corruption controls have been implemented.

5   **Training and awareness programmes**

Awareness of fraud and corruption risks is a key component of fraud and corruption prevention. Training programmes should be practical in nature, cover a wide spectrum of risks and apply to all employees as well as involved third parties. Training programmes should form part of the organization's ongoing practices and should allow feedback and sharing of information and best practices. The purpose of this element is to measure the degree and evaluate the effectiveness of the organization's fraud and corruption training and awareness programmes.

6   **Risk follow-up**

A system should exist to ensure that fraud and corruption risks are regularly followed up by the correct level of management based on the risk level. Fraud risks should also be re-evaluated whenever major change initiatives are introduced, for example, new or re-engineered products or processes. A mechanism should be in place for situations where line managers believe that a change initiative has created unacceptable fraud risks. The purpose of this element is to measure the degree and effectiveness of how fraud and corruption risks are being followed up.

7   **Internal audit process**

All organizations require some form of independent function to ensure that controls are working and that anti-fraud and -corruption measures are functioning as intended. This function is usually referred to as 'internal audit'. The internal audit function should have a clear mandate, be staffed by appropriately experienced and qualified personnel, and spend a proportion of its time on anti-fraud and -corruption activities. The purpose of this element is to measure the degree and effectiveness of the internal audit processes with respect to fraud and corruption controls.

8   **Monitoring of the executive board**

The board of directors has primary responsibility for setting the fraud and corruption risk management strategy. The audit committee is responsible for actively overseeing the effectiveness of implementation of that strategy. The audit committee is also responsible for arranging and reviewing an annual fraud and corruption risk

Element	Name and description

assessment covering the board of directors and senior management. The purpose of this element is to measure and evaluate the degree of monitoring of the executive board and senior management.

9   **(Proactive) Monitoring and detection**

Proactive fraud and corruption detection is a key element in the risk management strategy, either to prevent illicit activity succeeding in the first place or to catch it in its infancy. Tests and triggers, which assist in the early detection of the symptoms of fraud and corruption, should be embedded into the organization's communication policies as well as procedures and systems. The purpose of this element is to measure the degree and effectiveness of the monitoring and detection processes.

10   **Management of incidents**

Management of incidents involves the methodical investigation and examination of incidents of potential fraud and corruption as well as the actions taken to remedy the problems observed. This should also include identifying and treating the root causes of problems and not just the symptoms. The purpose of this element is to measure and evaluate the degree and effectiveness of management systems and practices for managing incidents of potential fraud and corruption.

11   **Learning from events**

All recognized incidents of fraud and corruption provide the organization and its management with opportunities for improvements. By evaluating how and why incidents of fraud and corruption occurred the organization can learn what is required to prevent them recurring. The purpose of this element is to assess the extent and effectiveness of the systems for recording and follow-up of incidents, feedback to key support functions, and the methods of dissemination of information and experiences.

12   **Measuring results and review of actions**

All stakeholders including owners, audit committees, non-executive directors, regulators, financial institutions, governments and non-governmental organizations have different requirements and interests in respect of the prevention, management and reporting of fraud and corruption. The purpose of this element is to measure the quality, extent, effectiveness and consistency of the reporting of fraud- and corruption-related risks, incidents and follow up actions to the stakeholders.

10 *Fraud and Corruption Library*

Fraud and Corruption Library

Library of common generic methods of fraud and corruption

How to use this library

The Fraud and Corruption Library is an aide-memoire to the assessor guidelines for the fraud and corruption resistance rating protocol. The library has been distilled from hundreds of different methods of fraud and corruption which have occurred in the past. In order to understand which methods of fraud and corruption would work best in the company, it is necessary for assessors to put themselves in the position of a potential criminal (insider/outsider or both) and identify methods which would bypass any defences (or controls) which exist. This 'thinking like a thief' concept is fundamental to being able to evaluate which methods of fraud would work best, and whether these actually have been recognized by the organisation. The generic methods in this library should provide the assessor with a starting point for evaluating some of the most common frauds and how these would be committed against the company which they are reviewing. *This library should not be used as a definitive checklist: assessors should continually look for variations or new methods not listed.*

Method of fraud/corruption

Method of fraud/corruption	1 – Corporate (includes share and investment transactions, major acquisitions and disposals, etc)	2 – Accounting (manipulation of the financial records)	3 – Property and major asset management	4 – Human resources, recruiting, payroll and use of consultants	5 – Procurement and purchasing	6 – Outsourcing / large service contracts	7 – Treasury and corporate finance	8 – Payments (to suppliers, employees, etc)	9 – Inventory	10 – Logistics and transportation	11 – Sales and marketing	12 – Information technology and systems	13 – Other, to be added as required – Inflation of figures / assets
Employees inflate project budget and submits invoices from their own company without any budget overrun.		X						X					
Overcharging by a long-term supplier(s) which the company is dependent on.					X			X	X				
Subcontractors or employees register excess hours on projects to achieve fraudulent payment of overtime.				X				X					
Supplier overcharging for 'ghost hours', which are spent working on private projects for employees.				X				X					
Insertion by suppliers of additional hidden costs which are not part of contracts. The company does not identify the overcharging, which is kept within budget.					X	X							
Supplier uses group invoicing where costs allocated to different projects are included on the same invoice, in order to be able to hide false costs.					X			X	X	X			
Payment of false invoices/costs, due to lack of specification on a supplier invoice.								X		X			
Payment of duplicate invoices from a supplier to another bank account.							X	X					

© Hibis Scandinavia A/S / Det Norske Veritas

Method of fraud/corruption

Method of fraud/corruption	1	2	3	4	5	6	7	8	9	10	11	12	13
Internal customer orders are made for a higher amount than necessary. The supplier and the internal customer split the surplus.											■		■
Internal employees and external suppliers or consultants cooperate and systematically overcharge the company.				■	■								
Highly specialized consultants are easily able to add to real hours spent, budget increases, etc., because of a lack of knowledge of the particular discipline in the company.				■			■	■					
An agreement between an employee and a supplier that 2-3% of a payment or order amount wil be transferred to an offshore bank account.								■					
An employee ensures a dependent relationship between a 'friendly' supplier and the company.				■	■								
Employees with approval rights collude and submit fictitious invoices or invoices from suppliers owned by employees.		■						■					
Employee from accounts receivable department writes false credit notes to customers with number of personal account or of an account of a company controlled by the employee.						■	■				■		

Column key:

1 - Corporate (includes share and investment transactions, major acquisitions and disposals, etc)
2 - Accounting (manipulation of the financial records)
3 - Property and major asset management
4 - Human resources, recruiting, payroll and use of consultants
5 - Procurement and purchasing
6 - Outsourcing / large service contracts
7 - Treasury and corporate finance
8 - Payments (to suppliers, employees, etc)
9 - Inventory
10 - Logistics and transportation
11 - Sales and marketing
12 - Information technology and systems
13 - Other, to be added as required - Inflation of figures / assets

© Hibis Scandinavia A/S / Det Norske Veritas

Method of fraud/corruption	1 - Corporate (includes share and investment transactions, major acquisitions and disposals, etc)	2 - Accounting (manipulation of the financial records)	3 - Property and major asset management	4 - Human resources, recruiting, payroll and use of consultants	5 - Procurement and purchasing	6 - Outsourcing / large service contracts	7 - Treasury and corporate finance	8 - Payments (to suppliers, employees, etc)	9 - Inventory	10 - Logistics and transportation	11 - Sales and marketing	12 - Information technology and systems	13 - Other, to be added as required - Inflation of figures / assets
Fictitious invoices are created, sent in, inserted into the payment stream approved. (As long as invoices are either installed, meet certain electronic approval criteria and are for relatively small amounts, they get paid automatically and get lost in the budgets).								■					
An employee hires a fictitious person and directs payments to own account.				■									
Payment of purchases made by a non-employee.				■				■					
An external or internal person creates a false fax by pasting genuine signatures on and then sends it to the bank to make a payment to an account set up to look like a genuine account.						■	■	■					
An internal person steals passwords to payment systems and then inputs a series of payments to own account.						■	■	■					
An internal person creates a false payment instruction with forged signatures and submits it for processing. Similarly, an external person sends in a false payment instruction as if it was from a genuine supplier or customer.						■	■						
An external or internal person steals blank cheques, forges the signatures and cashes the cheques through an account set up to look like a genuine account.						■	■	■					

Method of fraud/corruption

Method of fraud/corruption	1 - Corporate (includes share and investment transactions, major acquisitions and disposals, etc)	2 - Accounting (manipulation of the financial records)	3 - Property and major asset management	4 - Human resources, recruiting, payroll and use of consultants	5 - Procurement and purchasing	6 - Outsourcing / large service contracts	7 - Treasury and corporate finance	8 - Payments (to suppliers, employees, etc)	9 - Inventory	10 - Logistics and transportation	11 - Sales and marketing	12 - Information technology and systems	13 - Other, to be added as required - Inflation of figures / assets
Stealing incoming cheques and cash through an account set up to look like a bona fide payee.							■						
A person sends a false email payment request together with a hard-copy printout with a forged approval signature for processing.							■	■					
A manager instructs staff to transfer maturing funds to his or her own bank account set up to look like a company account.		■					■						
Taking advantage of the lack of time which typically occurs during book closing to get fake invoices approved and paid.		■			■			■					
Employee establishes and uses own consultancy company (for personal gain) which conflicts with the company's interests.				■	■								
Private expenses added to travel expense claims or invoices.				■				■					
Purchase of additional (unnecessary) items that can be sold to third parties or used privately.				■	■				■	■			
Private use of company cars and other vehicles.									■	■			
Private use of tools and other material.									■				
Approval of invoices of private expenses by an employee.				■				■					

Method of fraud/corruption

Categories:

1 - Corporate (includes share and investment transactions, major acquisitions and disposals, etc)
2 - Accounting (manipulation of the financial records)
3 - Property and major asset management
4 - Human resources, recruiting, payroll and use of consultants
5 - Procurement and purchasing
6 - Outsourcing / large service contracts
7 - Treasury and corporate finance
8 - Payments (to suppliers, employees, etc)
9 - Inventory
10 - Logistics and transportation
11 - Sales and marketing
12 - Information technology and systems
13 - Other, to be added as required - Inflation of figures / assets

Method of fraud/corruption	1	2	3	4	5	6	7	8	9	10	11	12	13
In an application process a manager chooses to hire someone very close (husband, brother, etc) over another qualified applicant.				■									
Purchasing company cars at a low price and selling them at a higher price.					■				■				
Inadvertant leakage of sensitive information by giving people the opportunity to look at company documents at airports, on airplanes, in taxis or other public places (like the Internet).	■												
Sale of critical bid information, contract details or other sensitive information to a competitor.	■				■								■
Selling or providing critical bid information to a potential bidder in a tender process.					■								
Transfer of knowledge to a competitor by an employee who eventually joins the competitor's company.													■
Use of inside privileged knowledge for trading of shares in either the company or a partner, supplier, customer or other associated listed company.	■												
Payment of agency / facilitation fees (also known as bribes) in order to secure a contract.	■				■					■			
Payments (bribery) to customs officials, tax inspectors, etc.								■					

© Hibis Scandinavia A/S / Det Norske Veritas

Method of fraud/corruption

Business area / category columns:

1 – Corporate (includes share and investment transactions, major acquisitions and disposals, etc)
2 – Accounting (manipulation of the financial records)
3 – Property and major asset management
4 – Human resources, recruiting, payroll and use of consultants
5 – Procurement and purchasing
6 – Outsourcing / large service contracts
7 – Treasury and corporate finance
8 – Payments (to suppliers, employees, etc)
9 – Inventory
10 – Logistics and transportation
11 – Sales and marketing
12 – Information technology and systems
13 – Other, to be added as required – Inflation of figures / assets

Method of fraud/corruption	1	2	3	4	5	6	7	8	9	10	11	12	13
Kickbacks paid to senior management in relation to the acquisition of a new business or company.	■												
Kickbacks paid to senior management in relation to disposal / sale of a part of the business.	■												
An employee agrees to sell company-owned property at a value below market value either to receive a kickback in return or in order to sell to the company at a higher price in the future.			■										
Purchase of property at a value which is higher than market value in exchange for a kickback.			■										
Supplier and employee collude in connection with procurement and award of contracts and orders.					■								
Sale (or theft) of the company's services or products below market price.											■		
Selling products (for example specific parts used for industrial purposes) at a very low price to an arranged network of buyers.											■		
IT person or other employee accesses a batch file of payment instructions being transferred from an accounting system to a payment system and alters bank account details to divert the payments to own account.							■					■	

Method of fraud/corruption	1 - Corporate (includes share and investment transactions, major acquisitions and disposals, etc)	2 - Accounting (manipulation of the financial records)	3 - Property and major asset management	4 - Human resources, recruiting, payroll and use of consultants	5 - Procurement and purchasing	6 - Outsourcing / large service contracts	7 - Treasury and corporate finance	8 - Payments (to suppliers, employees, etc)	9 - Inventory	10 - Logistics and transportation	11 - Sales and marketing	12 - Information technology and systems	13 - Other, to be added as required - Inflation of figures / assets
An IT person (or other suitable skilled employee) accesses a file containing static data and alters the bank account details to divert payments to own account.							■					■	
Inflation of sales figures which are credited out after the year end.	■	■											
Inflation of balance sheet asset values.	■	■											

© Hibis Scandinavia A/S / Det Norske Veritas

References

Association of Certified Fraud Examiners (2002, 2004, 2006), 'Report to the Nation on Occupational Fraud and Abuse'.

Basle Committee on Banking Supervision (2003), *Sound Practices for the Management and Supervision of Operational Risk*, Bank for International Settlements.

Bosshard, Peter (2005), 'The environment at risk from monuments of corruption', *Global Corruption Report 2005: Corruption in the Construction Industry*, Transparency International, <http://www.transparency.org>. See also <http://www.globalcorruptionreport.org>.

Clarke, John (2005), *Working with Monsters*, Random House Australia.

Comer, Michael J. (2003), *Investigating Corporate Fraud*, Gower Publishing Limited.

Comer, Michael J. and Stephens, Timothy E. (2004), *Deception at Work: Investigating and Countering Lies and Fraud Strategies*, Gower Publishing Limited.

Committee of Sponsoring Organisations of the Treadway Commission (COSO) (1992), *Internal Control – Integrated Framework*, COSO.

Dunnett, Robert S., Levy, Cindy B. and Simoes, Antonio P. (2005), *The Hidden Costs of Operational Risk*, McKinsey & Company.

FTSE Group (2006), FTSE4Good Index, see also http://www.ftse.com/ftse4good.

Hare, Robert D. (2003), *Without Conscience*, The Guilford Press.

Huther, Jeff and Shah, Anwar (2000), 'Anti-corruption Policies and Programs: a Framework for Evaluation', Policy Research Working Paper 2501, The World Bank.

International Auditing and Assurance Standards Board, (2004), International Standard on Auditing 240, 'The Auditor's Responsibility To Consider Fraud In An Audit Of Financial Statements', International Federation of Accountants.

Kaufmann, Daniel (11 Dec 2003), 'Trillion-dollar scourge of corruption under attack', UN Press Release at the United Nations Convention against Corruption, Mérida, México.

Leech, Tim and Gupta, Parveen P. (1 April 2005), Letter to the US Securities and Exchange Commission regarding experiences with implementing and evaluating Section 404 of the Sarbanes-Oxley Act of 2002. See <http://www.sec.gov>.

Levitt, Stephen D. and Dubner, Stephen J. (2005), *Freakonomics*, HarperCollins Publishers Inc.

Mackenzie, Craig and Mallon, Patrick (2005), 'Rewarding virtue: effective board action on corporate responsibility', see also http://www.insightinvestment.com/responsibility/rewardingvirtue.asp.

PriceWaterhouseCoopers (12 March 2004), 'Investigation into foreign exchange losses at the National Australia Bank'.

Promontory Financial Group LLC and Wachtell, Lipton, Rosen & Katz (12 March 2002), 'Report to the Boards of Directors of Allied Irish Banks, PLC, Allfirst Financial Inc., and Allfirst Bank concerning currency trading losses'.

Public Company Accounting Oversight Board (2004), 'Auditing Standard No. 2 - An Audit of Internal Control Performed in Conjunction with an Audit of Financial Statements'.

Reingold, Jennifer (17 April 2000), 'Executive Pay', *Business Week Online*, http://www.businessweek.com>.

Stansbury, Neil (2005), 'Exposing the Foundations of Corruption in Construction', *Global Corruption Report 2005: Corruption in the Construction Industry*, Transparency International, <http://www.transparency.org>. See also <http://www.globalcorruptionreport.org>.

United Nations Global Compact (2004), Principle 10: 'Businesses should work against corruption in all its forms, including extortion and bribery', see also http://www.unglobalcompact.org.

US-China Business Council (2006), 'Foreign Investment in China', http://www.uschina.org/info/china-briefing-book/chops/fdi-2005.html.

White, Andrew (2001), 'Flow on effects of Recent Collapses', *Collapse Incorporated: Tales, Safeguards and Responsibilities of Corporate Australia*, CCH Australia Limited, Sydney.

White, Ben (20 September 2005), 'Ex-Tyco Officers Sentenced', *Washington Post*, <http://www.washingtonpost.com>.

Index

Tables and figures are indicated by **bold** type.

The Tightrope

A Story of Fraud and Corruption

NIGEL IYER
and
MARTIN SAMOCIUK

Table of Contents

Preface

The story provides answers in plain text to the following questions:

- What are fraud and corruption and who is involved?
- What are typical responses to dealing with fraud and corruption?
- Why is very little done in most cases and why is this the case?
- What are the many, almost insurmountable obstacles to dealing properly and effectively with fraud and corruption?

Using realistic characters the story demonstrates the nature of fraud and corruption as well as the challenges in actually doing something and describes the sheer determination and passion which are needed if a lasting solution is to be found.

The methods of fraud and forms of corruption in this case study are based on an amalgamation of hundreds of cases of corporate fraud and corruption which the authors have seen and investigated. The methods used to manage the risk are also taken from reality and the authors' experience of those which work and those which don't. However the characters in this case study are fictional. Any references to persons alive or dead are purely coincidental.

Acknowledgements for *The Tightrope*

Numerous people from various walks of life provided input, inspired or reviewed the text of *The Tightrope*, making it topical, realistic and hopefully useful in conveying the message. Special thanks go to:

Atle Andreassen, Bengt Arvidsson, Chris Bowes, Robin Brunskill, Crawford Chalmers, Michael Comer, Helge de Fine, John Devaraj, Nathalie Dushesne, Christopher Flint, Bjørn Frang, George Ghinnes, Laurent Giezendanner, Carl-Olov Halvarsson, Sara Miranda Iyer, Anil Iyer, Hilde Susan Jægtnes, Petter Kaareng, Marius Kolbenstvedt, Kimmo Lehtosuo, Ken Matthews, Allan McDonagh, Gary Miller, Richard Minogue, Veronica Morino, Jonathan Norman, Maria Puhr, Tim Puhr, Karen Samociuk, Simon Scales, Henrik Seip, Espen Uvholt, Peter Wieland and all the other people who in some way contributed to this text.

N-Trex

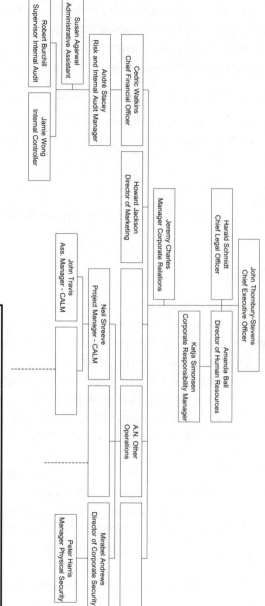

John Thornbury-Stevens
Chief Executive Officer

Harald Schmidt
Chief Legal Officer

Amanda Ball
Director of Human Resources

Katja Simonsen
Corporate Responsibility Manager

Jeremy Charles
Manager Corporate Relations

Cedric Watkins
Chief Financial Officer

Susan Agarwal
Administrative Assistant

André Stacey
Risk and Internal Audit Manager

Robert Burchill
Supervisor Internal Audit

Jamie Wong
Internal Controller

Howard Jackson
Director of Marketing

John Travis
Ass. Manager - CALM

Neil Shreeve
Project Manager - CALM

A.N. Other
Operations

Mirabel Andrews
Director of Corporate Security

Peter Harris
Manager Physical Security

OTHER CAST MEMBERS

Max de Gras	Founder of Xamdos
Deepak Roy	Investigation Manager Xamdos
Sarah Lutz	Investigator Xamdos
Chris Kowalowski	Director RDS Corporation
Conrad Burge	Director Analogy Software Corporation
Georgios	Former sales manager at N-Trex
Marilena Stacey	Wife of André Stacey
Tim Stacey	Son of André and Marilena Stacey (aged 9_)

Act 1: The Awakening

Chapter 1

The simultaneous tapping on my interior office window and ringing of my office phone bring my thoughts abruptly back into the real world.

I am working on my response to draft 14 of the revised N-Trex Code of Conduct which Harald Schmidt of the legal department has sent to me for comment. The so-called Ethics Committee consisting of Harald, our Chief Legal Counsel, Amanda Ball of Human Resources and various other hangers-on like me are responsible for finalising it. If we are to do this properly we should send a really clear message, a message that people will want to follow. I started early today so I could get some peace and quiet to finish this. I have to leave at 3.30 p.m. sharp and take my son Timmy to his football tournament.

Since the arrival of the new Chief Executive John Thornbury-Stevens a couple of years back, flexi-time is now tolerated. 'I pay you to get your job done, not to be chained to your desks,' is one of JTS's stock phrases. Actually he doesn't pay us. The owners do, but like many chief executives of his generation, he sort of feels he owns the company.

I check my mobile. It says 08.27 and already I have three missed calls. Thankfully the phone has been on silent the whole time!

I respond to the tapping on my door and am greeted by Suzy, my secretary … correction … our Departmental Administrator (another JTS modernisation). Our Risk and Internal Audit department consists of the grand total of three people plus Suzy. She's still got her coat on. 'Cedric rang me to say he has been sending you emails and trying you on your mobile since eight o'clock this morning and is worried why you are not responding.' Cedric Watkins, the Chief Financial Officer of N-Trex, moved from National Power a couple of months after John took over here.

'Idiot,' I mutter to myself. Why can't he walk down two flights of stairs and come and tap on my office door like Suzy. He expects that everybody who reports to him is permanently plugged into emails, and will respond instantly day or night. Besides, he could use the exercise.

'What's it about?' I ask Suzy wearily.

'It sounds like he is all worked up about something, though I don't think it is your fault,' she replies.

Good. Cedric is usually worked up on Thursdays, as he certainly puts the hours in during the week and is desperately in need of a holiday. He is probably too scared that John will replace him. Poor guy!

I quickly save the draft of my position paper, grab a coffee, my notebook and mobile and walk up the interior staircase up to Cedric's office.

He greets me: 'André, nice to see you. Glad Suzy got hold of you in the end. Have you been hiding in your office, incommunicado as usual?'

He is all smiles, an ominous sign that I am going to have something dumped on me shortly. 'Shut the door and sit down,' he continues briskly. 'John and I tried to get hold of you yesterday afternoon when we got this, but Suzy said you were at the doctors with your kid. Anyway it wasn't so urgent. John told me to discuss it with you this morning as you are Director of Risk and Compliance, so you are probably the right man to take care of the problem.'

Here it comes, I think, with a sinking feeling in my stomach.

'John is preparing for the meeting this afternoon with that governmental delegation from Minsk … he said it should be OK if you and I sort this out … don't know why Howard got this … he says just ignore it … .' Cedric appears to be talking to himself now while simultaneously fiddling with his PC. He hits a few keys and seconds later his latest laser printer bursts into life. With a hint of gusto he whips off a sheet and hands me the single page as if it was just hot off the press.

To:	john.thornbury-stevens@N-Trex.com;
Cc:	cedric.watkins@N-Trex.com; howard.jackson@N-Trex.com
Subject:	Life is anything BUT c.a.l.m
From:	john.smith9999@hotmail.com
Date:	10.04.20XX

Dear respected gentlemen

I would like to apologise that I am sending you an anonymous email in this way but after you appeared to not have received (or ignored) my previous letter, I would like to put my thoughts down more succinctly and on record. I hope you will see these as constructive comments and also appreciate the fact that until you have taken this matter seriously and dealt with it, I am unlikely to disclose my name for fear of retribution.

Let me re-iterate my main points again:

1. We have strong indications that at least three main suppliers on the CALM project have been grossly overcharging N-Trex through inflated invoices, unnecessary work and numerous other clever and corrupt schemes

2. You are of course aware that the CALM project is now over budget by 125 million and there is still no real proof that the system will be delivered on time and will work. (I know that you and your colleagues have already had discussions about scrapping CALM). I think that 1 and 2 are related

3. Competent honest employees and suppliers are being squeezed out of the project, mainly because they have the skills to make the system work on time and in budget. However the 'Big Three' suppliers and their friends still believe that N-Trex will throw more good money after bad money. They prefer to milk you just a bit more.

Since my last letter I have also found out that at least one of N-Trex's project

managers (it should not be too difficult to work out who...) is in the pocket of the Big Three. You have fallen into the trap that everybody believes that system projects like CALM always go vastly over budget. Our analysis, which we are happy to share with you later on, shows that CALM could have been completed if the correct programming languages had been used at an overrun of just 20% on your original budget.

I suggest you ask your auditors to look much more carefully over the bills that are going through CALM and start taking some action to stop the haemorrhaging!

Will be in touch again shortly and good luck until then

Friend(s) of the CALM project

Ps. my colleagues and I stand to lose a lot if CALM is scrapped and many of them are getting really frustrated. One of them is even off sick and is seeing a psychologist for depression. I hope you can do something because short of exposing this story in the press there is not much we can do without your help.

I have just time to skim the page when Cedric starts up again. 'Seems like an honest enough chap but I just hate it so much when they want to be anonymous,' he muses. 'It gives them a feeling of power over us. Anyway John and I have decided that we need to take this one seriously. After all, the sender knows something about CALM and even knows our discussions about scrapping the project. Can you look into this one and see if there is any truth in it and also find out who this chap is and who his friends are? I wanted also to talk to Neil about it but the boss said that we should wait a little until we have done our homework and I have talked to you. I think that as Neil is the project manager, he has a right to know, but John disagrees. What do you think?'

It's so difficult when he goes into verbal overdrive leaving me no space for questions (let alone breathing). Cedric is pretty overworked and tends to over-react at times like this. At least he has stopped talking.

Several questions pop into my head like 'What previous letter?', 'Why was this email dated two days ago?' and 'Didn't I warn you about Neil's spending six months ago?', but I think it better to keep quiet for now. Cedric has a habit of sticking his head in the sand if he feels somebody is attacking him and this is not the best moment anyway. 'Could be serious', I say 'but I'd like to study it again and check up on some invoices we were looking into before putting some thoughts in writing to you. I'll be back to you by three this afternoon'.

This seems to work as he replies, 'Fine, but I just don't want this sort of thing putting yet another spoke in the wheel of the project. Neil's got enough problems with CALM as it is and this may just push him over the edge. If this John Smith goes to the media, it could give us a real headache just when we don't need it, truth or no truth. For example, take these visitors from Minsk. I don't think they would be too impressed if they found out that our new logistics platform was a shambles.'

Good job I kept quiet! He's really over-reacting now. How he connects the proposed Byelorussian joint venture and an over-budget IT project are beyond me, but I guess it is just that Cedric is paranoid about bad publicity.

My vision of watching Timmy the goalkeeper is fading slightly, but I think I'll be done in time. Actually I must make the football. Marilena, my wife, is speaking at one of her periodontal (or for simpletons like me, dental) conferences and I am picking our daughter Maria up at the kindergarten before Timmy's football.

'OK – see you at three then'. Cedric picks up the phone, probably to summon another of his firefighters, smiles at me and waves for me to shut the door as I exit. He looks happy! I think he actually enjoys his job, but I hate to think what his home life is like, if he actually has a home!

Back in my office I temporarily shelve the Code of Conduct for another day. It seems that ever since I got this job all I do is comment on and redraft new papers and policies. Last month it was a pre-draft on Corporate Responsibility and before Christmas it was a paper on the new SOX provisions (Sarbanes-Oxley Act of 2002 for the lucky souls who have never heard of it). Before that it was a paper on Fraud Risk Management. It is strange, but in the past, I had a really hard time convincing the management that fraud ever took place at all. The usual riposte of our former chief executive was that 'the N-Trex culture should keep everybody honest'. Now, judging by the number of position papers I have to produce, it seems that the words fraud and corruption, or at least the regulatory aspects, are continuously being talked about all the time in the boardroom. What is frustrating for me is that all people seem to do is talk. All of my practical suggestions on how to combat fraud and corruption always seem to be postponed.

I use some time to study the John Smith email, while doodling a mind map of ideas on my scratch pad. After a few minutes, with a slight smile beginning to form on my face, I summarise my thoughts.

EVALUATION OF 'JOHN.SMITH9999' LETTER DATED 10.04.20XX

What do I know?

- *Someone* either inside or outside the project has tried to warn the management of major fraud but has been ignored the first time and is now escalating. Use of 'I' and 'we' in the mail – probably more than one person.
- They may or not have a motive (honest or malicious) but we need to find this out.
- CALM is definitely a mess – we know that but nobody wants to admit the scale of the mess – we keep on pumping money in and hoping (more like praying) for some results.
- I warned Cedric and his audit committee about the problems about 6 months ago after an audit which found the project director Neil Shreeve and his team authorising some pretty vague expenditures on consultancies and other odd invoices. Neil had some unusual personal expenditure too. What happened? No response from Cedric except that he felt that upsetting Neil at this crucial stage in the project might not be a good idea.

- I have had very little time to spend personally on CALM because Cedric and JTS have constantly bombarded me with requests for position papers, documentation of internal controls, risk maps and other similar stuff.

How are management going to take this?

- N-Trex's profits are down and shareholders are screaming for improvements so if this letter points to anything even half true, management are not going to like it.
- JTS and Cedric have been telling the non-executive board that the Corporate Governance and CSR initiatives are there to combat fraud and corruption, so in a sense they need to act. Now is their chance.
- I think Cedric has given Neil Shreeve his support for now so that might be a tough one to crack. (Note: I need to be careful with Neil. After the last audit he is not my #1 fan.)
- I suspect, although I have no proof of this, that Cedric, and maybe John, want this one to go away – they are happy to scrap CALM as long as they can lay the finger of blame on somebody else (like Neil or worse still, me!) – note: better delete this point!

How should I respond to Cedric?

- Positively. In spite of Cedric's palpitations this letter has come at a very good time. N-Trex's management has been broadcasting anti-fraud and -corruption messages for some time, but I don't think the people in the company really believe they mean it – they see it as just another thing we have to do because we are a big company. This could be the test case, which demonstrates Senior Management are willing to walk the walk.
- I will have to tell C. that I need some resources to perform a thorough and objective investigation – then I can see if there is any truth behind this email.
- Advise Cedric not to tell Neil yet as he would only be defensive (but I don't need to tell Cedric that). Better tell him that it would only upset Neil and make him think we did not trust him. At least the first part of this investigation, I can perform very discreetly.
- How am I going to do the investigation – don't know yet but will meditate on this one.

At lunch I end up sitting with Neil and a couple of chaps from the CALM project team whose names I always forget. They are all obsessed with the test launch and seem to be taking bets as to which subcontractors are going to deliver on time or not. Neil seems a bit quiet and withdrawn. 'Lot on your mind Neil?' I ask in the most sympathetic voice I can muster.

'Yeah, just the usual stuff,' he says, and pointing at the ceiling, 'they don't seem to

understand'. Strange he pointed up, as recently the canteen was relocated to the top floor. Maybe he is talking about angels. 'Fancy doing another audit of me then do you André?' – he half smiles and I can't work out whether he is joking or he knows about yesterday's email.

I make my excuses and head back to my office where I am greeted by a collage of post-it messages and a string of unopened emails. Requests for assistance with the new internal controls documentation tool, follow up of a systems audit, request for my presence at meetings and a lecture on how N-Trex is fighting corruption at the HR managers forum. Suddenly, some large dark-suited shapes in sunglasses move past my window and I peek out. The 'men from Minsk' have arrived. Apparently Howard Jackson, N-Trex's head of marketing is showing them around with an interpreter. We really need this Byelorussian contract and Howard is taking them out to show them the delights of our hottest nightspots later tonight. Somehow, I don't think I will be allowed anywhere near those particular expense reports.

❖   ❖   ❖

Three o'clock and I'm back in Cedric's office. He bustles in ten minutes later. 'OK what do you reckon? We need to move fast on this one as John called me again.'

I outline my ideas and he mostly nods, except for the part when I tell him we should first conduct a covert investigation and not tell anyone in the project, not even Neil. 'OK, put something down on paper for first thing tomorrow specifying what, how, when and how much, and I will get John to OK it. I don't think he will like you shutting Neil out like this but let us see.'

Cedric can be OK at times.

The trouble is, I haven't got a clue where I am going to find the resources for this investigation. I can't do it myself. However, for now, I have to rush if I am going to get to the kindergarten in time.

I am just packing up when I look up and catch the blonde highlights of Mirabel Andrews, N-Trex's Head of Security, going past my open door. Mirabel is a couple of years older than me but that's hard to believe. She has been at N-Trex for nearly ten years and worked her way up from being a site security manager. Before that she was in the police. Mirabel is tough, takes no nonsense and is efficient. Some N-Trex managers find her a little bit frightening and that's probably why she is occasionally excluded from some meetings. She has always been supportive with me though, especially since fraud and corruption came under my remit. Mirabel is much more hands on than I am. She works with physical security and electronic security and runs all the executive protection and country risk programs. She also reports to HR so she does not have to put up with Cedric and his pet projects. However she does not get too involved with fraud and corruption and professes to have little experience with financial matters. 'Sticking to the knitting', that's her motto. It's just that I can't see Mirabel sitting by the fire knitting woolly jumpers, though from what I know of her husband, he might do it.

'Hi, have you got a second?' I beckon her into my office.

'Sure, what's up?' she replies and she sits down, looking slightly curious.

I recap over the morning's events and what I just proposed to Cedric. She ponders for a moment and, as if reading my thought, replies 'They would not ask me, probably because I might find something out about Neil. I think Cedric wants to keep it in his team. Anyway overcharging is much more your area. But this may involve potential criminal activity, so you will need some investigative help from the outside. Remember my old police boss, Max, whom I mentioned to you? He set up his own investigation company about five years back. They do good work and help us with screening of some of the high-level staff and also investigations into counterfeiting and intellectual property theft, so he is no stranger to N-Trex. Give him a call. I will text you his details on the way back.'

'Thanks for that. I will call him,' I reply.

'I suppose you are running to get the kid as usual? Get an au pair, it will let you relax like me.'

Relax, with two small kids? Some hope of that. But Mirabel is fun and also a friend, I think.

Chapter 2

As I enter the offices of the Xamdos Group I can sense the smoke permeating through the walls and doors. Mirabel has already warned me that her former boss Max de Gras refuses to give up his pipe even for asthmatics like me. Luckily I am well stocked up with inhalers.

I had called Max on the number Mirabel had given me and he told me he was only returning from the USA on Saturday. He would arrive at his office around lunchtime on Monday and considering that I had rung him at 3.30 in the morning stateside time, he sounded surprisingly alert!

I am led by the receptionist through a number of doors into Max's inner office, a large old-fashioned room with wood-panelled walls. The wall behind where he sits is adorned with several framed certificates and a variety of law-enforcement plaques from around the world. As he gets up from behind an enormous desk strewn with files, papers and electronic gadgets I see a man in his mid 50s, a little worse for wear, short for his weight and balding. The apparent chaos in his office, however, does seem to have a sort of hidden order to it. He looks at me (or should I say through me) with sympathetic but sharp eyes.

'Max de Gras,' he says, almost breaking my hand although I guess he does this to everybody. 'I thought I would finally meet you. Bella tells me you're the one at N-Trex who has had this case dumped on you.' I am not sure if he is being ironic or even knows more than me but I decide to let the introductions continue. Let's find out what he says so I can decide whether I should use him before I disclose too many details.

'Thanks for making the time to see me, Mr de Gras. Mirabel speaks very highly of you.'

Max shrugs.

'She said that you could help us out with the external investigation work. I couldn't really go to the external auditors because I suspect that if this is something big, they should have picked it up in the first place,' I continue.

'Potential conflict aside, there's another reason you shouldn't use them,' he replies. 'Auditors rarely make good investigators. Their job is to find excuses, sorry I mean reasons, why everything is OK and then support it with figures and bits of paper. Sorry, but years of this work has made me a bit too cynical for the likes of you, I guess, but from my experience, fraud and corruption boils down to people and behaviour. If I can give you your first piece of advice, you'll need to think much more laterally to understand what the real state of play is this time.'

Impressive, if not a touch arrogant. I suspect that Mirabel and he are quite close and she has already filled him in about what is going on.

He continues, 'Oh and just call me Max, I'm not too keen on the "de Gras" bit. My great-great-grandfather came over from southern Europe about 200 years ago so I'm stuck with this pretentious surname. I believe he was on the run from the law.' He pauses and then adds with a hint of irony and an over-pronounced French accent, 'Café au lait pour vous?'

This could be interesting. On his first 90 seconds I would say that Max was anything but pretentious.

I decide to open up about what has happened recently and also my previous collisions with Neil. This includes what I think of CALM, how nobody has really allowed me to audit the project expenditure and of course the anonymous letters. I only managed to extract the original typed letter from Cedric's clutches last week.

Max listens quietly and patiently while drawing on his pipe now and then, watching me all the time.

Over the weekend I had been copying archived documents such as audit reports, memos, emails, sample supplier invoices and those questionable expense vouchers from the last audit. I even found the time to do a little summary of key issues as well as a more detailed analysis of supplier costs charged to CALM.

As if Max was reading my mind, he asks me if I have brought any documentation with me. I take the file out of my bag and he enquires politely if he could take a look.

Immediately he grabs his reading glasses off the desk and starts poring over my handiwork with a concentration that ill befits his demeanour.

My report and the anonymous letter he gives no more than a cursory glance to; he flicks through the invoices and then dives into the spreadsheet analysis of supplier costs analysis and the expense vouchers. About five minutes later his eyes home in on my analysis of supplier invoices, and in particular two supplier groupings.

'Where is the background research on this Shreeve character and his team?' he asks, almost a little shocked not to have found it on page one. My bemused look prompts him to say 'I'm sorry, you must forgive me. You've done a good job for a freshman. It's just that I treat everyone as if they were one of my own staff.' He points to his pipe as I cough again. 'Yet another of my bad habits. Anyway it would be interesting to see where our Mr Shreeve has been.'

I'm not exactly sure what he means here but it seems he is just talking to himself until he suddenly asks 'Would you mind if I draw on this?' pointing to my spreadsheets and picking up a red pen.

'It's OK with me but I've got a copy of the spreadsheet on my laptop if you want to play with the figures,' I reply.

He is writing almost immediately, completely ignoring my offer of the use of modern technology. For somebody who just a few minutes ago told me he despised auditors for their obsession with figures and bits of paper, he isn't doing too bad a job of it himself.

'What do you know about this Object Talk company?' he asks after a few minutes, this time remembering to be polite.

'Not that much actually,' I reply.

I had identified them as the fifteenth-largest supplier on the CALM project so I did not feel that they merited that much scrutiny. I look closer at the printout. 'Judging by the WBS, I mean Work Breakdown Structure they are allocated to, I guess they are body shoppers. That's to say they provide supply consultants when we need them. Why the special interest in the company?'

'I would say the Isle of Man address gives us a bit of a clue. Many body-shoppers use a tax haven so that they can effectively invoice higher rates and pay as little tax as possible. It's one way of them staying as consultants for longer, and also avoiding paying so much tax.' He replies as this should have been self-evident. 'Then look at their invoice numbers. They give a lot away.'

Sup_no	Supplier	Rank		Total Spend (12 months)
C73229356	Object Talk International	18		2,482,733.00
	PO Box 5432			
	Athol House			
	Douglas, Isle of Man			

WBS	Date	Invoice		Amount	Paid
DEV05001	13.02.200X	OT20040 100		17,089.00	14.03.200X
DEV05001	14.02.200X	OT2004 0200		29,000.00	14.03.200X
DEV05001	12.03.200X	OT2004 0400		120,200.00	13.04.200X
DEV05001	29.03.200X	OT2004 0700		350,373.00	10.05.200X
LOG09400	10.04.200X	OT2004 0500		356,000.00	10.05.200X
DEV05001	10.05.200X	OT2004 0900		234,591.00	09.06.200X

Max has already ringed in red around invoice numbers 100, 200, 400, 500, 700 and 900. 'That's a pretty little sequence there unless you believe in coincidences. I bet you they don't have too many other customers either.'

I admitted that I had not heard of Object Talk until I did my research last weekend. Like all the suppliers I tried to look them up on Google but in this case I could not find anything about them at all, not even the Internet or in the phone book at the address they had. Even though they are not that big in the scheme of things I would at least have expected to find something.

Max nods, this time apparently pleased that I tried to look them up and resumes his preaching: 'Attention to detail is what you need to remember. The red flags are always there. We just choose to ignore them, so like footprints in an arctic winter they get covered up by the snow.'

'And this one, RDS Systems Partnership, also looks a little interesting.'

'They are a much larger supplier too. I wonder who they are paying off?' he continues.

RDS and their invoices looked reasonable enough to me on Sunday. Noticing my puzzled expression, Max decides to enlighten me: 'It is not much to go on so far but they are quite sequential, there are lots of large round number invoices compared to the other

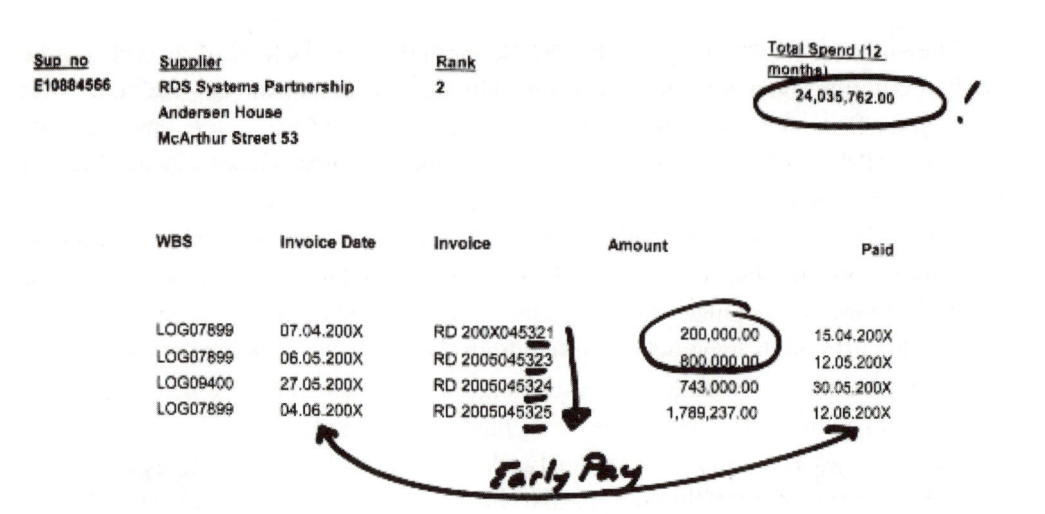

Sup no	Supplier	Rank	Total Spend (12 months)
E10884566	RDS Systems Partnership	2	24,035,762.00
	Andersen House		
	McArthur Street 53		

WBS	Invoice Date	Invoice	Amount	Paid
LOG07899	07.04.200X	RD 200X045321	200,000.00	15.04.200X
LOG07899	06.05.200X	RD 2005045323	800,000.00	12.05.200X
LOG09400	27.05.200X	RD 2005045324	743,000.00	30.05.200X
LOG07899	04.06.200X	RD 2005045325	1,789,237.00	12.06.200X

Early Pay

logistics suppliers and you seem to be paying them a bit quickly too. I would say that you are quite a big customer of theirs and they could be charging you whatever they can get away with.'

I am about to answer that most suppliers would do that if they could, but before I can he continues. 'Some of the invoices I saw from this lot have something about them that I can't quite put my finger on yet, but I'll tell you as soon as I work it out.'

Two frothy cappuccinos are set in front of us by a smart lady. 'Dip the biscotti in the coffee so you won't break your teeth,' Max adds.

'RDS is one of the big logistics developers we use,' I continue. 'Everybody knows of them and they have been one of the suppliers at the heart of this system for some time. Now you mention it though, I can't see a reason for paying them early, especially if other suppliers are not getting this treatment.'

Max nods and gestures for me to continue.

'OK, I admit RDS and Object Talk may be a little bit interesting but I don't see any evidence here which can allow you to point the finger of guilt as yet. We don't exactly have a smoking gun.'

'Of course not', Max replies, 'and that's not the point at this stage. All I am trying to say is that there are some red flags there which are worth exploring.'

'I can see where you are coming from but in the normal course of things, if there was anything unusual, then these invoices would have been queried by the accounts payable staff and taken through the normal escalation procedure. I assume that Neil would have to get the larger ones counter-signed by another N-Trex director as he doesn't have such a high authority level. I remember seeing at least one other signature on some of those invoices.'

Max frowns. 'Maybe someone else did countersign them or it was queried. My point is that there is only any value in checks or procedures if the people doing them understand why they are doing them. Correct me if I am wrong, but in Neil's project there must be hundreds of these invoices each month and your accounting clerks have a

mountain of these to get through each week. If another director who is busy with his own work simply signs them after Neil, are they really interested in raising questions?'

I can see his point, partly anyway.

'Well let's just say your procedures, checks and controls exist in form but not in reality,' he continues. 'As long as we go on believing that the correct checks are being done then we believe that very little can go wrong. At the same time none of us wants to go around being suspicious do we? Everybody sees it in their interest to mind their own business so they stay popular.'

His down-to-earth approach is unfamiliarly refreshing to me as for the past 12 months I have been surrounded by sycophantic consultants who have been content to praise me in return for a slice of my risk management and internal controls budget. Max's challenges to things I had previously taken for granted are quite interesting.

'Whenever you believe the controls and checks are working, you become blind to the few but highly dangerous hidden loopholes which are available to a fraudster. The essence of a successful fraud is that honest people like you are trained not to suspect. However, once you open your eyes and recognise the potential for fraud in any person's job, it is much easier to see the loopholes and opportunities that exist.'

For the time being, I let most of what he just said drift over my head and, as I take a much needed comfort break, I make a mental note to ask him about this later after I have shared with him some other reflections on the project. I select the toilet door marked 'Guardia di Finanza' rather than the one with an FBI badge on it and the words 'Fairly Bad Investigators' scrawled just below.

I had four missed calls on my mobile and received a text message from my wife Marilena reminding me again to pick up the kids because she has a dental officers' meeting tonight. With typical efficiency Marilena had backed up the text with a voicemail just in case. There was another pointless message from Cedric: 'André … er …', followed by the rustling of papers, 'er its not urgent, just want to re-schedule the compliance control meeting. We can discuss it tomorrow.' Poor guy. His head is buried so deep in his papers that he can't see what is happening around him.

The last message, rather unexpectedly, is from John Thornbury-Stevens in his famous booming voice: 'André, awfully sorry I've been so busy and not able to speak with you personally. Cedric tells me you are doing an excellent …'. This sounds like it is going to be a long one, so I save it for later.

On my return from the bathroom Max is looking at his watch. 'One and a half minutes, not bad. Some of my investigators are in there for up to half an hour mulling over a case. I found this paper on the net from the Helsinki Institute for Workplace Research which demonstrates that toilets can be very conducive to creative thinking and problem solving. Something about the combination of a confined space and the ability to purge the body of waste. I am thinking of having another toilet put in to help increase productivity and reduce queues. Have you any suggestions as to what we should christen the new one?'

I don't think I am ready for this yet. Years of accountancy has dulled my brain and

suppressed my sense of humour. I tell him I'll think about it and describe some of my experiences the last time I tried to audit the CALM project. I told him about Cedric's response when I took up the lack of proper documentation of expenditure, circumvention of rules and ever-expanding budgets: 'Cedric told me that I had to bear in mind that Neil and I played on the same team. Despite my good intentions the language in my report could be interpreted as if I was trying to slow the project down. Neil is under a lot of pressure to deliver and an audit report like mine might just tip him over the edge resulting in even more delays. Cedric said that he couldn't see any upside in issuing a report like this at this moment. We would then all lose. I was not to get into a slanging match with Neil when there were so many more important things which I needed to address.'

Cedric had then edited my draft report making quite a number of changes to improve the political correctness of it as well as portray my department in a positive and constructive light, as he put it. The final report had gone out last year without any of my carefully prepared appendices and examples and was still awaiting a written response from Neil and his team.

When I had reminded Neil a few months ago he had replied that he had a project to run at the moment but would get back to me in due course. I had almost given up hope of getting a response and had all but forgotten about the report. However for some reason I had kept a copy of the full pre-Cedric draft at home which I had now brought with me to Xamdos.

Max leafs through the thick file, pausing to scrutinise invoices, taxi, hotel receipts and expenses, including a rather substantial one marked 'team kick-off' from a company called Frankie's Girls. I could see him grin about that one, especially the company logo on the invoice. I think he spotted another red flag, or should we say red light.

'You did well my young pit bull, but like nearly everyone else you gave up in the end.' He laughs. 'The problem with an audit like yours, is that it is not about presenting the truth, but about finding an opinion which pleases everybody. Any remaining contentious issues can then be debated ad nauseam until the last man standing either gives up or moves on.'

Max's warning signs, or red flags, have been around for some time. He can sense my discomfort with the situation, especially the fact that he knows I gave up.

'How has Neil been with you since then?' asks Max.

'Neil has been blowing hot and cold with me ever since but basically he has been trying to avoid me when he can. Suzy, my secre ... I mean assistant, told me that all the CALM staff are now a bit scared whenever I question their entertaining expenses. I strongly suspect that Cedric, who was the only one who knew what we did, discussed my suspicions with Neil and so warned the team. I think both of them are a bit defensive but don't want to show it.'

'What's your opinion about Neil and Cedric's honesty?' asks Max quietly.

It's a bit of an odd question but I can see his point. 'I don't believe either of them are dishonest if that's what you mean. In Neil's case he was doing his job, the best way he

could. Everybody at N-Trex tries to sneak in a little expenditure if they can. Neil has morale problems in his team and needed to boost it. As for Cedric, he's too boring to do anything criminal. Seriously though, when he butchered my report I think he really believed that he was doing the best thing for the company by toning things down. He probably had a quiet word with Neil afterwards. If Cedric is a fraudster, I'll eat one of your hats.' I gesture at the neat selection on Max's hat stand in the corner. 'Anyway why do you ask?'

'Oh, I was just interested in how you evaluated honesty, that's all,' replies Max casually. He claps his hands together. 'Anyway enough detail for now. Lets go for the bigger picture and how we get to the bottom of all this before you have to go to another meeting.'

I glance at my watch, it's only five to three and I feel that he is completely dominating the discussion. Also, I'm not sure if I like being referred to as a pit bull.

I try to move it back on track. 'I'd first rather like to understand where you are coming from, before we go any further. You paint the picture so black that, from your point of view, everybody at N-Trex is either stupid or a criminal. One anonymous letter might disclose a series of weaknesses in our systems and processes, but at the end of the day we will probably find logical explanations for everything. There is a big difference between bad housekeeping and corruption. It's easy for ex-policemen like you to be paranoid and suspect the worst but if I went around thinking like that in my job I wouldn't last long.' Surprisingly he doesn't argue, but shrugs sympathetically and gestures for me to go on.

I compose my thoughts before continuing: 'More specifically I was not sure what you meant when you said that we were being exploited and that we were trained not to suspect. Each year we are audited internally and externally. If anything really big was wrong it's bound to get noticed. Also, although I would not describe our people as paranoid, we are not naïve either and we are certainly not trained to deliberately ignore problems.'

Before Max can reply his phone rings and a fresh tray with coffee arrives at the same time. He smiles and waves at the coffee girl as he picks up the phone. 'Pronto ... good or bad news? ... Benissimo, bravo ... in a meeting right now. Parlare at six? ... great, ciao.' He hangs up and gestures to the coffee. 'Sorry about that. Italian case we have been working on for some time now. We got a nice breakthrough. Sarah here, pointing to the coffee girl, has been working on this one. The supplier told her colleague that he was forced by the maintenance manager to buy him a home cinema and charge it as technical equipment to our client. If he didn't, he would lose the maintenance contract. I sympathise with the poor chap. Apparently he is very religious and broke down in the interview. I think one of the bigger contractors has succeeded in building a non-existent warehouse. He hasn't confessed yet and probably won't but it doesn't matter. The client might be a bit shocked at this so I'll wait until I am a bit calmer before I tell him.' Max leans back in his chair. 'I love the Italians. Excellent food, wonderful opera and highly creative opponents. Sometimes a bit too creative but they put up a great show.'

As we down the second coffee together I am treated to the world of fraud and corruption à la Max.

'You see, André, many people don't realise that fraud is actually the second oldest profession in the world', and adds with a grin, 'and the oldest one is not the legal profession either although there are some striking similarities. Secondly although there have been many studies, your off-the-shelf corporate manager is either unaware, or will not accept, that fraud and corruption typically costs in the region of two to five per cent of a company's sales.'

'Two to five per cent of sales. I've heard those figures too but aren't those just for companies that actually have serious problems? I don't believe that N-Trex can be losing 5 per cent of its sales,' I interject.

'Well, nobody really knows the accuracy of the studies. It could be less, or more likely, even more. One thing I can say though is that I haven't seen too many companies where fraud and corruption is absent. They just absorb it into their costs.' He pauses so I indicate for him to continue.

'Fraud takes place because there are always opportunities and people are sufficiently motivated to take advantage. Part of their motivation is due to the fact that the risk of being caught is so low. You can't argue with that. I even read that in an accounting standard of yours.'

Ignoring the little dig at my professional qualifications, I reply, 'I think you are referring to International Auditing Standard IAS 240.'

'Whatever,' continues Max with a dismissive wave of the hands. 'Who then do you think has the greatest opportunity to become a fraudster, those at the top or those near the bottom of the corporate worlds?' He flips over an envelope on his desk and draws a symbolic pyramid.

'Well, I guess those near the top with all the decision-making power have more opportunity, at least the bigger opportunities,' I reply, not quite sure where all this is leading.

'And now onto motivation,' Max adds. 'People with lots of money and power. What do they want most?'

I reply 'More money and more power, but that's just human nature,' I reply.

'I know. We are all human.' He smiles a small self-satisfied smile as if he has just won at poker, but I am not supposed to know that yet. 'So what you are telling me then is the people most likely to become involved in fraud are people like Neil Shreeve and Cedric at N-Trex as well as powerful players outside your company like suppliers, customers, competitors and the like.'

'That's a bit of an oversimplification.'

'Is it?' He lets his words hang in the air for a moment.

I try again. 'I mean we don't just hand out cash like sweets at N-Trex. We have budgets, rules, controls, internal audits and finally an external audit which will stop anything getting out of … '.

Max is smiling and I see where this is leading now. Neither one of us has to say the word 'CALM' to realise that Max has won this little debate.

'It makes some sense to me now but I am still going to have a hard job convincing the management. If all of this stuff about the cost of fraud and corruption is really true, then why haven't the management textbooks and gurus picked up on it. John and Cedric are going to want some facts, not just your philosophy.'

'In a company there is little room for bad news and cynicism. It's not a quality managers are supposed to have. As for their textbooks and the gurus, they write to please. If you don't believe me, look at all the corruption and fraud scandals in the papers and compare this to the textbooks. Some mismatch if you ask me.'

'You are probably right,' I reply. 'Auditors are told to be professionally sceptical, but they probably are as sceptical as the client's budget wants them to be.'

He sketches what looks like an extended noughts and crosses board.

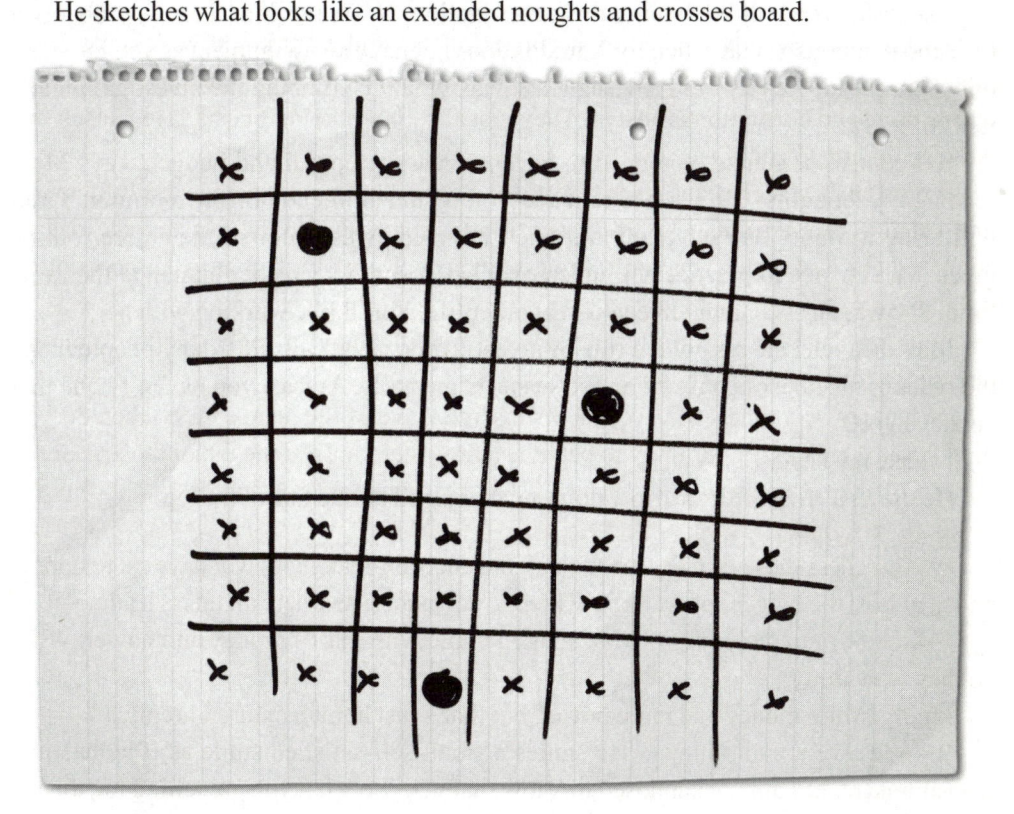

'If the square represents your company, then those crosses are your controls. That's what you auditors get excited about.' I'm not sure how much more of this auditor-baiting I can take. 'Provided you have enough controls or crosses then most auditors and management are pretty happy bunnies.'

'We need controls – otherwise everything would fall apart.'

'Exactly', says Max emphatically, thumping his hand on the table, 'and you don't fall apart that often. You just get worn down a lot. Those little circles are loopholes, or in our language, opportunities which bypass all of the controls.'

'So what you are telling me is that people are as honest as the controls allow them to be and not much more?'

'You've got it,' says Max grinning. 'And my and your job, if you still see we have a job to do, is to …'. I put up my hands in submission as if to tell him 'no problem, carry on'.

'… is to discover what actually happened, clear the innocent from suspicion, root out all the fraud and take action to correct the problem and prevent it happening again. But before you start you should remember that honest human beings can easily turn dishonest if they meet the right temptation.'

'Put that way it sounds a lot more palatable and much less paranoid. Where do we go from here?' I am anxious for Max to provide me with a concrete roadmap and not just theory.

Max asks who will be running this investigation, N-Trex or him. I reply, probably a little too pompously, that officially Xamdos does not have an assignment as yet, but were this to go ahead, then I would envisage that Max would be running the investigation and reporting to me.

'Of course, of course, you need to have a written proposal and budget,' says Max, reading my thoughts. 'I'll get one round to you by lunchtime tomorrow morning. Sarah will bring it round. She's actually a trained forensic investigator so the coffee routine gives her a chance to practice her undercover skills and it keeps her human at the same time. She was an accountant like you in another life. You'll like working with her.'

Max then tells me his golden rule of investigation as he calls it: 'Many people make the hideous mistake of confronting the suspects too early. At least you haven't done that yet have you?'

I shake my head.

He draws a cross with an arrow pointing down and a little flag at the top.

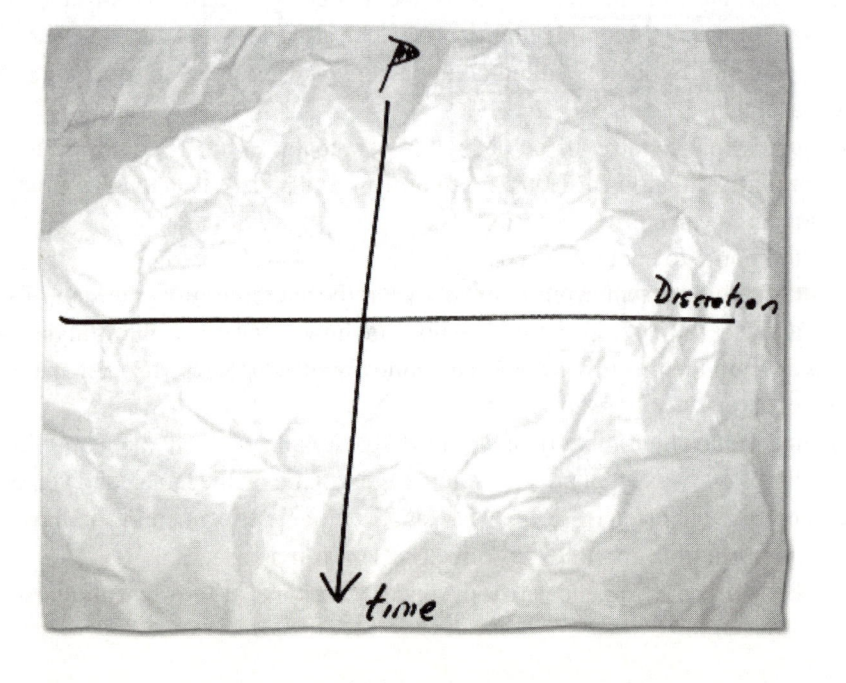

'The flag represents your initial suspicion. The arrow pointing down marks time and the horizontal line is your all-important line of discretion. Cross that too early and you are dead in the water and you will fail in your objectives. Before we cross the line and interview the subjects and suspects, we must first do all we can to collect material from inside and outside the company in a discrete and covert manner.' Max looks up. 'With me so far?'

'Yes, makes sense. But is the information we are going to collect legal?'

'That's an important question,' replies Max. 'In the old days, we investigators used to bend the rules, and some of us went too far, I am sorry to say. You always get caught out in the end. I can assure you we don't do anything illegal, and you mustn't either. It'll all be in the paper I am sending you, along with objectives, a clear strategy and also how we plan to do it, using legal techniques.'

Just then I remember the rumours which had been circulating concerning Neil and his relation to an IT company, I float these past Max.

'It all adds up,' he adds, 'You want to look at your company policy on computer and email use to see whether we can monitor and read his emails as well as image his hard disk.' As I am writing a list for myself he adds, 'Oh and remember to ask Cedric for the previous annonymous letter if he hasn't thrown it away. And see if you can't remember the name of that IT company our Mr Shreeve was supposed to be related to and get details of that too.'

'I guess you will also want the whole file of supplier invoices charged to the CALM project from the accounting system. It is a big project so there are hundreds of suppliers and thousands of invoices.'

'As much as you can give us please. Can I borrow these copies?' he asks, thumbing through them again and holding them as if he was going to fight me if I said no. 'I have already signed N-Trex's confidentiality policy,' he adds.

'No problem, if you don't mind taking a copy. I want to avoid sneaking around the archives as much as I can.'

He agrees that Sarah will be at N-Trex's reception with a proposal and strategy document for my attention at 1.00 p.m. tomorrow and adds, 'It's a tough journey you are embarking on. It can consume you and destroy your family life.'

I am too polite to enquire exactly what he means here as it sounds like he is making some sort of reference to himself.

It is just after 4.00 p.m. when I am done with Max and I am going straight to pick up the kids. I've got them on my own this evening, but it will also really help me switch off from this case.

Just as I am leaving my curiosity gets the better of me. 'Why the name Xamdos?' I ask him.

'I wondered when you were going to ask,' he laughs. 'Its something my boss said just after I walked out of the police five years ago.' I'm still puzzled,

'Backwards,' he adds as he waves me and my taxi off.

In the taxi I recheck my mobile. No new voicemails so I listen to the long one from JTS.

'André, sorry I've been so busy and not able to speak with you personally. Cedric tells me you are doing an excellent job. Well done. I just wanted to have a chat with you about this dreadful letter business. If you get this message by four then you can give me a call back. Otherwise I will be on the plane to New York and we'll have to catch up later. Appreciate what you are doing to sort things out in spite of all your other commitments. Cedric flaps a bit, but I really want us to get to the bottom of this. As I said, I will be in New York until Thursday but if you have any issues, then just call me.'

I press the number one on my phone to call back but I just get his voicemail. Strange that he should call me directly when most of the time he issues his directives through Cedric.

The kids are great and Max and the work day are already far from my mind.

Marilena arrives back at ten. I have prepared a salad with some nice cheese from the deli for us to share.

'Sounds like an interesting character this Max.' She's in a good mood. The dental officers' meeting must have been stimulating, if that is at all possible. 'You know in our profession we also have fraud and corruption. There was this dentist who once took out most of this patient's teeth because he could claim for each extraction. The patient complained and the investigation showed that he only needed two fillings rather than a full set of dentures.'

'What happened to the dentist?' I ask

'He got a strong warning and a fine, that's all. The poor patient lost his teeth at the age of 42. I don't think he was terribly pleased.'

'No not really,' I reply trying to repress my laughter.

'And the way my colleagues cheat on expenses; I mean nobody checks them so they get away with it.'

'That rings a bell,' I am thinking of what Max told me 'So why don't the Dental Association do anything then?'

'Well I guess it is like that doctor, Shipman, who killed hundreds of his patients. All the signals were there: abnormally high death rates on call outs, stockpiling of diamorphine. We are honest so we think the best and ignore the signs. After all we don't want to suspect one of our own even if they could be a psychopathic killer. It's the same with you corporate people I guess. You don't see it when it is under your nose.'

Not bad for a dentist. The conversation is interrupted by loud crying from the bedroom. Maria, our two year old, just woke up.

Chapter 3

I meet for a few minutes with John Thornbury-Stevens after he returns from the USA. He listens with great interest to my progress report and makes positive noises about his support for what I am doing. He tells me that I have the full backing of Cedric and himself even though Cedric could be, in his words, a bit of a stick in the mud.

'André, this revised code of conduct, which I know you all are working on, will reflect the values in this company and reinforce the ethical high ground which we at N-Trex stand for. Absolutely everybody needs to absorb the message so that they do not put the company at risk.'

'I totally agree with you,' I replied.

'I think you should spend some more time with that new girl heading up Corporate Responsibility,' he glances down at a paper on his desk.

'You mean Katja Simonsen?'

'Katja, that's her name. I think she is very bright and driven.'

I nod in agreement. I know that JTS has a soft spot for Katja having hand-picked her from Human Resources to head up the new Corporate Responsibility function.

'I also like their idea for this Code of Conduct helpline, you know the one we are thinking of calling U-Count. I think you need to get involved there too.'

I try not to wince at the name U-Count, or the prospect of more work.

'Now as for this case, if any N-Trex people are misbehaving then they will have to face the consequences of their actions. I am relying on you on this case, André, but if you run into trouble then my door is open to you, OK?'

He turns to look at something on his screen as if to indicate the cosy little chat is over so I give a mock salute of thanks and re-enter his outer office. At his old job in National Power, JTS was famous for his moral-boosting five-minute chats.

I make a mental note to spend more time with Katja. She talks a lot about the evils of bribery and corruption although I still haven't figured out what she really knows. I reckon that I should give her a chance because maybe JTS really means what he says.

Cedric has been more lukewarm with me recently but to my surprise never hostile. I think it takes a lot to get him excited. It took a lot of effort to convince him that what we had now was circumstantial evidence at best and confronting Neil at this stage would be a bad idea. In the end I persuaded him that we should wait until we had a better picture. I strongly suspect that Cedric would like things swept under the carpet but he would never openly contradict John.

The next few days are hectic. I have had Suzy liasing with Sarah (Max's multitalented lady), pulling documents and dropping stuff around which they need. Max is rather particular and wants originals or good quality copies. I'm not sure why but

Cedric has requested that I should not involve Mirabel or her people too much in the investigation.

At the same time I am getting regular progress updates from Max and Sarah. They are also bombarding me with requests for more invoices, expense vouchers, other documentation and information. I ordered an extract from IT of all the incoming and outgoing CALM emails for the past twelve months. This took some time to arrange and I had to ensure that both the legal and Human Relations departments were happy. It amazed me that the size of the emails was over three gigabytes. Suzy dutifully delivered six specially prepared CDs to Max's offices.

Rather embarrassingly I also found out that about two years ago we had purchased a copy of the same data-analysis software for auditors which Max had recommended. The box was still shrink-wrapped. After a quick self-study course I found myself sitting up late night after night sifting through hundreds of thousands of CALM invoices looking for red flags, unusual payments and tax-haven-based companies using Max's idiot's guide to red flags in accounts payable systems.

Finding Fraud

(Max's "rough guide" to red flags
in account payable systems)

What to look for…

U Payments to front companies or companies in tax havens

U Dependent or significantly dependent suppliers where invoice numbers are sequential or <u>nearly</u> sequential. These can indicate a supplier which is getting lazy (or alternatively is desperate)

U A high percentage of round numbers in the payments or invoices

U A lack of reference to purchase orders, contracts or agreements behind the payment

U Keyword for payments "Mr.", "Global", …

U Round sums of reference, authorisation matrix or payment

Max said that it is worth shaking the tree whilst we are at it. I am having fun here and feeding the results and copies of the invoices back to him.

Judging by the huge number of suppliers we have used, there seems to be a lack of strategy in CALM. Everyone is panic-buying by the looks of it. On a couple of occasions, I became curious about a supplier and so I looked it up on the Internet. Interestingly, I would have expected that an events company would have marketed itself but this one seemed to be operating from a small private house. One consultancy invoice for €250 which had the text 'diverse software licences' was so strange that my curiosity got the better of me. After about an hour on the Internet I finally found that the address and telephone number routed through to Aldgate Nominees, a company formation agent run apparently by a Mr Pantelis Barbaris. Searches on this name pointed to an associated law office in Larnaca, Cyprus, which was a bit of a dead end. I made a note on a post-it, stuck it on the invoice and passed it on to Max.

From my regular updates, Max's investigation is progressing. He certainly is not putting his head over the parapet and is the master of discretion. We have pencilled in a meeting a week on Thursday with Cedric and John to review progress. As I only need to get involved from time to time I am free to get on with the rest of my job. This includes getting my head around the latest corporate governance and internal controls legislation which N-Trex needs to comply with. In addition to this, N-Trex's risk management model badly needs updating and our Code of Conduct and Conflict of Interest Policy needs revitalising. What has been annoying me is the apathy shown by my colleagues although I can't really blame them. It is pretty dry and soul-destroying stuff. Maybe the results of this investigation will galvanise them into action. Wishful thinking.

I can feel my finely balanced home life taking a turn for the worse as N-Trex once again consumes my life. I am not seeing the children as much I would like and I tend to meet Marilena in the hall at handover times. When I am with the children my mind is far away as Timmy pointed out to me last night. 'Dad, you are not listening to me any more,' he remarked with that wonderful child's honesty. Maybe I should try to explain to him what I am working on some time.

On a positive note, Cedric is behaving much more civilly again. He even had the bright idea to find the best international definitions of fraud and corruption so we can incorporate them into N-Trex-speak and our risk management model. However this is proving more of a challenge than I thought. It seems that on one side, the accountants and lawyers talk about fraud whereas on the other, macroeconomists, people in corporate responsibility and the non-governmental organisations use the term corruption, often synonymously with the term bribery. To me, the terms overlap quite a bit. After some pretty exhaustive Internet trawling I have selected two definitions which I quite like:

Fraud: An intentional act by one or more individuals amongst management, those charged with governance, employees, or third parties involving the use of deception to obtain an unjust or illegal advantage.

International Standards on Auditing ISA 240

Corruption: *The abuse of public office for private gain.*

OECD/World Bank working definition

One of the sites I find is run by Transparency International which is a vociferous and by all accounts very successful anti-corruption lobbyist. The website and numerous papers highlight the problems of both public and private sector bribery and also give some useful guidance on how to combat it. They even publish a regular Corruption Perception Index of countries and also a Bribe Payers Index, which look pretty impressive.

The fraud definition in its widest sense seems to cover any unethical act in business, done by any party. As I see it this definition covers most things including theft, conflicts of interest, embezzlement, overcharging, misuse of expenses, hacking and viruses as well as most of the aspects of corruption.

I am still wrestling with Max's statements on the true cost of fraud and corruption and find it hard to believe that the real cost is in the region on 2 to 6 per cent of our turnover. However if you can accept that nobody is 100 per cent honest then this might be true. Max told me that about 5 years back he was asked to lecture to an industry group of finance directors and chief executives on the subject of white-collar crime. He had started by asking all of them to raise one hand in the air and keep it raised. He then told them to put their hand down if they had ever inflated a private insurance claim, not declared all income for tax purposes, stretched an expense budget to include family members or friends and a series of other questions. Apparently he had raised a lot of laughs and smirks but what was interesting was that at the end of his questions, nobody had their hands up any more.

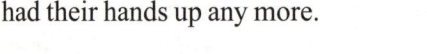

The worst thing about trying to sleep when you have ideas swimming around in your head is that you are unable to switch off until you have written them down. Marilena has, in the past few weeks, grown accustomed to me leaning over her in bed and scribbling things down in the notebook I keep in the bedside table which is next to her side of the bed. I was going to switch sides. Initially I think she saw the leaning over as a return to passion in our relationship. Now she accepts my eccentric ways, for the moment.

'Why don't you get some help from the people you like at work instead of tossing and turning all the time?' she suggested one night, after I had switched on the bedside light for the third time.

I guess today's informal meeting to resolve some of the thoughts is as a result of Marilena's suggestion. I have booked a meeting room and ordered coffee and sandwiches all under the name of a corporate governance brainstorming session. Rob and Jamie who work a lot with me are there, as is Suzy who is keen to get involved. I did

not need to invite Cedric as he poo-poos brainstorming. Suzy has discovered a new mind-mapping program and says it will be a great way to capture our ideas. Also I have invited Katya as she is still doing some of her old Human Resources job in addition to Corporate Responsibility. JTS had made her the HR liaison for the CALM investigation. I am just kicking off and bringing them all up to date on the investigation and what we may expect when the door opens and Mirabel pokes her head around.

'Am I late?' she asks promptly sitting down at a corner. I am surprised she can make it given her busy schedule and forthcoming short-term secondment to N-Trex USA.

'Well, I usually lock the door after starting my meetings,' I reply, attempting to conceal my delight that she came.

This free-for-all meeting to discuss and agree on the definitions and identify the main fraud and corruption risks to which we are exposed is a breath of fresh air. I am kicking myself for playing my cards so close to my chest up till now. Mirabel has already taken charge of the whiteboard and Rob, Jamie, Suzy are contributing most enthusiastically. Katja is a bit quiet; the jolt into the real world is still a bit hard for her.

We agree that the definitions I pulled out need to be seen together and Mirabel has used the whiteboard to sow the seeds of a model for understanding the different types of fraud and corruption which exist and then we highlight those which can affect N-Trex.

We go through the exercise of defining N-Trex's assets and opponents, followed by a open session to come up with as many methods as possible.

'Remember, think loopholes, not controls,' I say.

'When you put yourself in the position of a criminal it is actually much easier,' remarks Jamie.

'We used to do that in the police sometimes,' observes Mirabel.

After a while brainstorming, Katja, Rob and Jamie have to leave but it's been a good session and the board is full.

'Not bad for a couple of hours work,' I say, rather pleased with how it's gone. 'Suzy, you don't mind writing all this up do you?'

Suzy promises to write up the meeting and action points and distribute the material. One of the action points is to do an Internet trawl of the financial press to see what sort of fraud and corruption has affected similar companies. I am interested to know if they have the same issues as we believe we have.

I turn to Mirabel as we leave. 'Thanks so much for coming, you really have helped both me and the others get some perspective on this. I wish I'd asked you before. Max is great but he doesn't really understand all the battering I have to take in the corporate world.'

'I would always watch your back, André. It all seems so clear and simple when we are working on the whiteboard. If you are really serious about taking this case on, then you had better know that things could get pretty black before they get better again. I reckon there are some people here who do not want you to succeed.'

'Thanks for the advice,' I say, not really wanting her to throw any more cold water over my enthusiasm.

'Anyway, best of luck. I am off to the States soon but if you need a shoulder to cry on use my private Gmail address won't you,' as she scribbles down an email address.

I nod, only half sure of what she meant as she leaves.

Max has asked for a pre-meeting with me before lunch to go over the preliminary results once more. He arrives at 10.30 carrying a bulging case with several files under his arm.

Max believes that certain suppliers have managed to get Neil and a couple of the other project managers in their pockets. His conclusions are interesting but he warns me that much of what he has is circumstantial and there is still quite a lot of work to do to obtain any hard evidence. Some of this work can only be done after we conduct interviews. He is already proposing about four or five simultaneous interviews with Neil, one other manager and three suppliers. These interviews would be conducted without warning although, of course, care would be taken so that they were performed in a proper and legal manner.

'You've read my preliminary report I presume, but if you like I can give you a quick run down on the main findings,' he says.

'The floor is yours,' I gesture to him. I received the report yesterday afternoon and have only skim-read it.

'OK then. Your CALM project is crawling with suspicious supplier relationships. Virtually nothing has gone out to tender so you are probably paying through the nose anyway. However like our Mr X in his letter we have concentrated on three suppliers to start with.'

'Did you find out who our informant was?' I interrupt

'We have a pretty good hunch but going any further would probably compromise our investigation. We have enough to go on anyway at this stage as it is. Anyway as I was saying, we have concentrated first on three supplier relationships, two of which you already know about and one new one called Analogy Software.'

I am pretty surprised because Analogy is our main software development partner and a well-known company.

'It seems that Neil has become very good friends with a Mr Conrad Burge the senior director in Analogy as all this e-mail correspondence shows.' Max waves a ream of paper. 'It looks like the friendship has been developing over time what with dinners, club visits, social events and the whatnot. Anyway Neil authorises anything Analogy throw at us. Basically he is in their pocket and has given them a licence to print money. All the signs are there.'

'Have you any proof as yet that Neil has taken a bribe from them?' I am trying to tie Max down.

'No, not yet but we are getting close. The mobile phone logs and emails indicate almost everything except the money itself. I think the bribes will be in the books of Analogy once we can do the audit there. For what it's worth Neil has recently moved his children to a smart private school where Mr Burge sends his kids. Burge controls Neil, believe me.'

I hold up my hands as if to say 'go on, go on; I won't stop you'.

'As for RDS, it is much the same picture except RDS would go bankrupt without the N-Trex account. RDS are really milking you. I think they have a long history with a couple of your managers from previous projects and Neil is just in on the tail end of it. It seems as if the project needs them so much that they just send in any invoice and it gets paid. Look at these.' He shows me a pile of vaguely specified round-sum invoices, which pretty much illustrate the point he is making. 'At least one of the owners of RDS used to work at N-Trex before as a software developer and is very close to your people.'

'What about Object Talk?' I ask, keen to get as broad as picture as possible before the meeting with Cedric and John.

'I wondered when you'd ask about that.' Max chews his pen top so hard that he almost bites through it. 'We have reason to believe that Neil has a stake in this company along with a couple of other N-Trex guys and our man Kowalowski from RDS. It's difficult to prove because it's offshore but the email correspondence hints at it, as does the make-up and nature of the invoices. I think it all ties into Aldgate nominees, that consultancy invoice you found and Kyriakidou in Cyprus. Leave it with us. We are working on a pretext approach here.'

I resist asking him what this pretext actually is.

'There's lots more interesting stuff here and loose ends to tie in still but we have tried to focus on what we can start to prove. This is just a small part of the documentation we have been working on and referencing up,' Max continues, pointing to his open case and the pile of files.

'As for expenses, we haven't found that much yet. I think the suppliers are wining and dining your boys and paying for their trips. However there were some large nightclub bills which were put down to team kick offs.'

Max then picks up a thin file marked Conflicts of Interest. 'Only one of your project guys, someone called Travis, was a director of an active company. It's a consultancy which was set up a year back and it is relevant. It's all in the files. I think the offshore companies are where the relationships are hidden. Give us time.'

'Anything else,' I ask, realising that Max's job has not been easy so far.

'We had a close look at Neil's lifestyle. There's nothing special to note in this country. He lives quite well but then I guess your salaries are not that bad. He's pretty free with his email correspondence too.'

'He won't want to attract unnecessary attention to himself will he,' I add, 'otherwise people at N-Trex would notice?'

'I think he's more interested in not attracting attention from his wife actually. You see his wife, Jane, is a schoolteacher and a nice girl who is really dedicated to her job and the kids. I think they are having some pretty big marital problems. I don't think she likes the way Neil became very materialistic a couple of years back. Look at this.'

Max shows me photo of a nearly completed gleaming white villa and a marina in the background. 'Neil just had that built. Oh his wife knows about it and she is not pleased. So far she has told him she doesn't want a villa in Marbella, nor a boat and refuses to go down there. I think good old Mrs Shreeve is suspicious of where the money came from and so are we. Neil thinks she'll come round eventually. Funny transaction also regarding the land which we are looking into. Looks like he got the land for next to nothing.'

'Who did he get it from?' I demand almost authoritatively.

'Patience.' says Max smiling. 'These things take time, especially since we must obtain everything totally legally. 'You know Neil paid a pretty hefty cash deposit on the flat.'

'You are deliberately saving the most interesting bits till last. You'd make a good storyteller.'

He laughs. I'm impressed and also a bit surprised.

'Come on, let's grab some lunch.'

Over lunch in the company canteen we are able to find a quiet table. 'What are the next steps then, Max?' I ask, assuming of course that he has thought of this.

Max outlines how these investigations usually progress. 'Basically, I think we are in a position to have four or five interviews, that is Neil Shreeve and John Travis, his sidekick, as well as Burge from Analogy and probably Chris Kowalowski from RDS although I am not sure about this yet. That should be enough and if we interview without warning and simultaneously then I am sure that we will get sufficient confessions and evidence.'

'And the fifth one?' I ask.

'Yes I forgot the fifth one. That could be our suspected informant and letter writer. We are considering throwing the informant in for good luck. I am sure they'll help once they know we have taken them seriously.'

'Do the suspects tell you anything in these interviews?'

'As long as we are well prepared, the interviews are done at the same time and the interviewer knows what the hell he is doing, then yes, most of them will tell us a bit. We'll also have a control centre; that's Sarah's speciality. Then we can relay information between the different interviews.'

'But you said earlier that the interviews were voluntary. If I was Shreeve or even Burge, I would just say nothing.'

'You'd think so, wouldn't you? You've got to remember that these people are not hardened criminals. They are just like you and me. They're too curious to walk away. A really good interviewer will persuade them that they will feel better by telling the truth.'

Seeing me looking a bit shocked he adds, 'Don't worry, we'll train you up – it's not that tough really. Maybe Bellatrix, sorry Mirabel, will help out with the interviews to keep your costs down. After the interviews and statements we would then get copies of the internal suspects' computers and search their offices, all with their written permission of course. We should also press for an audit of the main suppliers too. It really depends on what comes up of course.'

He sees the look of horror on my face. 'If it makes it any easier you should stop thinking of the criminals as something out there.' He points through the window. 'It's something I learnt at the police. Most of them are just like us and you need to build rapport with them. We are all just somewhere on the slippery slope, somewhere between the angels and the devils. Anyone will break the rules if they have the opportunity and also the motivation, even you.'

'Definitely me. Its just that I have no opportunity and not much motivation,' I reply with a touch of irony.

'Yeah motivation; a funny thing that is. You know who are the most motivated, not the poor starving ones like we would expect but often those climbing at the top. Tell me what do people with lots of money want most?'

'We've done that one already,' I reply .

'Bene,' replies Max giving me a fatherly pat on the shoulder, 'take the Bagels test then.'

As I don't want to delay us any more I save my question about bagels for a rainy day.

After a long and rather interesting lunch followed by coffee we return to my office to prepare for the meeting. Max has brought with him a large diagram called a link-analysis chart showing all the different persons involved, the suppliers and the various financial and interpersonal relationships.

'Cedric should love that,' I say as Suzy knocks on the door.

'Hiya Snoozy, how are you doing,' says Max, surprising me how familiar he has become with my assistant. Suzy has brought with her a thick dossier of recent fraud and corruption cases which she has trawled from the Internet, categorised and indexed.

'Thanks Suzy that's great. I'll look at it tonight,' I say putting the file into my bag. As she slowly walks off I catch myself looking at her legs just a little bit too much. Am I kidding myself that she thinks I am her hero? Anyway I better check myself here. It would not be the best for anything.

Max and I walk up the stairs to Cedric's office. Max is wearing a suit and tie today and is already sweating by the time we reach the second flight. Cedric's new assistant ushers us into Cedric's private conference room adjoining his office. The assistant tells us they are a few minutes late and offers us coffee. I explain to Max that Cedric gets through assistants at the rate of about four a year. They all come through an agency now. I am not sure whether he works or bores them to death. Max looks at me sternly as if to say 'grow up!'.

The side door opens and to my slight surprise in walks Howard Jackson followed by Cedric.

Cedric makes the introductions.

'Nice to meet you Mr de Gras, I have heard a lot of good things about you. Allow me to present our Director of Sales and Marketing, Mr Howard Jackson'.

Max and Howard shake hands. Howard looks like he has just come back from one of his boozy sales lunches. Howard just about acknowledges my presence. I am wondering why he is here and not John.

As if Cedric is reading my mind he continues. 'John was called away urgently and sends his apologies. I invited Howard to join us as we need to keep a tight control on this case. Howard being the director for Marketing and Sales is very interested in our customer relations. If something comes out on this then we would like our customers to see it in a positive light'.

I wish Cedric had told me this so that I could have prepared Max in advance. Howard can sometimes be very annoying and obstreperous, especially after one of his boozy lunches. Recently Howard has been known to shout his mouth off about CALM and how if he had managed the project it would not have got into this mess.

The meeting goes smoothly to start with as I recap on the starting point, our initial suspicions and how we developed the investigation. Cedric is tapping his fingers on the table as if he is desperate to go off and read a taxation journal and Howard is all smiles for the moment.

So far so good.

I then suggest that Max takes us through the main findings so far and the actions that he is recommending.

'You've kept this investigation very quiet so it should be very interesting to see if you have found anything at all,' interjects Howard. 'Of course any further actions will have to be ratified by the executive management.'

'We wouldn't do anything without the approval of John and Cedric', I say as Howard frowns, so I add with a forced smile, 'and the rest of the executive.'

We listen in silence as Max goes through the findings much the same way as he did in my office, pausing for dramatic effect before describing the villa in Marbella.

However the reaction this time round is definitely different. Cedric still looks quite bored and Howard is now smiling.

'So what?' is his opening remark. I see bad omens as Max ploughs on with his proposed strategy. Howard is smiling at Cedric who is looking a little warned now.

'I can't see that there is that much here to go on at all in fact,' says Howard once Max has finished. 'All that you can prove is that CALM is a bit out of control and a few of our suppliers have been rather clever at legally exploiting us. I would have done the same in their position. We know this already.' I see Max starting to reply, but Howard continues. 'The rest of what you have shown me is pretty circumstantial, you have to admit. You can't tell me that a few dodgy expense reports prove that a man is a hardened criminal. As for your plan, you would need something a lot more convincing than this before I vote to have our people being given the Spanish Inquisition by your sort.'

'So far we are looking for indications, not evidence. That comes later … ' starts Max patiently, but Howard cuts him off.

Howard looks at Cedric 'In my opinion we have paid a lot of money for very little here and frankly I am disappointed. We haven't even found the person who wrote the letter.'

'The intelligence we have gathered to date is substantial and in my experience of many other cases, will lead to solid evidence,' says Max. 'Also, all our invoices and charges are justified and fully supported by documentation.'

Howard ignores him. 'Was that your BMW X5 in the visitors spot? If so we are definitely paying you too much.'

'Gentlemen, please. We must look at this from all angles.' Cedric has stood up in a rare moment of, for him, decisiveness. 'André and Max have now presented the findings and have recommended a way forward, and now it is up to us with André of course to evaluate them. I suggest that we take a time-out now and get back to you. Thank you for your time Mr de Gras, I am sure André will show you out.' Cedric is polite and shakes Max's hand. Howard is already busy checking email messages on his latest digital toy and ignores him.

It is difficult to know what Cedric is thinking. He was impassive throughout only showing signs of slight irritation when Howard and Max started sparring with each other. If he has a fence in his garden I'm sure he spends most of his time sitting on it.

'We have a lot of things which smell but nothing that is evidently rotten enough for these guys.' Max gives me a look like he's seen it all before.

One thing is pretty obvious. We have some fairly big problems at N-Trex. When we

have a difficult situation we specialise in bickering about it instead of focussing on understanding it and deciding what action to take. Today was just another example.

On my way home it should be easy for me to take my mind off N-Trex. Recently I haven't had much time for just myself like reading a good paper from cover to cover. Today I pick up a *Financial Times* and also a *Herald Tribune* which was on one of those free stands at the station. I have had enough of CALM for the day so I launch into the *Herald* and its excellent news section, making a mental note that I must try to keep up with what's happening in the world more often.

On the front page is a headline about the conviction against an accounting firm for its role in perpetrating and concealing a well-known fraud being overturned on a technicality. The prosecutors are appealing and the case goes on. Then there is a report on an ongoing case where two aircraft manufacturers are accusing each other over illegal subsidies.

Most interesting is a well-known Russian tycoon who is just my age. After a dramatic commando-style capture which was followed by a drawn-out court case he was sentenced today to nine years in a prison camp for fraud and tax evasion. If he survives jail and can still get to his offshore cash I guess he will celebrate by throwing a big fiftieth birthday party.

Three out of the seven front-page stories have something to do with corrupt, illegal or fraudulent businesses. Maybe Cedric and his friends ought to have learnt something about the real world at business school.

When it looks as if the inside pages have more stories about fraud and corruption I wonder whether I too am being infected by Max's paranoia.

I flick through Suzy's dossier and compare the cases to our N-Trex categories. She's done a great job. It looks like we are not alone at N-Trex.

I have the day off tomorrow. We are taking a family break on a farm in the countryside and apart from the phone, which I have to keep switched on, I resolve to close my mind from work until Sunday night.

The kids love the animals and despite the rain it is very refreshing to spend time playing with the children again and getting two proper nights' sleep. Not that we're fighting in any way, but I can't help noticing that Marilena and I have not had that much to say to each other lately. I think I accidentally called her Mirabel once, too.

By Sunday evening I feel that my reflections have crystallised sufficiently to put them down and I decide it is time to bounce them off Mirabel. At 10.30 with Marilena and the kids safely in bed and a glass of chilled white wine in hand I go down to the basement and the Internet PC for my first consultation with the Oracle at Delphi.

To:	Mirabel.Andrews@gmail.com
From:	Andrestacy01@yahoo.com
Cc:	
Subject	'Shoulder crying'
Date:	11.05.20XX

Hello Mirabel,

How are things going in the States and when are you back? I need some help and pointers as to the direction I am heading in.

The investigation is not going too badly in spite of a little hiccup when Cedric invited Howard to ambush the status meeting. I didn't have time to warn Max about him either. Anyway we kept calm and I think it is all going to be OK in the end. What Cedric was playing at I just don't know. I hope he was just naïve! Anyway I won't bore you with the details. Watch this space!

After our little brainstorming I can't help thinking how everyone keeps trying to overcomplicate the subject of fraud and corruption. Basically it looks as if fraud and corruption is the single largest unmanaged risk we face – the serious newspapers are full of it.

However, I don't think management wants to see the shock that this CALM issue and the letter has caused. That's probably why everyone is either keeping their heads buried or looking for someone to blame when it blows up. I feel like shouting 'the enemy is not in this room'. They are supposed to be tough managers but even JTS is not as tough here as he should be.

Something about Howard's attitude disturbs me. The way he laid into Max was totally unnecessary. However Cedric says he's a top marketer and we need him badly especially at a time when we are expanding into emerging markets. Am I becoming like our paranoid friend at Xamdos?

I know I am out of my depth in all this but with yours and Max's backing I am willing to stick my neck out. It makes a refreshing change from checklists and form filling. Let me know if you have any suggestions. I could also do with some tips on how to sell my ideas to Cedric and JTS.

It would be nice to hear if you think I've lost the plot.

Thanks

André

Chapter 4

Like all passing storms the last meeting with Howard was not such a disaster. Cedric mentioned to me in passing that John was reading Max's report with great interest. It looks like John wants a re-run of the meeting with just Cedric, Max and me present. He has also via Cedric given us the go-ahead to continue the investigation as planned and prepare the action plan.

Max is also back to his effervescent self again. His emails to me are getting more and more obtuse though.

To:	Andre.Stacey@N-Trex.com
From:	Max.de.Gras@gmail.com
Cc:	
Subject:	Fraud Detection
Date:	12.05.20XX

Although, like you I prefer solid red flags like black money and hookey invoices I still believe in a few of the subjective ones. I presume you have heard the well-founded theory that the male fraudster's giveaway is that his shoes are often more expensive than the sum of the rest of his attire. As for women nobody knew what was their most common trait – until now. I have been doing some research and it seems that the female fraudsters go for those black leather shiny shoes with about 5 centimetres of unused point on the toes. So far the results are pretty consistent.

So whether they are male or female look down, not up beancounter-boy!

MdG

Ps: Mirabel sometimes wears pointy shoes but they are for self-defence – trust me!

Pps: And by the way, I think your man is into cheap land transfers along with Burge. Will show you the evidence when we meet. How's my favourite salesman doing? Give him my regards when he next bumps into you.

I make a mental note to ask mad Max to use my Yahoo address as Suzy often reads my mail. I show it to Suzy anyhow when I thank her for her excellent dossier that she has prepared. She laughs and shows me her shoes – which incidentally are black leather and quite sharp. So much for Max's stupid theory but I am intrigued that he actually used the word 'evidence' when referring to Neil.

Apparently a new report from Max is on the way and he promised me that it would be evidential. He also said something about Howard which made me stop and think. I see a

text message on my phone 'You've got mail: Yahoo'. It's from Mirabel so I check my private account.

To: Andrestacey01@yahoo.com
From: MirabelAndrews@gmail.com
Subject: Shoulder Crying
Date: 15.05.200X

André
At the Internet café at Newark so must be brief (and frank). You are thinking along the right lines.

Avoid H for now – I'll tell you more when we meet. My flight back is boarding. Want to have lunch tomorrow? If so just book Il Franco Rossi – table for 2 at 12 and I will join you direct from the airport and my jetlag.

Ciao

M

Ps: Sometimes you have to take Max's advice with a pinch of salt. Sometimes he can be full of ****

❖   ❖   ❖

When I arrive at Il Ristorante Franco Rossi it is already past twelve. The waiter takes me over to the table booked in the name of Ms Andrews.

'What kept you?' asks Mirabel.

'Investigation is taking over my life. It's just one thing after another. I'm beginning to wonder whether I actually work for Max.'

'I used to work for him, once upon a time,' she says to no one in particular.

'I know that, you recommended him to me.'

Mirabel has a reputation of being a connoisseur of Italian food so I let her do the ordering. It suits her too. 'The chef is from Bologna and does the best *tortellini in salsa di fiori di zucca*.'

'OK, I'll try it.' I am a little suspicious that the word '*fiori*' means flowers or something.

She tells me she has been thinking after she got my email. 'When you start investigating, it also exposes the people who don't like you. It's like those people who love to hate the police.'

I decide to let her in on my little secret. 'When I returned from my voluntary service in India, I wanted to join the police, do three years and then do my degree and join the fraud squad,' I say.

I have hardly talked to anybody about my voluntary service stint in India. I was quite an idealist then, and in love.

'Why didn't you then?' asks Mirabel.

'Didn't what?'

'Why didn't you join the police then?'

'I wasn't tall enough!'

Mirabel laughs. 'Pity you didn't join up. It would have given you a taste of what is coming to you now.'

'I think I can manage Cedric but Howard is hard work and so is Harald. In their own ways they are always trying to pull the rug from under my feet. Howard looks for the opportunity to prove himself right and Harald is, well, he's just so dull.'

'That's something, coming from an accountant,' she jibes.

'Thanks.'

'My pleasure. Hey, whether it's N-Trex or anywhere else most people don't care about fraud and corruption in companies. It's not on their agenda. The men at the top are actually scared of it but too macho to admit it. But I'm a woman, right, what do I know?'

'But you're the Head of Corporate Security; they respect you.'

'Yeah, right!'

'What's that supposed to mean?'

She just shrugs her shoulders.

'You don't like Howard much either do you?' I say.

'Between you and me, there's more grease on him than an oil slick but he brings in the money so we shouldn't complain.'

I laugh. It's nice to see Mirabel not being so politically correct for once.

I decide to push my luck. 'We do a lot of business in developing countries where bribes are paid to get business. What's his view on bribery and corruption given N-Trex's official standpoint on this?'

'That's an interesting question. I think Howard will do whatever he can get away with and what can be denied later on. What exactly do you mean by corruption?'

'I've seen for some time that some of the countries we are developing business in like the former Soviet Union and some African nations are perceived to be the most corrupt in the world according to Transparency International's Corruption Perception Index.'

'And their Bribe Payer's Index is something like the Corruption Perception Index turned on its head,' she adds.

'I suppose so,' I reply, having only just heard a few days ago that there was a Bribe Payer's Index too.

'The magazines in business class on the flight back from New York had loads of figures in them. I couldn't sleep so I used them to do some calculations,' she says. 'Look I'll show you. I have them in my jacket.' She pulls out a neatly folded napkin. 'I had to guess the percentages of the cost of fraud and corruption but they are in line with most estimates and surveys. Some people may say Nigeria is a bit on the low side,' she jokes.

It's an impressive table, all the more so because she didn't use her laptop! I turn the paper through 180 and point to the last column. 'So what you are saying is that the real

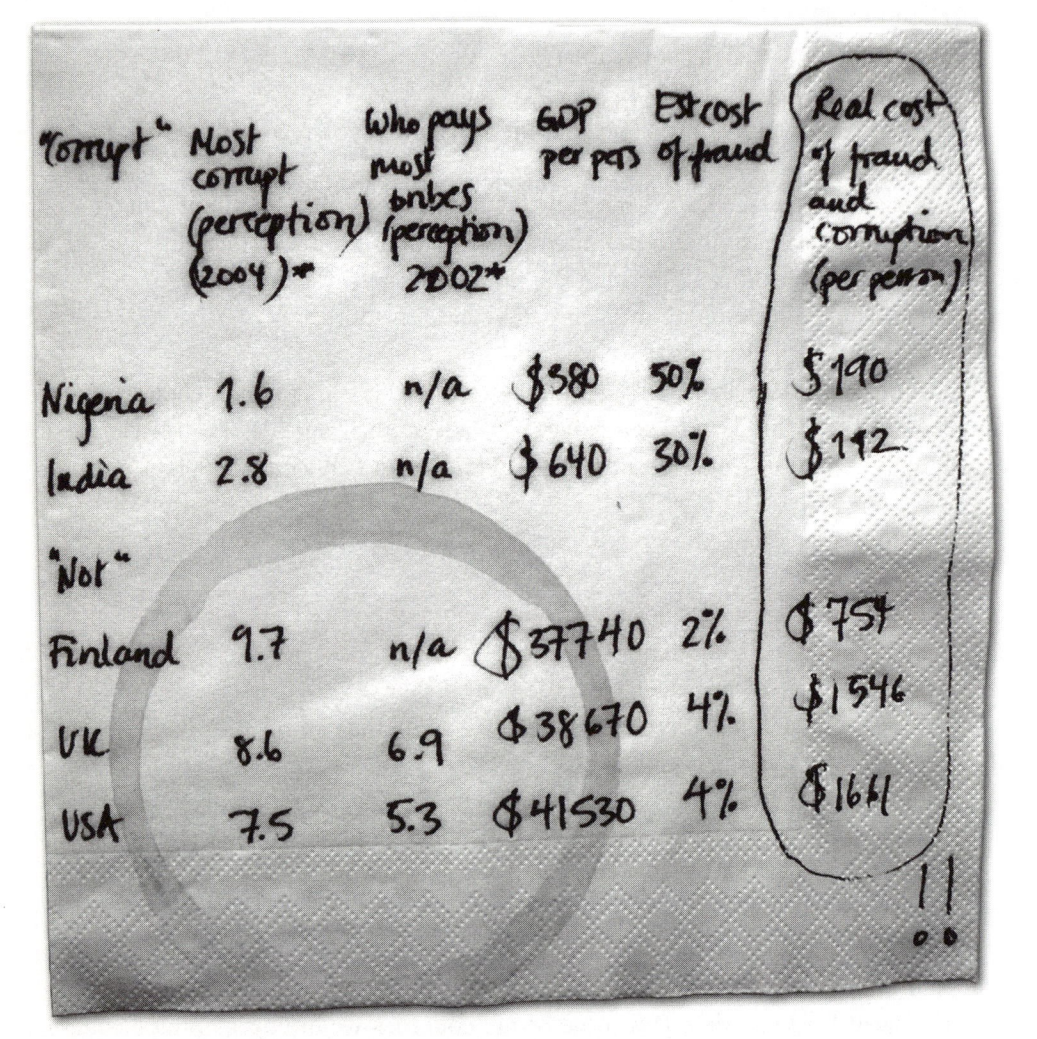

"corrupt"	Most corrupt (perception) (2004)*	Who pays most bribes (perception) 2002*	GDP per pers	Est cost of fraud	Real cost of fraud and corruption (per person)
Nigeria	1.6	n/a	$580	50%	$190
India	2.8	n/a	$640	30%	$192
"Not"					
Finland	9.7	n/a	$37740	2%	$757
UK	8.6	6.9	$38670	4%	$1546
USA	7.5	5.3	$41530	4%	$1661

cost of corruption and fraud is highest in the countries which we perceive to be least corrupt. It is just that they are so rich they don't notice it.'

'You got it baby,' she quips, imitating an American, 'and if you want to be even more cynical, we are probably the ones paying the bribes that keep the other ones corrupt.'

'But why don't Finland, India and Nigeria score as bribe payers?' I ask

'My guess is that the Finns were not asked and the Indians and Nigerians aren't able to pay the size of bribes to win business that we so-called developed countries can. Who knows but don't quote me on this one.'

'Why not? That is some serviette. You should show it to the management.'

Mirabel laughs. 'Are you crazy or what? You would have been less naïve if you had been taller and been a cop. The management would laugh this off as the doodlings of a silly girl who thinks she's a manager.'

She sees by my reaction that she has touched a raw nerve. 'Sorry, I didn't mean to be heightist,' she says. 'You are doing a great job – much better than becoming everybody's

favourite lapdog. Just don't get all worked up about the report. Max is working on it now and it will be fine, he told me.'

'Thanks, I believe you.'

'Just don't go putting out fires for ever,' and then she shouts *'Due espressi e il conto per favore'* to the waiter who turns out to be hovering just behind me.

'You speak Italian!'

'Not really,' she says, with her mind clearly on something else.

This afternoon I have to catch a flight to Poland. I'm supposed to be presenting the risk management model to the recently established local management team. Cedric also wants me to look around the operation. It is new, and devouring money.

There's no food in economy on this Boeing 757. That is if you don't classify the rather nasty dry sandwich as food. I forgot my reading material so am stuck with the in-flight magazine, which I think I read already. Leafing through I notice that the back pages are crammed with adverts for hair replacement, liposuction, and at least ten announcements for offshore companies or bank accounts. Somebody must answer these advertisements. I guess the ones in business class or in suits.

The trip was quite uneventful otherwise. They wouldn't let me near anything of interest in the Polish company. However, when I return, Max's updated report is waiting for me. I tear open the double-wrapped envelope and start to read.

I leaf through the report. It is well structured and indexed containing invoices, corporate documents showing the conflicts of interest, photos and land-registry documents of Neil's house in Spain and emails. It is pretty impressive considering where we were a couple of weeks ago.

I decide to call Max. 'Not a bad report, Max,' I say.

'It was quite a lot of work. Decided to do it really thoroughly after that last meeting with your friend Howard. How was Poland?'

'Pretty uneventful – they did not let me near any files. The food was surprisingly good though.'

'That's something then.'

'Max, those land-registry documents from Spain are pretty convincing and I don't speak Spanish. Its very clear Burge transferred that land over to Neil for next to nothing. And you've done a good job on the email analysis too. I'm curious to find out how you got these documents about Object Talk with Neil's name on the invoice for administration fees for the company?'

'That was a hard one,' says Max

'But you told me those offshore companies were impossible to get behind,' I say.

Xamdos
Privileged and Confidential

Investigation report: N-Trex CALM 01

Date: 22.05.200X

Executive Summary

The preliminary investigation work performed to date and evidence uncovered supports the following findings.

A number of suppliers including RDS and Analogy appear to have been grossly overcharging N-Trex for services provided.

An Isle of Man-based company, Object Talk Ltd, has been used by a consortium of persons, including representatives of suppliers and at least one N-Trex employee to systematically overcharge N-Trex.

A senior employee (Travis) established and is one of two directors of an active UK-based company. This is contrary to declarations signed early this year by him that he was not involved in any external businesses.

Several N-Trex senior managers working on the CALM project have misused company expenses for private purposes.

In addition there are strong indications of the following:

•That a personal friendship between Mr Shreeve and the director of a supplier (Burge) has led to personal gain for both parties to the detriment of N-Trex and possibly also the supplier company

•Bribes have been paid in various forms by at least two suppliers to senior CALM project managers

•A number of sub-contractors and consultants have inflated figures and timesheets

•The existence of other conduits which have been used to pay or receive bribes

It appears that certain managers of the CALM project have been prioritising personal enrichment in favour of their duties as employees. This could be one of the identifiable causes as to why the CALM project has experienced significant delays and budget overruns.

Xamdos' recommendations with regard to follow up action are provided in the following section. The key findings plus a number of other issues and open items are explained in detail in sections 3 to 7 of the report. Supporting documentation is provided in Appendices 1 to 52.   1

'Well they are usually, but not always for us. We used a pretext to find the weak point. Then we bluffed a few impoverished incorporation agents that they were going to get paid. You see Mr Neil Shreeve is not that good with money and forgets to pay his bills.'

'Is what you did legal?'

'You bet it is. If you ask your in-house people they will probably say no, but any reputable city attorney will see that we simply used a loophole in the law to obtain it.'

'I'll take your word for it. Hey, one other thing; there's nothing in here about Aldgate or any of the other offshore companies. Why did you leave that one out?'

'Politics André, politics,' says Max. 'I have a hunch that Aldgate and the other offshore companies we have been sniffing at may possibly be known about higher up the tree. If I put any suspicions about them into this report, then there is a chance that this whole project may get closed down pretty quickly. I'm just being cautious.'

'Who do you think is involved?' I ask, my curiosity getting the better of me.

'I don't know. Maybe nobody from N-Trex but since we don't have anything concrete, I thought it better not to include it. Anyway we have more than enough to go to interview with your two guys and the two suppliers.'

'Is that who you are suggesting we interview simultaneously?'

'For starters yes. I've drafted a proposed interview plan as an appendix to the report. Lets see what your bosses say and then we can talk.'

'OK.'

Max has sent two copies of the report so I take one up to Cedric. He's not in so I leave it with his new secretary, who I've not seen before.

The meeting with John is scheduled for Friday at three o'clock.

On my way up to the meeting I pass Pete, Mirabel's head of personal and physical security, a 55-year-old battle-scarred ex-policeman.

'Eh what's up Stacey?' he says imitating a New York policeman.

'Not much Big P, catch you later.' We have developed a habit of grunting at each other to liven up the day. Pete's OK and I think he likes me.

We are waiting for John in the boardroom – Max and I on one side of the big conference table and Cedric and Harald on the other. Harald, Max and I are talking about holidays while Cedric is playing with his latest digital organiser. He wouldn't probably understand the meaning of the word holiday anyway. John as usual is late.

At ten past John breezes in with a ream of documents and takes his seat at the head of the table nearest to Cedric and myself. He looks unusually happy.

'Right gents, sorry I'm late but I guess you've all had a chance to study André and Max's reports. While I might not say it was pleasant reading, it certainly kept me awake last night.'

Nobody says anything but John is used to this.

'Well done', he says, looking at Max and I. 'I can see a lot of hard work has gone into this.' I feel like adding 'and a lot of the company's money', but I refrain from doing so.

It's evident as he flicks the pages that he has been reading as there are underlinings, annotations and exclamation marks everywhere.

'I have a few questions but first I want to say that the case looks pretty clear to me. The rot has set in without us knowing and the only cure is firm action. Do you agree?'

There are murmurs of 'yes' and 'absolutely' in the room.

'And I like the strategy you propose,' John says looking at me although the strategy was all Max's idea. 'We stay discreet and then next Tuesday hit the main culprits with simultaneous interviews – voluntary ones of course. I remember a teacher at school doing this to some boys who were found pinching chemicals from the labs at my school. It worked a treat. One day of disruption only and it earned him lots of respect.' He says this with a slight twinkle in his eye. I guess he was one of the boys who was caught.

'Any legal problems with this approach in the company?' he says looking at Harald

'None that I can see so far. I am much more in favour of doing the office searches of the key employees with their permission, after the interviews,' replies Harald. He looks as if this is one meeting he'd rather not be in.

Cedric pipes up. 'Isn't Howard joining us?' asks Cedric.

'No, he's in one of those former Soviet states working on a new deal,' replies John smoothly.

We spend some time going through the evidence and John's queries. Max has all the answers. Cedric is open-mouthed. Only Harald throws in the occasional challenge, but is quickly swept aside.

'Cedric, will you be able to make the time to follow this one through? As the CFO it will be good for you to see some action as well as the money we should be saving if we avoid getting into these messes. One way of making money is to stop losing it!'

'I can't agree more,' says Cedric. Given the way the meeting is going, I think Cedric would have agreed even if John had asked him to fire Harald.

'And Harald, the law is on our side but make sure these guys', he points to Max and I, 'don't do anything naughty or stupid as I'd hate to have my next meeting with you and André in prison. Their coffee is awful.'

Harald laughs a little less heartily than the rest of us. Only three-quarters of an hour has gone and the meeting is over. John leaves followed quickly by Harald and then Cedric who half-smiles saying, 'Lets talk about the plan tomorrow then.'

'That was a bit of a turn-around, don't you think?' I say to Max.

'He hasn't turned as yet, André.'

Once again I'm left trying to decipher the De Gras code.

Even if Max sometimes looks like a slob, you can't fault him on his meticulous planning. Everybody involved in the simultaneous interviews has a briefing pack with a complete set of relevant documents, background information and specific sections covering their particular interview object.

We all meet on the Monday evening to review the next day's plan. Two of Max's colleagues, Dan and Deepak, who I've never met before, are present as well as Sarah, Max, Mirabel and Suzy, who has volunteered to type up the interviews. Everyone is very focussed.

Max is not letting me do an interview. Instead I will be in the temporary control

Xamdos

Privileged and Confidential

Interview object	Interviewer	Comment
Neil Shreeve	Max	To start 9.00 a.m.
John Travis	Dan (Xamdos)	To begin immediately after interview with Neil Shreeve
Conrad Burge (Analogy)	Mirabel	Letters of authority requesting co-operation from the supplier to be signed by JTS
Chris Kowalowski (RDS)	Deepak (Xamdos)	Letters of authority (see above)
Control	André, Suzy, Sarah	Meeting Room N-208

12.06.20XX

centre taking information as it comes in, keeping a log of events and relaying information out to the individual interviewers where needed. It is an approach which is unfamiliar to me but it seems to make sense. Cedric is on hand to control the situation, Harald has checked our legal position and all the appropriate letters of permission have been signed.

On the day of the interviews we arrive at eight but there is little to do, probably because of the meticulous planning. Things are going smoothly and according to plan. Cedric is in and out. Harald has called in sick and sent an assistant who is so nervous that eventually Cedric relieves him and tells him to be on call. I think the assistant relieved himself immediately.

Mirabel rings just after ten to say she is done with her supplier already and is on her way back.

Then 12 pages of a handwritten statement arrives on the specially set up fax machines with a cover note saying 'Type up asap and bring in to me. More follows.'

Suzy gets to work typing it up. After a while she says, 'Looks like Neil's painted himself into a corner. He's lied too many times about things which we know are true.'

'If I know Max it sounds like Neil's going to tell the truth pretty soon,' says Sarah.

Mirabel arrives back. 'They threw me out, politely of course, but not before they had told me a lot. They are really scared at Analogy that they are going to lose our business.'

'Which they probably will after this,' I add.

'But they are so desperate, you know what they told me?' We wait for Mirabel. She is enjoying this. 'Burge told me that after he made an offer for 122 000 to N-Trex, Shreeve and Travis turned up telling him that he had won a contract for 135 000. Burge said that he didn't understand what they meant at first …'

'I bet he did,' interrupts Suzy.

'… and they finally spelled it out that 13 000 was for them. Burge said he protested but in the end he said he was very sorry but caved in to pressure. He gave me a sob story about how they have massive debts and had no choice, so I asked him if that was his Mercedes sports car in the car park. He told me that I should go now and make an appointment and that was that. Anyway I got a statement and a copy of the two contracts. Suzy, can you pass this piece of information to Max and also Dan. It might help them.'

Deepak rings in next. 'He's gone to the loo but thank god for that. This guy just won't stop talking, and I think he's a pathological liar. He's tied himself in knots but won't sign anything. He says that N-Trex completely lost control of the project and we are lucky that he, the Great Kowalowski, is actually the de facto project manager. When I asked him why every project budget matched exactly, he eventually confessed that they used a system called living budgets where they delivered the budget for sign-off after the project. Look guys, I'm not an accountant but have you every heard of a living …?'

'No!' cuts in Cedric. He's rather worked up. Maybe because for a second he thought somebody mentioned an accounting term he had never heard of.

After numerous faxes, statements, corrections, requests for lunch, coffee and water and all, Max finally comes in at half-past four looking tired.

'It took him a while to get his head around it, but eventually he admitted the truth. He's tired and demoralised. I'm trying to get him to eat something. He looks ill. Can someone from personnel join me for a few moments, or at least somebody here who still likes him. He does not know what's going to happen to him, but I guess on the strength of this', Max waves a sheaf of handwritten notes and papers, 'you will need to dismiss him tomorrow.'

'Did he confess?' asks Cedric.

'Pretty much, I guess. Go easy on him, he's not a bad guy.'

Nobody believes him.

The day ends at nine, but not before Travis has resigned and been escorted off the premises by Pete, who rather enjoyed being called up to do this. John had popped by at eight to see how things were going, and was so pleased that he brought down four boxes of exclusive company chocolates. The last person back was an exhausted Deepak complaining of tendonitis.

The next day Cedric and Harald handle the formal dismissals of Neil and Travis. I never even saw Neil before he went.

There is a lot of additional information to be analysed such as the files and computers. It is likely that we will be putting a case for recoveries, although RDS will probably declare bankruptcy soon.

John, Cedric and Harald are working on an internal memo to explain what happened and how the business is back to normal.

A week later John, Cedric and I are back in the boardroom. Harald has been called away, Max is busy. To my surprise John has invited Mirabel to join us.

'I just want to say well done to you two and also to you Maribel for your team's work behind the scenes.'

'Thanks for your support – it was a hell of a job,' I reply on behalf of us all ignoring John's mispronunciation of Mirabel's name.

'Good. We can now close this case down and focus on turning the logistics function around. Cedric and I have already discussed the replacement management team which we will announce shortly. You will be one of the first to know.'

'Should we not follow up on some of the other remarks Neil made about other frauds?' I interject.

'Neil who?' says John, with an expression of disinterest.

We all laugh, but I am not sure if John was only joking as he resumes his stride.

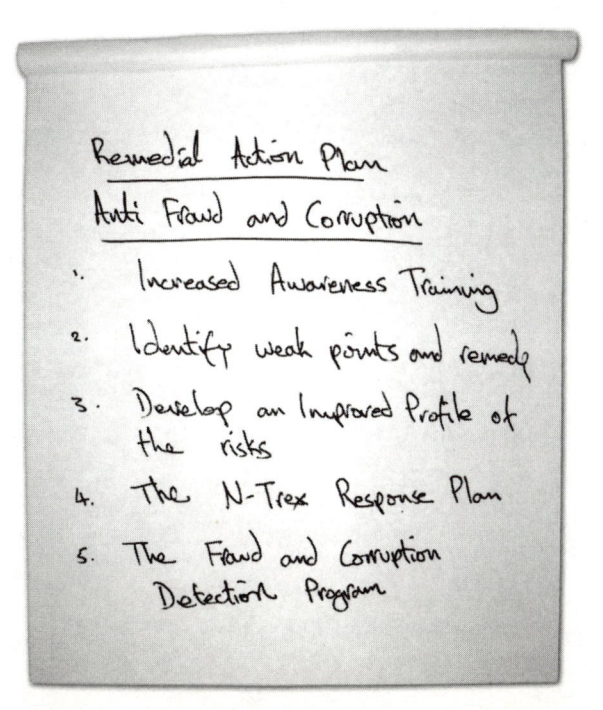

'I want to put in place a remedial action plan which will help us prevent this sort of thing happening anywhere else.' He looks at me. 'André, what do you think?'

I have already been briefed by Cedric and turn the flip chart.

'Excellent – though I'm a little uncertain about that last point but let's mull it over shall we?' says John. 'Anyway ladies and gents, what do you think?'

As we ratify the plan and discuss how it will contribute to improving and protecting N-Trex's value, reputation and culture, Mirabel is beaming over the recognition she is getting.

'I want you to take the lead on this project, André, with a dotted reporting line to me.' Cedric smiles. It is obvious that he and John have discussed this in advance.

After the meeting Max rings.

'How did it go?'

'Fine – well brilliant actually,' I say 'He bought the plan. I think we can really make a difference.'

'Maybe but there's always a bigger fish out there,' is all Max says.

'You cynic,' I say.

Max just laughs it off.

THE CODE
OF CONDUCT

Setting the standard at N-Trex

We at N-Trex have the highest standards in:

1. Respecting the freedom and basic human rights of each and every individual
2. Stopping the spread of corruption and bribery by adopting a zero-tolerance policy within N-Trex
3. Free competition and open and transparent business
4. Actively contributing to a cleaner and healthier environment
5. Equally respecting different races, creeds, cultures and religions
6. Doing business with ethical partners
7. Taking strong action to prevent the occurrence of fraud, corruption and abuse of the company's values
8. Avoiding and wherever required exposing abusive practices such as child or forced labour, harassment or false propaganda
9. Supporting the fight again drugs and alcohol abuse
10. Making a positive contribution in the communities where N-Trex operates

Any suspected violations of the N-Trex Code of Conduct should be reported to your supervisor or divisional HR manager or via the U-Count! helpline.

For further details go to **http://ntrex.ucount.helpline**

Act 2: The Dilemma

Chapter 5

After the excitement of CALM nine months ago, once again I find myself still wading through the standards for COSO, our de facto internal control standards. COSO stands for Committee Of Sponsoring Organisations, which published a control framework in the early 1990s.

Since the post Enron-WorldCom legislation in the United States the epidemic problem of management fraud and corruption has at last been recognised; it's not just 'a few rotten apples' as a politician once said. The inherently dull subject of internal control and the COSO report is enjoying a bit of a renaissance. It's good solid stuff, but I can't help wishing they had thought of a more imaginative title.

Nine months ago when we were sorting out CALM, many of us were thrilled about the launch of the new Code of Conduct and the U-Count helpline. I can't help thinking that there has been less of a sense of urgency recently as I gather my papers for my debut at the Audit Committee meeting this afternoon.

Audit Committee meeting # 3 – Agenda

15.06.20XX

1. Apologies for absence
2. CALM follow up investigation – status
3. Remedial action plan and Anti-Fraud and -Corruption measures:

    a. Awareness training
    b Profiling
    c. Ethics help line
    d. Fraud and Corruption Detection programme
    e. Fraud Response Plan

4. Status of other ongoing investigations
5. Corporate Social Responsibility and Code of Conduct
6. Any other business

Although most of the participants haven't yet warmed their seats this is an important meeting. This committee has the power to ratify many of the initiatives we have been working on during the past nine months.

The chairman opens the meeting. 'John Thornbury-Stevens has sent his apologies for absence and on behalf of the committee I would like to welcome André Stacey who is heading up our remedial action plan and anti-fraud initiative. André will be presenting the plans at this special meeting.'

The people around the table actually clap!

The chairman hands over to Cedric who launches into the formalities. Two other non-executive directors, a man and woman are already looking bored. The lead external audit partner is also in the room. He looks more attentive, probably because he charges by the hour.

'If everybody is happy', continues Cedric, 'then I suggest we simply cover the items on the agenda in order. André can you bring us up to date with the CALM investigation?'

I launch into my prepared speech: 'CALM is finally living up to its name. The system is working well now and all the glitches are being ironed out. Cedric and I just received a copy of the latest progress report from the new project director who is also very satisfied with the new suppliers. The court case against Mr Shreeve ...'. One of the non-executives is whispering something to Cedric so I pause.

I hear Cedric say 'the fraudster' to him and suddenly he looks more alert.

I continue: 'The case against Mr Shreeve is due in court very soon. He is fighting back more than we originally anticipated and his lawyer is claiming that he was the victim of a witch hunt. Our side is being coordinated by our legal counsel Harald Schmidt and N-Trex's external legal advisors. Although I am a potential witness I hope they don't need to call me. Our documentary evidence was pretty clear and Harald is confident we will win.'

'Excellent. Good news. I hope we have seen the back end of that,' says one of the non-executives, whose name I have already forgotten.

Cedric then outlines how we are taking measures to prevent recurrence in projects like CALM and after about fifteen minutes we get to point three, my blue-print for our anti-fraud and -corruption initiatives.

'As part of N-Trex's anti-fraud and -corruption plan we are currently revamping the Code of Conduct and Fraud Policy, launching an ethics helpline ...'

'Is that the one called U Turn?' asks the woman. Someone stifles a laugh.

'Its called U-Count actually,' says Cedric with a faint smile. 'Go on André.'

'In addition we are launching Fraud and Corruption Awareness Programmes, a series of Profiling Workshops and our proposed Fraud and Corruption Detection Programme.'

'For everybody's benefit can you take us through what profiling is once again please André?' asks Cedric.

'Profiling is the process of understanding what methods of fraud and corruption could affect N-Trex. Through group brainstorming sessions we develop a sort of radar

plot of what things could hit us and then try to evaluate the likelihood of them succeeding and the impact it could have.'

'What sort of impact do you mean,' asks the woman.

'Well, profit, reputation, share price, our culture – anything negative for us I guess.'

'Things which would get us sued for negligence,' adds the chairman.

'Probably,' I say, not knowing what response is appropriate. 'Anyway, the only real way to understand the risk of fraud is to look at N-Trex from the point of view of a fraudster. If we can think like a thief, we avoid the complacency that often sets into big companies.'

There are some raised eyebrows from the non-executives, probably at the phrase 'think like a thief'.

Cedric comes to the rescue: 'Profiling is in important part of understanding our operational risks. What André is saying is that for years our operational risk processes have paid too little attention to fraud and corruption and we need a methodology to get the threats onto the risk map.'

Now Cedric is speaking a language which they understand. He goes on to talk about the need to find a balance between opportunity and abuse of privilege. 'At N-Trex we empower our managers to take decisions and thereby provide them with the opportunity to make things happen. We also need to motivate them, and that also means giving them something to reach for that would be good for them personally and not just the company. Our job, no actually your job, is to make sure that we provide enough guidance and controls to prevent people straying from the ethical path. At the same time we should not get carried away with conspiracy theories and see everything as doom and gloom.'

At least after this little speech they are back on track. I know that Cedric is not wild about my proposals for the Fraud and Corruption Detection Programme. He feels it smells too much of 'big brother', the Orwellian version, that is.

The awareness programmes seem to be popular though and even the helpline gets the nod.

After the coffee and comfort break the Chairman says to Cedric and myself, 'Can you explain your vision for this Fraud and Corruption Detection Programme?'

'What we are trying to achieve is a way of continuously monitoring the business for the early warning signs of fraud and corruption, in line with COSO. We learnt from the CALM investigations that these red flags are already there but in the normal course of our work we tend to ignore them. It needs a healthy sceptical mind and some smart work to find them.'

I pause to judge their reactions, but already I can see that I am not winning many friends around the table. I decide not to mention some of the work which we are already doing such as analysing the senior management's expense accounts and searching the accounts payable system for evidence of kickbacks and other fraudulent invoices. Even as we speak, Rob is performing a morality test looking at what expenses N-Trex is paying to fifty top managers. I mentioned it in passing to Cedric about these pilot tests and he did not seem to object. The results are very interesting especially in sales and

marketing. Jamie has been slower with the accounts payable pilot work. We've bought some analysis software and he is learning how to use it.

'The programme is really doing something concrete against fraud and corruption rather than just complying with regulations. The difficulty in implementing a real Fraud and Corruption Detection Programme is to monitor without looking like the police,' I add.

There are nervous smiles all around the table. Everyone looks uncomfortable, even Cedric. He glances at his watch.

'Ladies and gentlemen, we're already in extra time. Maybe we can take another look at André's programme at the next meeting in three months time together with the Fraud Response Plan. Is that OK with you André?'

'Sure.' I take the hint as I don't think this last part was going too well.

With hindsight, the audit committee meeting seems to have gone well enough although I feel with some irony that there is a certain reluctance from this committee to really commit to anything concrete. I think that they are keener to watch me from a distance. Surprisingly, Cedric has been much more supportive than I expected.

He said it was better that I did not tell them too much about the results of my pilot reviews. With some simple digging on the Internet, skimming through business magazines and a little help from Max, I put together a list of over 200 tax-haven jurisdictions and front-company addresses and then cross-match them with the supplier master files and supplier bank accounts. I also look for large round-number payments to unusual destinations or payments outside the European Union if the country where the payee was based and the country of their bank account did not match.

I look at the files laid out over my little conference table. I have so far collected a number of potential red flags.

There are a few large round-sum payments to tax havens which look very much like commissions or facilitation payments. This includes a curious little company called Finance Holding Enterprises in Liechtenstein. The company has a Swiss bank account. I can't find any trace of it in the international yellow pages or elsewhere on the Internet. The only reference I can find are the words 'Ice Hockey Project' on the invoices. Rob tells me that this is a cryptic reference to Howard's Minsk project; the president of the country is apparently a very big ice hockey fan.

There are some suppliers which look suspiciously like front companies and at least five smaller invoices which definitely should have not been paid, not to mention the rather shocking findings from my management expenses review.

As if my mind is being monitored, Howard pokes his head around the door of my office.

'I see you've been doing some digging,' he remarks casually, gesturing at the piles on my table.

'What makes you ask that?' My voice is tight and defensive.

'A little bird in my office told me you had borrowed the Finance Holding files. You could have asked your Uncle Howard you know.'

'I thought you weren't that interested in routine audit work.' I am really hoping he will go soon, but it looks as if Howard is here for a purpose.

'André, I just would like to say that we in the management are very impressed by what you are doing about fraud. Just remember that everything is not black and white and you could end up catching the wrong guy if you are not careful.'

'What exactly do you mean?' I am not sure how much he knows, so I tread cautiously.

'Well, if you agree that our Code of Conduct and policies are designed to protect the company, then you should also recognise that they should not be turned into something which could harm the company.'

'So?' The less I say the better I think.

'To put it bluntly too much of a good thing could be a bad thing. Are you tracking with me?'

'Maybe.'

'Look André,' he says putting a paternalistic hand on my shoulder, 'to get certain things done in this company, you occasionally have to bend the rules. Otherwise we would be all out of a job. Say we need a particular supplier and he wants his payment offshore, then what business of ours is it? He delivers the goods to us and everything is transparent. What he then does with the money is his business, don't you agree? Maybe he is even friends with one of our guys, but that's where it stops, believe me. The most important thing is that we have the best and often cheapest supplier wouldn't you agree?'

'Yes but …', I try but don't get far as Howard is now in full flow.

'Take my job for instance. In some of the countries we are operating there is no way we could sell if we did not lubricate the wheels. I know our competitors all do it, and they have codes of conduct just like us. Come on, I don't like it any more than you, but we are no worse than the competition.' Howard sees I am not entirely convinced. 'In some ways I like to think we are better, after all our Code of Conduct is much clearer than many and, of course, we have given you the chance to clean up.'

I try and ignore his condescending attitude as I retort, 'But what about the ethics of it, and how can we be sure that the money we are paying is actually going to the people it is?' I make an inverted commas sign in the air with my fingers. 'Supposed to go to, rather than going to either some other criminals or even our own dishonest employees?'

'I've been thinking about that too. If we did not sell into those countries then they would not have the benefits of N-Trex products. Our agency and facilitation payments, I think the word bribery is over-used, actually help to build up their economies. Of course I would like it to be less concealed but that's the way of the world. And if you are concerned that anyone here is pocketing the money then I can assure you that there are controls at levels of which you are not aware.'

He won't convince even Timmy with arguments like that. However he has a point. What concerns me is whether the other senior managers think like he does.

I think, or at least I hope, he only knows of the Finance Holding Enterprise file and not all the red flags which are beginning to accumulate in my office.

Howard rests his hand on the handle of my office. I think he's finally going to leave. But then he turns to face me.

'Oh and I know about your little infiltrations into the senior management expense accounts. You are taking your job very seriously. I'm surprised you got John's approval?'

'It's implied in my new mandate.' My voice is strained. I did not ask John, but I am pretty sure I mentioned it to Cedric at some point.

'Those club receipts of mine you've been looking at – they were customers I took there you know.' He gives me a look almost of pity.

'Were they?'

I didn't really intend to challenge him like that but some of the director's expenses were very eye-opening. Max had told me to how to spot them: high-value, simple-looking receipts from anonymous-looking companies. It turned out for example, from Max's digging, that the $715 Howard paid on the credit card to GPS Admin Services BV was an erotic bar and the $400 to Anita and Jane Inc was for an escort agency.

He looks displeased with my challenge. 'It was just business,' he says emphatically.

'That's what all the girls say.' I say it before I can stop myself.

'Come on André, get real and don't tell me you are that naïve. Our customers like to be wined and dined and more. It's my job here to do this. You really think I would bother otherwise?'

I decide to reserve my judgement here.

'Anyway I can't see what all the fuss is about,' continues Howard. 'We were in Copenhagen where it is legal.'

My enquiries have shown that it wasn't just Copenhagen and I know some of the visits were just with the internal sales team. I keep quiet as can see I have touched a raw nerve here.

'André your digging could really hurt this company. If the papers found out who some of my customers really were, they would have a field day, and that would be before the repercussions of the odd ministerial resignation.'

I cannot agree with his attitude or actions: they make a complete mockery of our code of conduct.

Nevertheless, I try to bring a tone of civility back into the discussion 'Howard, I hear what you say but from a personal standpoint I guess we will have to differ on this one.'

He fixes me with a stare. 'Don't mess with things you don't understand André,' he says coldly, and promptly walks out of my office.

Chapter 6

'I'm not going to be put off by veiled threats,' I tell Jamie after describing the episode with Howard. 'How's the audit software coming along?'

'It's taking some time to get to grips with but there are some really neat tests you can do. I took Max's red flag paper and have started implementing it in accounts receivables.'

'Great, keep me posted. Don't go too far though. I still need formal approval for this project,' I say.

'Are you ever going to get that?' asks Jamie.

'God knows. Anything remotely controversial gets buried in a sea of meetings and redrafted proposals. When anyone smells something potentially nasty, their enthusiasm for doing things just seems to evaporate.'

'André, I love your proposals – lets run it past the committee.' I do an imitation of Cedric. 'What about JTS then? I'm sure he backs you up,' asks Jamie.

'I believe he does, but getting an appointment with him is not easy these days. He's got bigger problems facing him than our detection programme.'

'Like that article in the newspapers recently?'

Some journalist has latched onto the CALM case and has interviewed some of the suppliers. It looks like there's been a leak and some people are even pointing the finger at me, which is preposterous.

The headline is:

Thornbury Stevens unable to C.A.L.M things down at N-Trex – an insider talks …

This is followed by an article which uses phrases like 'culture of deceit' and 'hands in the till'.

'At least they refer to you as a special investigator,' says Jamie laughing. 'It'll make your kids think daddy's some sort of James Bond figure.'

'They don't watch James Bond, they're eight and two remember.'

'Right,' says Jamie. 'What would I know about kids.'

'Anyway, luckily I'm not dealing with the press. JTS thought I have too much on my plate already.'

'There's also our Polish market,' I continue. 'The board has been asking a number of awkward questions as to why we are closing down our marketing company there. You know the one I visited last May, when they didn't want to let me look around. We had to write off a big chunk of our investment there.' The reason I know about Poland is because something came into the U-Count mailbox about this, but I haven't shared it

with the rest of the team as yet. 'I suspect that JTS is having second thoughts about lifting the lid on this can of worms,' I say as I get back to my desk and the report I'm working on.

❖   ❖   ❖

A short while later Suzy puts her head around the door. She looks like she is about to cry.

'What's up?' I ask.

She doesn't say anything at first but shuts the door and sits down opposite me.

'Come on Suzy, if something's come up, you know I've got all the time for you whatever problem you have.'

She's holding a couple of sheets of paper, but they're face down so I can't see what's written on them.

'It's not me, André, it's you,' she says still not making much sense.

'If I've offended you in any way then it was uninten … '

She cuts me off. 'Not me, stupid, it's what they're saying about you.' She hands me the papers she is holding. 'I think I got this email which was meant to have been copied to Susan Abson in Marketing, but was accidentally sent to me by mistake.'

I turn over the paper and begin to read.

To:	\<HJ-Sales-Managers-mailing-list\>
From:	Howard.Jackson@N-Trex.com
Cc:	Debbie.Jackson@N-Trex.com; Susan.Agarwal@N-Trex.com;
Subject:	Expenses – Highly Confidential
Date:	21.03.20X4

Friends,

Since our last sales meeting in Hamburg, I have just discovered that our over-zealous Risk Manager at Head office has been reviewing our travel expenses using the online system.

While we are doing our best for the company, this jumped up little s**t is poking his inordinately large nose into our affairs believing he has support for his snooping and breach of our privacy from his fairy godfather at the top of this company.

I don't see any immediate problems but if Mr Stasi and his band of amateur sleuths continue to poke around and take up our time with useless questions, it might affect our ability to close deals and, hence to make profits for the company.

I plan to put a stop to his activities once and for all. In the meantime, if he approaches any of you, just refer him to me.

Your 'Uncle Howard'

Ps: Keep calm and watch out for 'the Stasi' (see attached jpg).

I look at Suzy and for a moment I am unable to say anything.

'Thanks for telling me,' I say quietly.

'I think you should tell John. This is just not fair. After all we've been doing … '

I raise a finger to my lips. 'I'll sort this out. It's my battle. Can you get me a cup of coffee. I just need to think for a bit.'

'Ok, do it your way but I think you are taking too much on yourself personally.' She pauses. 'Oh and Neil Shreeve called for you.'

'What did he want? I thought the court case was nearly over.'

'He didn't say. He just said he'd call back.'

'OK, thanks,' I say distractedly as she shuts the door behind her.

I flip to page two of the email and there is a photo of a Nazi guard standing to attention with my picture crudely superimposed onto the face.

In spite of my calm response to Suzy, I feel the emotions and questions are churning in my brain. A knot is forming in my stomach. Is that what they really think? Why is he doing this? I am only doing my job.

A sudden surge of anger envelops me. I am going to face down Howard and sort this out.

As I walk down the stairs to Sales and Marketing I am shaking. It is uncharacteristic of me but a voice in my head tells me I am going to have it out with him here and now.

Through the glass panels of a meeting room, I can see that Howard is holding a presentation for some of the local sales team.

I knock hard on the door.

He opens it and flashes a smile at me. 'I'll be done in an hour or so. Can it wait Mr Stacey?' he says, emphasising my last name.

'If you don't mind I'd like a word now'. I pause. 'Outside if you don't mind.'

He looks at his audience. 'Hang in there guys, I'll just be a couple of minutes,' and steps outside shutting the door behind him.

'You look terrible. What is it that can't wait?' he says.

'I thought you'd know that already.' I grip the nearby filing cabinet to stop myself shaking with anger.

'Know what?' He's not giving anything away.

'Emails perhaps?' He doesn't flinch. 'Slandering your colleagues?'

'Oh that email,' he says nonchalantly.

'You've got a bloody nerve! You've been undermining me all along and now this'. I wave the offending email in his face but he doesn't answer me. 'I thought those club visits were pretty low, but you've shown me new depths to which you can sink.'

My voice is raised and faces are now peering out of the meeting room window.

'I remind you who you are talking to André.'

My voice is rising at his repeated provocations. 'I know who I'm talking to. You're a fat salesman with no morals and conscience like the inebriated bastard who put my brother in a wheelchair nine years ago.' I feel a momentary release of tension as I ignore all company protocol and tear into him.

He drops his voice to a whisper and brings his face closer to mine so I can smell the

alcohol and stale tobacco. 'If you are planning to make accusations I'd advise you to get the evidence first. Otherwise I'd watch your mouth, Stasi-boy.'

Then he peers over my shoulder, smiles, turns and walks back into his meeting, shutting the door behind him. I turn to see what he was looking at and find Cedric and John a few meters behind me, staring at me and the space Howard occupied, looking horrified.

Chapter 7

After the turbulent events of last week it feels good to get away. I know the reason I lost control is that I have been internalising my frustrations for too long. After my little outburst at Howard, rather than hide away, I had a chat with Cedric. JTS had been accosted by an angry Howard. Cedric told me that the situation needed urgent defusing and it would be a good idea if I took a week to cool down. At first, I tried to protest as I did not want to look like the one who was running away. At the same time, I felt that it would be good for my family situation to put a break between myself and the pressures at N-Trex.

With a little bit of reshuffling I have been able to clear away or reassign all my tasks for next week. Timmy is off school this week anyway and even Marilena has promised to come up on Wednesday evening.

This mountain cottage is just the thing. There are some beautiful trails in the forest and crystal-clear water in the lake, although it is too cold for swimming. I have one of those baby-rucksacks for carrying Maria along the numerous hiking trails. Although Timmy is not that used to walking he seems to enjoy it more and more and is helping by carrying our lunch in his little rucksack. The cows look as if they don't have a care in the world, but the sheep remind me too much of people at work.

'I'm sorry I missed your football match the other day. Everybody was blaming me for things I didn't do, so I was unable to just run away.'

He comes over and gives me a hug. 'It's OK Dad, we lost the match anyway. I was also being blamed by my team for letting in three goals.'

With Maria chipping in from time to time and pulling at my ears and hair as we walk, I tell Timmy more about what I do in my work than I have ever done before, including my run-in with Howard and the events leading up to it. I even manage to tell him the story about the drunk salesman and why Uncle Richard ended up in a wheelchair.

'But Dad, even Howard can't be just bad. I know you are right but there is meant to be some good in everybody. We are all born nice and then things happen in our life that makes us become more and more bad. If we get away with being bad then next time it is easier to be more bad.'

Timmy's honesty is most refreshing, especially his views about not winning at all costs. He makes me promise to him that I will not fight Howard when I get back, but try to find a way to do what is right without fighting.

It is wonderful to have so much time here with my kids. Timmy's vivid descriptions

of his own experiences spark my own thoughts and reflections, taking me back to the choices I made at school and in my career. Where would I be if I had taken history and literature instead of maths and economics. What would have happened if I had followed my heart and stayed another six months in India doing voluntary service when I was 19. Would my kids have been half-Indian? Who would I have been if I had followed my ideals and changed paths after university?

Thoughts of Neil, Cedric and Howard are pushed to the back of my mind and I am able to see the person inside who I still am rather than the one which everybody, including myself, thinks that I have become. At the age of forty-one, I believe that I have become rigid and dull – totally resigned to the fact that it is not possible to make a difference. That is probably why the teasing at work hurt me more than I would like to admit. Nothing has changed since school.

I am also surprised how much Rick's accident still plays on my mind and how, subconsciously, I see Howard as the drunk driver who was treated too leniently by the courts because he professed that his drinks were laced at a sales promotion event. I remember that day in court with Rick just out of hospital and me pushing his wheelchair and how the driver blatantly lied about not knowing that his drinks had been spiked with vodka.

I see that I have another message on my mobile. My one concession to the company, or was it myself, was to take my phone with me. I must have missed two calls.

'Dad why don't you just switch that thing off,' says Timmy.

'I can't completely walk away from the problems; that would be cowardly,' I reply, knowing myself that it is not true.

Although the phone is on silent the display is flashing.

It's a message from Mirabel: 'Guten Abend Herr Honecker. I hope the mountain air is helping and you're not crying over last week. Found out some interesting things which are going to cheer you up but I'll save them for next week. Pete is dying to know how you did it. Ciao you cult hero.'

Seeing me laughing for the first time after a call Timmy asks me who it was.

'The iron lady,' I reply.

'Mum?' he asks eagerly.

'A different one.'

Timmy looks suspicious.

'At work,' I add.

Timmy is happy that I don't ring back. Mirabel will call again if there is anything really important.

Dinner at the lodge is a wonderful affair. We are having our evening meals there and tonight is trout caught the same day from the lake, served with cucumber salad, potatoes, broccoli and home-made mayonnaise. Since Marilena has not yet arrived I allow Timmy

to try a very small glass of white wine mixed with mineral water. Despite being very enthusiastic to try it I don't believe he was impressed.

When Marilena comes up I am allowed a few hours each day of solitude. Walking around the lake I see a man in a shabby hat and anorak complete with fishing rod and bucket. I saw him on my walk with Timmy and Maria couple of days back too.

As I walk past I notice that he has what look like three trout in his bucket. 'Not bad,' I say with an appraising smile.

'Yes – today looks like being a good day,' he replies

Not being a fisherman myself I remark 'Guess it's just luck then?'

'I'm not sure. Didn't catch a thing for three days, but then the bloody mobile phone kept ringing. It fell out of my pocket yesterday evening while I was crossing that river.' He points into the distance. 'Either the ringing had frightened the fish away or I was not relaxed enough until I lost it.'

It turns out that my newfound companion is a partner in a city law firm. He came away to the mountains to get away from the stress, but like me made the one single and dangerous concession to his important job by bringing the phone.

'Now even the fish don't disturb me. I can really put things into perspective.'

Unlike most semi-important people who prefer to talk about themselves, he seems more interested to ask me about my job and is particularly interested in the little problem that occurred last week.

'So why don't you throw your phone too,' he asks me, revealing a little white lie he told me earlier. 'Go on, it will do you good and you can always tell them you lost it fishing. I'll throw in a couple of these fish too!'

'Surely the off button will suffice,' I reply, a little shocked at his sudden lapse into lunacy.

'But, you will keep checking it and then you'll never get that peace you need.'

The more I ponder the idea the more I realise how much more I am going to enjoy the remaining three days here and his offer of two fresh trout if I do.

As the ripples disappear from where it hit the water I am thinking only about fresh trout, homemade mayonnaise, peas and potatoes. After all I have my SIM card in my pocket and a backup of all the numbers in the office.

At first the family are a bit shocked when I tell them about the parabolic flight of the mobile and the man by the lake. However the taste of fresh fish more than pacifies them.

Without the phone and with no email I am finally able to think. The days even seem longer.

'It's nice to see you relaxed again. You were really losing it,' says Marilena one evening. 'You need to get a balance between your rediscovered idealism and the rest of life. Don't fight battles you can't win.'

'You're right. I really messed up at work as well as home this time.'

❖ ❖ ❖

'Haven't I seen you somewhere before?'

It's Monday morning and my first day back after the essential break. Mirabel has popped her head around the door. She's not usually in so early. She comes over and gives me a hug which is also out of character.

'André, why the long face? You are even more of a cult hero around here now. I told you I have some good news.' I can't determine the extent of her irony as yet.

'Fire away then.'

'Well your fight with Howard has done the rounds and the opinion polls put you as the clear front runner. Everyone wishes that they had had the guts to say what you said. Secondly Pete has found out through his contacts that that company you found, Finance Holding or something, is a vehicle for facilitation payments, and Harald made it semi-legal with the help of the external auditor's tax advisory arm. We think the Sales and Marketing Team dipped into it for their kick-offs and Harald is really mad at them. Lastly, I think they're scared of you.'

'Who is scared?'

'Oh, not just Howard, but all of them at the top. They don't know how much you know. Pete's really jealous of the respect you command but he'll never get it because he cannot write or add up like you.'

'Lucky Pete. Please Mirabel, if I wanted excitement like this I would have joined the secret service. I'm an accountant and risk manager. I just want to do my job and roll out the anti-fraud programmes as I agreed with John earlier.'

'You are doing that.' She says emphatically. 'What you don't realise, and the top guys don't realise either is that these programs are quite a radical change for this company and there is bound to be some pain and aggravation as we make the shift. But you still have JTS's support.'

'I really hope so or I might as well pack up and leave.'

'Listen André, you live in the corporate world which is not always the real one. John has to support you whether he likes it or not because after CALM he went out on a limb and told the shareholders that fighting fraud and corruption would increase shareholder value. I don't know what he personally thinks and frankly I don't care because it doesn't matter. You have a mandate.'

'And Howard?' I ask, not convinced.

'It doesn't matter what Howard thinks now. He ignored you before and now he hates you, but he'll do what JTS says. JTS had wanted him to sell so he did. If JTS tells him to do it differently then he will change, albeit reluctantly. Remember we are all servants to the goals of the company.'

'It just depends which goals you put first, right?'

'You got it. But first you need to make your ideas more politically correct. No offence meant, but your human relations skills can be pretty bad at times. And your Fraud Detection Programme and the sniffing round at management expenses doesn't sound good either. It's like selling foul-tasting medicine. In the USA they would find upbeat names like Wonder Fizz or even Prozac.'

'Yeah Prozac, that was good marketing,' I say sarcastically. 'So what do you suggest then?'

'Cut out the snooping, freshen up the goals of the programme and brand it the Corporate Health Check-up or Health Check. John will buy that I reckon.'

I roll the name around in my head for a while. Health Check. It does make sense. Mirabel's stints in the USA have obviously been very useful.

'Not bad for an ex-female cop,' I say after a while.

She ignores my Freudian slip. 'When I first met you André, I thought you were just another accountant climbing the tree. You can do much more than that; so don't waste your talents. I can't do it because I can never reach the boardroom or directors. You've got the academic background on your side too.'

'I wouldn't say that.'

'I'll get Pete to try to dig out more on those tax-haven companies and the rumours before I return to the USA. Oh, and you should have listened to what Neil had to say when he said there was more to tell,' she says with a smile and small wave of the hand.

'Thanks, Mirabel, you're a star.'

Before I have time to think, Suzy pops her head around the door. 'Cedric wants to see you if you have a moment.'

When I enter his office Cedric is on the phone. He beckons for me to sit down and after a few minutes he hangs up. 'Ah, André, are you relaxed now after the break?'

'Yeah, sure.'

'Good. I've spoken with John and he's cooled down. We're not planning to take any disciplinary action against either you or Howard, but we want you to make up. We simply can't have senior management brawling in public.'

I bite my lip. 'OK, will do.' It's probably best to say as little as possible.

'John also said he's happy to sanction the main parts of our anti-fraud and -corruption programmes,' adds Cedric.

'What part is he not pleased with?'

'He feels that the fraud detection element may give out the wrong signals. I tend to agree especially after your run-in with Howard,' he grimaces slightly but I am prepared for this.

'I am thinking of removing all the controversial elements, like looking at personal data, and renaming the programme the corporate health check.'

Cedric looks more relieved. 'That may work. Let me have a proposal tomorrow morning and I'll run it past John some time this week.'

'Thanks, is that it?'

'That's all. Just one more thing, André. Please don't let your personal feelings influence your professional conduct at work. You've been doing a good job lately, but when I saw you with Howard I thought you were going to hit him.'

'Sorry sir, won't happen again,' I say, saluting a smiling Cedric. The truth is if Howard hadn't walked off, I probably would have hit him.

Act 3: The Tone at the Top

Chapter 8

The lull after the storm is pleasant enough, now that my uncomfortable reconciliation lunch in the canteen with Howard is over. I have agreed to put the Finance Holding and employee expenses projects on hold until Howard comes back to me with plausible explanations.

The Training and Awareness Programme is developing nicely too. There are two distinct halves: a Code of Conduct Awareness Programme which reflects the spirit of the company, and a Fraud and Corruption Awareness Programme which educates all employees as to what can go wrong and how to stop it. I am leading the second programme with my team and have a seat on the working group for the first. Max's practical knowledge is coming in very handy though he is very busy with one investigation or another for us or other clients. If it's not Max doing the investigations, then it is a firm of accountants. I don't want firefighting to become my job.

N-Trex won the first round against Neil and others in court. At the start Neil's lawyer tried to call it a witch hunt. 'They all say that at the start,' was Mirabel's remark. I am curious if anyone is going to appeal against the verdict.

A few months back Harald initiated a fidelity insurance claim on our crime insurance policy and reckons we could get a sizeable payout. He has already rejected the insurance company's first offer to settle. 'Bloody useless policy if we can't get our money back,' were Harald's actual words.

Even Cedric is back to normal.

'Your little tantrum made me realise that I could be next.'

Apparently his wife threatened to leave him if he was not at home more often.

U-Count is taking off too. It's quite a job sorting out the different complaints which trickle in every week. One that caught my eye some weeks ago was from a former sales manager in Greece. He would not give many details but said that he was fired six months ago for telling the truth about corruption in N-Trex to his boss. Harald says that technically speaking we can ignore the message because he is not an employee and the incidents he is referring to took place before U-Count was launched. I'm not sure I agree, but it can't be my number one priority when there is so much else going on.

The focus on prevention, training and understanding the risks is much more satisfying than firefighting, in spite of sometimes getting bogged down in committee structures. My new team, which includes Suzy, Rob and Jamie, are doing well and they are forging better relationship with other departments, especially Corporate Security and Corporate Responsibility.

'Our work definitely contributed towards N-Trex's bottom line,' Jamie commented.

'I guess so', is my reply, 'but I still think investigations get the urgent attention.'

Rob, Jamie, Suzy and I are studying the latest iteration of the N-Trex Fraud and Corruption Profile which we now have been refining for some time; almost one hundred people have been involved in the brainstorming sessions. It doesn't matter if it never is perfect. So many people have now been involved, and Suzy is doing a great job of maintaining it. The responsibility to understand fraud and corruption and the risks they pose is more embedded in the organisation than ever before. Even the classifications and definitions are clearer now. The Fraud and Corruption Profile is like a radar plot of methods we expect could be used either by employees or external parties.

'Neil called again – he said it was important,' Suzy said coming in and handing me a phone number on a Post-it. The words 'not appealing' were scribbled next to the number.

The calendar alarm on my new, even more irritating organiser-phone is ringing. I am reminded that the Code of Conduct Awareness and Training Project conference call begins in five minutes. No time for glory here. This project is typical of what has been stuck in committees for months while representatives of Legal, Human Resources, Corporate Communications and the newly-formed Corporate Responsibility department argue amongst themselves about what form this training should take. Because of my role in revising the Code of Conduct nearly a year ago, John has insisted that I represent him in this project but very little has moved since it was published and I am thinking of telling him as much.

Almost everyone is based at or working in different locations so we have started to use telephone conferences a lot.

I press the button marked Internal Telephone Conference on my phone.

After a short burst of music I hear the synthesised voice: 'Welcome to the N-Trex teleconference centre. Please enter your conference ID number and press the hash mark.'

I enter the number 4936 from my instruction sheet and am prompted to enter my pin code which I enter. A couple of rapid pips indicate that I am in.

I just catch the measured tones of Harald, the head of the legal department. 'Before we formally begin Code of Conduct training conference number 19 we are just waiting for André and Pete …'.

As usual he is chairing the conference. 'Hello everybody,' I say. I hate the openings of these conferences. Either there are lots of pauses or everybody tries to speak at once.

After an unsynchronised chorus of 'Good afternoon André' there is a short pause while clearly everybody is waiting for Pete to arrive. He's usually late.

Harald breaks in: 'OK we'll start then and Pete will just have to catch up. Last time, which according to my notes was exactly two weeks ago, we discussed the form which the training should take and I do believe that there was a general consensus that the Code of Conduct training should focus on the positive aspects of our culture. Jeremy proposed an animated presentation of our ten messages with video clips of some key directors putting their own personal slant on their chosen messages.'

'Which directors do you have in mind Harald?' It's the dulcet tones of Amanda from HR. She always agrees with Harald anyway.

'Let me see.' Harald pauses as if he is consulting his notes. 'So far, Anne from HR is

happy to do a spot on human rights and fair employment, Ken Fletcher from the plant volunteered to talk about environmental developments, I am still waiting to hear more about Howard's slot on bribery and corruption.' There is more rustling of papers, 'Oh yes, just today over lunch John mentioned that he would be delighted to do a piece on N-Trex values.'

'That would be great,' bubbles Amanda as I try to stifle a cough. There are two rapid beeps and a 'Sorry I'm late guys and dolls – had a rather urgent matter to deal with.' It's Pete from Security.

After a few grunts of 'Hello Pete', Harald breaks in again. 'I know I'm jumping the gun here but, you, Katja and Jeremy, were developing some scenarios for the environmental and human rights videos. How is this going?'

Jeremy responds, 'Harald, I'm glad you asked that. Pretty good I think. We'll probably have something to send to you all by the back end of next week.'

Katja remains quiet.

'Wonderful,' says Amanda. I know from Katja that they have had a huge row over this one and she and Jeremy are not getting along that well.

'Anyhow', continues Jeremy, clearly trying to stamp his authority on the conversation as usual, 'what we have come up with is a Code of Conduct roadshow which disseminates knowledge. We need to communicate senior management's values to the troops. Of course the roadshow would really be an e-show, but I thought maybe we could arrange say five live ones in some of the major capitals where we operate. If we did these before the e-show then we might be able to build in some of the video clips from the live performances to make people feel that they were actually there. We would actually encourage people to watch the show in groups using projectors and big screens in meeting rooms. If you all look at your screens you can see a mock-up frame which was very kindly produced by our developers. I particularly like the oval buttons and the magenta frame around the visuals but that's just a matter of taste.'

Nobody comments. A vision of Howard pontificating about the evils of bribery and forced labour sneaks into my brain. In my mind a couple of exotic dancers are flanking Howard.

Jeremy continues, 'We have also considered getting a speaker on ethics to front the whole thing. Katja suggested the Dalai Lama but I don't think he would go down well with some of our Chinese customers.'

There are a few laughs in the background. I am guessing that Katja just bit her lip.

'I think we need to focus on content not colours right now,' I add.

'Of course, André. What would the main messages be Jeremy?' asks Amanda, as if on cue.

'We would pick out and animate the main messages in the Code of Conduct such as the ones on bribery and corruption. For example we thought of using the analogy of airport check-in counters where the N-Trex ones were much more stringent in what you were allowed onboard than the counter next door. The point we want to make is that we have a higher standard than the others.'

'Actually my view here is that we should say that we are aiming for a higher standard than others.' Katja has decided to make her point. 'There is a subtle difference.'

'I tend to agree; we need to understand whether the message of the Code of Conduct is something we really believes exists in N-Trex today or is it something we aspire to.' I want Katja to know I support her.

Jeremy seems quick to quash any debate here. 'Yes yes, but I think the only difference of opinion me and Katy have is that she thinks the N-Trex Code of Conduct is something we aspire to and I think it reflects the mood of the organisation today. I can't speak for the rank and file one hundred percent, but I can safely vouch for all of us senior managers.'

'I think it's a great idea Jeremy. To be totally honest with you I think this Code of Conduct has given a great lift to my department and it will be great to see the e-road show when you have done it,' coos Amanda.

'The mock-up storyboard is nearly done so I can mail them to you when you are ready,' adds Jeremy.

'Brilliant,' says Amanda.

'Copy me in too,' says Harald.

'I guess you'd better add my name to the list too. What do you reckon Pete?' In spite of his silence I sense discontent brewing in the mind of our security representative.

'I'm going to pass on this one. I'm afraid it sounds too airy-fairy and nebulous to me and I don't feel I can bring much to the table. Guess I live too much in the real world.'

There's a long, awkward pause. Outbursts like this are not supposed to happen in telephone conferences, especially not Harald's conferences.

Amanda just has to fill the gap. 'Peter, you surprise me. You've been involved in the project all the way and your views have been heard. It's just that the majority of us feel that a clear, positive message is much better than all your war stories of doom and gloom. We've taken a democratic decision.'

'Don't patronise me Amanda. If you want to live in dreamland then do so, but I'm out of here.' There is a single beep indicating that Pete has just hung up.

'I can't believe he just did that,' says Amanda.

'Well he just did.' It's Katja. 'Look he's the only one in this committee with any real experience of what goes wrong – sorry André you have some too – and we all just treat him as if he's on a different planet. Corporate Responsibility is about openness and transparency, not just broadcasting good news.'

'I am leaning in that direction too,' I add.

'Which direction you lean André I guess is your business,' says Jeremy to a few muffled laughs. 'We will broadcast good and bad news as long as we are able to put a positive spin on it, but what Pete is asking is tantamount to commercial suicide. He suggests that we open the debate on bribery by giving examples such as how we make facilitation payments to customers, but forbid the acceptance of bribes by our purchasing staff. I think his so-called true stories are the product of an over-zealous mind. What do you think guys?'

Amanda is about to speak but I just have to cut her off. I can't keep quiet any more especially since Katja will get a roasting if I don't support her. 'Look, Pete might not be the world's greatest diplomat but there is a lot of truth in what he says. We can't just assume the moral high ground if we don't know the reality that lies inside the hill beneath us. I've been in there a bit and it's far from perfect. Harald, as a lawyer you know better than most that it's a good idea to tread cautiously in a minefield. Too many companies have lost credibility because their codes of conduct are poor reflections of reality.' I surprise myself and wait for the onslaught, but it doesn't come.

'André, you've got a good point. I suggest that you spend some time thrashing this out with Jeremy but I'm afraid time's up for today and I need to rush. Katja can you circulate the minutes? We'll meet same time next week, OK?' Harald wants to defuse the situation but I can sense that Jeremy is fuming.

Four very quick goodbyes and beeps later and the conference is over. We didn't get on to the subject of whistle-blowing and N-Trex's U-Count Programme. Personally I don't know how this is going to work, or if it is going to work at all.

I look at the clock; it is ten past four. One and a quarter hours on the phone! My ear aches and my left arm is stiff as I put the phone down.

I have arranged a meeting with Neil in my favourite Indian restaurant for dinner at eight. He's late so I order some pakoras. It's strange but I've never really spoken that much with Neil, although I feel I know him from the investigation of his lifestyle. Max interviewed him and then I never saw him again.

'I'm sorry I'm late, André. I'm not living with Jane now and the connections from my flat to town are a bit unreliable. Thanks for coming, I really appreciate it.' Neil takes the seat opposite me. It is unnerving to see the man whose career I helped to end looking thinner and greyer, but somehow happy to see me.

'I'm sorry about that but I don't know if I should be meeting you at all,' I blurt out.

'It's OK, I can understand how you feel but I need someone to hear me out. I've been doing a lot of thinking lately.'

I hand him a menu. 'Shall we order?'

It's like India again. We share our curries and mop it up with naan. We go vegetarian in keeping with Neil's new regime. Funnily I can't help thinking how much more relaxed he seems. He tells me about his impending divorce, his new girlfriend and his new life. He's not going to appeal against N-Trex.

'It was rough for me André, but I don't blame you for what you did. Believe it or not I think I should say thanks for pulling me out.'

'Out of what? It was me who dropped you in the sh…'

He cuts me off. 'Not at all. I was a mess and heading for a crash before you stopped the nosedive.' He points to the meal. 'I couldn't enjoy a dinner like this. My stomach was so tight most of the time.'

I nod sympathetically.

'It happened. I'm not saying I wasn't to blame. I was greedy too, but it wasn't as simple as most people think. The project was in a mess, I was out of my depth and the contractors had me eating out of their hands. They made an offer and I accepted what they threw at me. Then things just got worse. They wanted more and more and I wanted to get to stay on top so much that I just complied. On so many occasions I thought of telling management about my problems, but was that what they wanted to hear? No chance! They only wanted good news so that's what I gave them.' There's a spark in his eyes which I have never seen before.

'There's a lot of yes men about,' I reply.

'You bet. It's all the corporate bullshit. Have you seen the new N-Trex Code of Conduct?'

'Actually some of that bullshit in the code is mine,' I reply. 'Maybe I believe it, sometimes.'

'Sorry.' But he actually looks like he is sorry for me.

'No problem,' is all I can say.

'I'm sorry that you were part of it. Listen, André, I knew a lot more about what really was going on and I told some of it to that fat ex-cop who interviewed me.'

'You mean Max?' I interject.

'Yes, that's him. Not a bad chap at all. Anyway after that nobody called me. I guess I wasn't a credible witness any more.'

'You're probably right about that.'

The waiter asks if we want dessert. Neil looks at me.

'Be my guest. It's on me, or should we say the company,' I say.

'Look André, there were lots of things going on higher up including bribes, payments to fake consulting companies. That sleaze-ball Jackson was in the thick of everything.'

'Let's just say that Howard and me are not best mates.'

'Well I'm glad about that. I admit, I was pretty sleazy too back then. Anyway, a few months after I left I got this call from one of the regional sales managers, Georgios. He said that it was unfair that I had been made the scapegoat for things which were not my fault. He was my logistics contact in sales when I used to be European ops manager. He's a good egg but likes to shoot his mouth off a bit when he gets upset.'

'I think I remember something coming in on U-Count. Didn't he get sacked for insubordination and suspected theft of information by the regional manager down there?'

'Well that's the party line but the truth of the matter is that he had been running his own investigation into corruption. When he presented his case to the country manager, they quickly got rid of him. He knew I'd been sacked and wanted me to help him with his industrial tribunal case.'

'And did you help him?'

'Not yet, but we chat a bit on the mail. Have a look at these,' he says, handing me a couple of copied documents.

The first is an invoice from a company I've never heard of called Thornbird Investment Holdings Ltd for marketing fees to one of the big logistics suppliers. The company is in Liechtenstein and it has a Swiss bank account in Lugano. Neil smiles as I read it, although I'm none the wiser. The second paper is a summary bank statement for a company called Windscale Inc, addressed care of a Greek firm of lawyers.

'OK, then tell me what it means then.' I wonder why he is showing me this.

'The invoices were given to me by some people I knew at Analogy. Why they gave them to me I don't know. They said that Thornbird is controlled by John and Howard, with the tacit approval of the board, but we can't prove that.'

'And where does Windscale fit in?'

'Windscale is related to Aldgate.'

Neil points to several large transfers out of the Windscale bank account to Thornbird Investment Holdings Ltd.

'Neil, this is all interesting but either I am stupid or this is not relevant. As far as I recollect John and the board reckoned there was no problem with Aldgate so we didn't follow up.'

'He had to do that didn't he? It would be too embarrassing. Rumour has it that Thornbird and others are offshore companies controlling funds used to pay off officials and also top up management bonuses. The Analogy invoice was just a top-up that they were ordered to pay. Look, I'm telling you this so that you don't deceive yourself about the squeaky clean tone at the top at your company. Have you ever wondered why they treat you like a hero at the top.'

'They don't,' I reply a little provoked by this. 'So if all this is true does it make what you did OK then?'

'Of course not. You don't get it do you? I was the new boy working sixteen hours a day with no life and I fell for the temptation of money and more. You're not on the operational side. Out there we have to make the business run and when you don't know how, you copy the people above you. You don't have time to question what is right or wrong. You just look for the opportunities. I got caught out and am paying for it now.'

I sense Neil's anger.

'It makes me sick that you all believe the new code of conduct. Georgios gets kicked for trying to put things right. Look at you. Now you've got a nice car, expensive suits and an entertainment budget just like Howard and John. Is that what you want – to join their club?'

'I'm sorry, I don't know what to say. I've got too much on to follow up everything.'

Neil pauses. 'I'm sorry too. That was out of order. I know you are trying. Just say you'll listen to what I have to say and look into it will you?'

'OK. I will, if I can.'

Over Indian ice cream and sweet spiced tea the atmosphere becomes more relaxed and Neil tells me that he and a few of the current and ex-managers like Georgios have discussed the 'tone at the top' as he calls it. He tells me that I will have to look further afield than the N-Trex archives.

'Why so late? What happened?' asks Marilena when I finally get home.

'A lot,' I reply.

'It's lucky I've got a well paid job then,' she says after I tell her what my next move may be.

Chapter 9

'It's your secret lover checking if you are still married on a Sunday evening,' says Marilena, handing me the phone with an odd smile.

I should have seen it coming what with the pressure I am putting on him and his unhealthy lifestyle. Mirabel's news that Max has been taken ill with a heart condition hits me all the same. I rely so much on the old fox and his team. Mirabel told me not to worry. Max will cope. He is a survivor like her. He just wasn't interested enough in his own health checks.

'I'm really sorry about that remark earlier André, I was mostly joking. It's just that I hardly know what you are thinking these days. Did she hear me?' Marilena says after I tell her the news.

'Mirabel wouldn't mind even if she did hear you.'

'It's just that since you started your crusade against corruption I am not always in touch with your thoughts; I know you snapped back into the world and are there for the kids again after the fish and phone episode but we still don't always connect. I have also lost myself in my work to compensate.'

'I know. We must do something about it,' is all I can muster.

Was I just about to cry?

I go in late the next day. Suzy and someone called Dave from Max's office are already there putting together a summary of where we are up to on all the various investigations.

'I know you are aware of most of these but I thought it would be good to have a summary in one place. Then you can help us prioritise which ones to focus on,' says Suzy.

I can see they are upset but there is something of a gritty determination about the two of them. Rob and Jamie are also helping, going through some packing boxes of files.

Suzy hands me a couple of sheets of paper fresh off my office printer. 'We have just made a start summarising things. Can you take a look?'

It's an impressive list in some ways. If I had to move one of them to the top it would be number six. It looks like an interesting one as the Southern Europe management team is based there and the regional manager seems to have become a very good friend of John. Also I would like to visit the Acropolis, even for just a few minutes.

I scan the list. Although there is a lot to do the situation seems under control. Case number seven catches my eye. I make an impulsive decision: 'Could you look into flights to Athens for me Suzy?'

Draft summary and status report – N-Trex ongoing investigation projects

Max de Gras / Sarah Lutz / Susan Agarwal for review by André Stacey – 25/05/200X

Case #	Description	Status
1	Grantham Biotechnology (customer) has been having liquidity problems for some time. N-Trex's regional sales director (Mike) has been selling increasingly large quantities to this customer, despite the fact the he was aware of these liquidity problems. It now looks like the customer will never pay	Background and internal research completed. Next step: Interviews
2	External Auditor's query on certain deferred costs which should have been expensed	Preliminary report completed. Awaiting response from External Auditor
3	Suspected misuse of N-Trex's trademark and logo by a competitor in the Far East (report came in from Mirabel's counterpart)	Awaiting report from local investigation company
4	Inflation of sales figure and various conflicts of interest in N-Trex Spain. Dismissals performed and court case pending	Local management are following up.
5	Investment in Poland – being written off – the external auditors are in Wroclaw now doing the post mortem and closing out the books. Possibility that this was a situation which quickly spun out of control and local management tried to cover things up	Need to look into whether there was any criminal behaviour either outside or inside of N-Trex which led to a) the investment decision and b) the eventual write off. First step. Follow up U-Count lead
6	Allegations of kickbacks in relation to award of shipping contract	To initiate preliminary investigations
7	Greek U-Count message. Allegations of management conflicts of interest and reporting frauds. Irate informant who has called and emailed several times	Max to interview informant in Athens asap. André to advise given current situation vis-à-vis Max
8	Events contract. The assistant events manager appears to have solicited a bribe. The supplier had told André that he had quoted 122 000 and the events manager had given an order for 133 000. The supplier had told André that he said that his pitch was for 122 000 and the events manager had said 'I know, the rest is my reward for giving you the contract.' The supplier said that this was such a huge contract that he could not refuse it and went along with the events manager. However he said it was one of the days in his life he felt least proud of.	Pending interviews
9	Audit of senior management expenses in Scandinavian countries reveals extensive representation (and 'recreation')	Pending
10.	Suspected theft of stock from warehouse (could be with help from insiders)	Awaiting report from local investigators
11	Investigation by the European Commission for Unfair Competition into a possible cartel involving N-Trex in Belgium.	Support being provided by Corporate Legal to EU investigators.
12	Suspicion of supplier overcharging in respect of a sub-component. May have led to faults and a huge indirect knock-on cost to N-Trex and its customers.	JTS priority. Xamdos working with local accountants and customers to contain situation. Certain products may need to be withdrawn from the market.

'For when?'

'Leaving on Wednesday afternoon around four and getting back early Thursday evening.'

Since my office has been taken over, I take the list and my diary and a couple of blank sheets of paper into a meeting room to try to take stock of things.

It's all a bit of a rush. Before I caught the plane to Athens Cedric called a meeting with some controllers and Legal to review the latest draft of my Health Check proposals. The good news is that they give it the green light but the meeting took ages. It was worthwhile as now the Audit Committee will probably rubber stamp it. I rush out to meet my waiting cab to take me to the airport.

'A courier left this for you Mr Stacey,' says the receptionist, handing me a package. Inside is a Xamdos folder labelled 'Athens – confidential'.

I hope the plane is not full because I have to read and digest this and a file of papers Suzy gave me before I meet Georgios. On the phone he just kept talking and talking, and the only way to get rid of him was to agree that he picked me up at the airport so he could take me for dinner.

Of course there is an accident on the motorway so I'm running late. At least I have time to call Marilena and Timmy and talk about something else.

'The Athens flight is overbooked and I'm afraid we only have middle seats left Mr Stacey,' the check-in attendant tells me.

Damn Georgios. I need to read these files.

The security lines are unusually long but I make it onto the Airbus A321 bound for Athens. Am I putting on weight or have middle seats always been this uncomfortable?

As soon as the plane levels off, I stuff the briefing packs under my shirt, squeeze past my neighbour into the aisle and walk towards the back of the plane. At least there are three toilets on this plane.

'I have had a bad stomach today, and may need to use the toilet for a little longer than usual,' I say to the stewardess.

She gives me a sympathetic look. 'Take your time. There's a call button inside if you need anything,' she replies, as if this sort of things happens regularly.

The first report from Suzy contains the various emails from Georgios to John, U-Count and others, some background on N-Trex's Southern European Marketing Operation, information she gleaned from the personnel files about Georgios and my notes and the documents from my conversation with Neil.

The emails don't tell me much other than that he is very persistent and worked for N-Trex in various roles for three and a half years until his dismissal six months ago. He is now thirty-seven. There are also current organisational charts of the operation. I have never met the Regional Manager Mr Lucas Kyriakidou, but I remember his marketing manager, a flashy lady called Paula. A Post-it from Suzy says that Rob and Jamie believe that Kyriakidou is a personal friend of JTS.

According to Georgios's profile report in the Xamdos file, he has his own consulting company in the Middle East which he set up before he left but tends to work mainly in

Greece. He has also filed preliminary court proceedings for wrongful dismissal against the company but nothing more has happened as yet on that front. There's also a picture of him. He looks well built.

Mr Kyriakidou's profile is longer and lists his various positions before N-Trex, his properties, all his telephone numbers and even includes pictures of a very nice house by the sea which I presume is his. A note at the bottom indicates that he is divorced and is believed to have moved in with the marketing manager, Paula.

The reports make interesting reading but my thoughts are interrupted by a tap on the door.

'Are you OK?' It is one of the stewardesses.

'I hope so.' My watch tells me I have now been in the bathroom for nearly half an hour.

As I make my way back down the aisle avoiding the strange looks from the other passengers I try not to laugh. Working in an aircraft lavatory. The phrase 'get a life' springs to mind. As I climb over my sleeping neighbour I notice that one of the briefing packs is protruding from under my shirt.

The heat and smell hit me as I walk out of customs but thankfully Georgios's car is air-conditioned.

He's not what I expected. He is genuinely pleased to see me and tell me his story, but his friendly manner is peppered with bouts of angry reflection about the way N-Trex has treated him, verging on the point of holding me personally responsible for everything which has happened to him.

'André, when I saw these false invoices I asked Kyriakidou for a meeting. He asked me what it was about and I told him about the bribes being paid in Paula's department and also the fact that I had found out that one of our partner companies was ripping us off. He seemed very concerned, said he valued me coming to him so I gave him all the documentation which I had to prove it. He then said he had to go, but we could set aside the time the next day at four to go through things. When I went back the next day Kyriakidou was sitting with Paula and some fancy lawyer. The lawyer said that making false accusations and stealing company documentation was a serious offence, but because I had been a good employee they would offer me €50 000 if I resigned'

'Did you take it?'

'Did I hell. I was so mad that I called him a liar, told him I was going to put them all behind bars, got what I could from my office and walked out. After that they had some jerk deliver this letter to me.' Amongst his papers he found and showed me an N-Trex letter of dismissal.

'Can you prove any of this?' I ask.

'Believe me it's true. But don't think I have been sitting around since then. After the initial meeting, I've been collecting documents for the last six months. I've written emails and tried to call Mr Stevens and Mr Watkins but they don't even bother to reply. Actually why are you here? Are you going to make me a bigger offer to shut up? Because if so I can tell you it won't work.'

'No I'm not.'

'Good, because then you could pay this bill and jump on that plane back. Nobody's paying me for helping you remember. You know what I think? Your Mr Stevens and probably Mr Watkins are trying to pretend that this never happened. They know, I'm telling you.'

I am about to tell him that I've personally gone out on a limb for him, but his ears are not switched on. I remember Max telling me once, 'Just let them talk. Never look at your watch.'

He carries on, 'Some time back that Howard guy told me that I should read the Sarbanes-Oxley Act to understand about ethics. What does he know? N-Trex is a mess. Kyriakidou controls a couple of suppliers and one customer through offshore companies and that girl Paula does his dirty work because he pays her well. She's not even pretty either and I should know. You know Senator Sarbanes is a Greek American? They even pronounce the name wrongly.'

The conversation, if you can call it that, swings violently from the governance of Ancient Greece to modern governance, from theft of stock to taramasalata, and from the ideology of the 17N movement to internal conflicts in N-Trex. It is like being in an action movie.

'Mr Stevens knows about Kyriakidou's dealings but they are friends you see. Anyway Kyriakidou used to make the biggest returns for N-Trex so nobody wanted to touch him. He just uses your money to bribe who he needs. Recently even that is not working so he is getting false sales put through and not writing off inventory which was thrown away months ago.'

I am wondering if most of this is made up. If it isn't, it's dynamite.

At just past midnight I am allowed to go to bed at the hotel, but not before I manage to extract a promise from Georgios that he will meet me tomorrow, with a clearer picture of events and also copies of any documents which he has to prove the allegations. In return I will see what I can do to support his case.

When I get to the hotel, I type one last email to Rob over the hotel's wireless LAN.

To: rob.burchill@n-trex.com
From: Andrestacey01@yahoo.com

Hi Rob

I need your help pretty quick. Can you go to the branch accounting system, company code NT0026 and pull off a list off sales to the ten biggest customers and call me to let me know who they are. Also use your Health Check data to look at any payments to the following companies (Aldgate, Windscale, Thornbird, Forenta Greece). Look everywhere and don't forget direct payments. Finally can you let me know if Greece has now migrated onto the global online travel system.

Thanks and call me asap
André

Ps. The Taramasalata you recommended me to try was pink and slimy. Will stick to souvlaki tomorrow!

The next day Georgios is waiting for me in the lobby. He is smiling and carrying a small document bag.

'I brought this for you, but you better not screw me or you know what will happen.'

I decide not to ask what will happen.

Georgios drives me back so I can catch the mid-afternoon flight. Although he is clearly traumatised by what happened, much of what he says adds up, especially after Rob rang me to confirm what I had suspected. The flaw is that the really hard-hitting stuff like the offshore companies, massive reporting frauds and the cover-up are mainly based on hearsay. If I don't think about it, I am sure a solution will present itself.

I use some time during the following two weeks to verify some of Georgios's allegations. Most of it is pretty much what one would expect, but there are also some surprises. In my mind there is only one possible course of action. Whatever the risks to my career, I need to take up the matter with John. I don't have enough evidence to go above his head to the board. It would probably go straight back to John anyway which would make my current position even worse.

Marilena and Mirabel independently agree with me. Funnily both of them tell me that I should take Max's advice first. I protest saying that he should not be disturbed while recovering.

'He would kill you and then me if you didn't ring,' says Mirabel. 'Here's his home number. I told his wife you'll be calling.'

'I half expected this' says Max. He tells me that he is OK but the doctor has told him to take at least two-months complete rest and no work. 'Watch John's eyes all the time. I always had a feeling that he knows or is involved in something.'

'You really think so?' I ask, although deep down I also had a feeling that John must know something about the bribes at least. After all, who else would take the risk of paying those sort of bribes without John's approval.

'Of course he knows', says Max, 'and I reckon that he approved the split salaries scheme for directors through offshore companies, as did that Harald character. It is most likely that he gets some money offshore too, maybe through Thornbird.'

'He probably thinks that there is nothing wrong with any of this, except the reporting fraud in southern Europe, which is difficult to prove that he knew anything about,' I say.

'In a way you are right. Some chief executives I have seen have a tendency to believe they are above the rules and also have already justified everything in their own minds.

Do you not remember the story in the press about the Swedish CEO – Barnaby or something?'

'Percy Barnavik,' I correct him.

'Yeah that guy. He didn't think he was doing anything wrong putting away millions of the company's money into his own private pension fund while hundreds of people were being made redundant did he?. He just thought it was what he was worth as a chief executive, I guess.'

'I suppose they have an over-glorified sense of themselves.'

'And more,' says Max.

'So I should not take up the three bottles of Chateau Haut-Brion 2004 at $200 a pop or any of his other outrageous expense bills,' I say with a laugh.

'Definitely not! Anyway,' Max's voice is steely, 'just stay away from the details. If he feels threatened he will to try to drag you into the details and then pick holes in your arguments until he can demonstrate that you are wrong. It's just a tactic, but you will come out believing that you did not do your homework. Stick to the principal issues like bribes, deception of the shareholders, split salaries and the use of offshore companies. If you've really got the guts, keep notes too.'

'I wish you would do this interview,' I say half hoping he will.

'You know I can't, and not because I'm in bed. It's your interview. Good luck,' he replies.

❖ ❖ ❖

This time John has made the time for me. Maybe because I told him I wanted to meet him alone and it couldn't wait.

I walk up the stairs carrying a file of papers with me. I only have it for comfort as I know everything that's in it anyway.

'Morning André, take a seat. How was the weather in Greece?' is the first thing he says as I walk into his spacious office and take a seat at the sofa.

John sits on the chair to my left and I put my heavy file on my right on the coffee table separating us.

'Warm,' I answer, not wanting to give anything away. I am surprised he knows that I went at all.

He smiles. 'I presume you haven't come to talk to me about the weather, André, so just fire away and I'll see if I can answer your questions. Sorry about Mr de Gras by the way, I hope he will be fine. Coffee?' I nod and he reaches over to the tray in front of us and pours me a coffee adding a little cream and one sugar.

I have planned how to tackle this meeting earlier but his manner, and knowing how I like my coffee is disarming. 'Keep calm and take it slowly. He's the one who should be nervous, not you,' was Max's last piece of advice.

'Well the reason I was in Greece was because we seem to have discovered a large reporting fraud.'

He looks genuinely shocked. 'Does Lucas know about this?'

'I believe Lucas Kyriakidou is responsible for it. They have been grossly overstating both inventory and sales in the whole of the Southern European region in order to cover up some large overspends.'

He looks concerned. 'André, I should tell you this. Lucas is one of my most trusted directors and a friend. Not that this will affect my judgement but you should only make such accusations if you can back them up with some pretty hefty evidence.'

I take a deep breath. 'There's enough evidence.'

'Fine then. We need to act in the usual way,' he replies coolly, obviously not pleased that I have brought this one up.

'Did you know anything about the false reporting in Southern Europe before now?' I ask.

'Of course not', he snaps, 'but now that I do, we need to get the bottom of it. Have you got a report on it?'

'You'll have one by Friday.'

'Good. Was there anything else you wanted to discuss?'

It is time for my second and, as I see it, much more crucial issue.

'When you signed off on the Code of Conduct did you really mean that we were to follow everything that was in there?'

'I think I am one hundred percent behind all the values in it, if that's what you're asking?'

I take a deep breath. 'Lets say then if you discover that we have been paying hundreds of thousands of pounds, euros and dollars in bribes, maybe even, millions to obtain business, what would you do then?'

'Judging by the nature of that question and that thick file you have with you, I presume you have found some transactions. Look André I will be totally honest with you because I know you have had a few run-ins with Howard on this issue before.'

He does not seem at all perturbed as he continues, 'I know and you know what these transactions are and just like you I want them to stop. However if we did not fulfil these orders somebody else would and we would have to lay off people. Isn't it better that we do them rather than our competitors? We probably pay less in facilitation than the others.'

That last remark angers me as he begins to sound like Howard. 'How the hell would you know that?' I blurt out.

He narrows his eyes. 'We don't, it's just we are committed to fighting corruption whereas many others have not made statements to that effect,' he adds.

'So what you are saying, is that bribery and corruption are legitimate as long as you make a statement against it. Isn't that just double standards?' I ask in the politest tone I can muster.

He leans back with him arms behind his head, trying to look relaxed but clearly very alert at the direction the conversation is taking. 'André, André, we are on the same side. Our code of conduct is something we are all aspiring to. Do you really expect the company to be a reflection of it from the word go?'

'No, sir. But if you are the first to condone breaking it then what chance do we have.'

He is taken aback by my sledgehammer approach but regains his composure. 'I see we will have to agree to differ on this, but let me tell you that all of the invoices in that file of yours were paid with the approval of the board. I am only the Chief Executive. My hands are tied and I cannot do very much without their approval.'

I don't reply.

He continues, 'Corruption is a fact of life and much as we want to avoid it, we have to accept it. That's probably why I did not go into politics. Look at who we have to pay in the former Soviet Union and the Far East. Sometimes we pay and pay and don't even get anywhere because the politicians change. We all have to make choices and I firmly believe that I can make better choices which eventually fight against child labour, human rights abuses and corruption, all from this chair as the CEO of a great corporation, rather than from the debating chamber. I believe that this century will be heralded as the century of the responsible corporation and we should all be pleased to be a part of this great change.'

I'm too tired for his pep talks and speeches at this stage. 'John, I know the world's corrupt as you say, but I've reason to believe that some of your directors have been taking some of the money intended for bribes.'

He's obviously well trained at hiding surprise or anger and answers, silkily smooth. 'If that's the case then we need to take action against them don't we. Can you show me your proof?'

I'm sure he knows that I don't have all the evidence

'I have strong indications, that's all.'

'Then for your sake be very careful what you say. It's good that you tell me privately, but others might not be happy with these insinuations.'

'Like Howard?' The name is out before I can stop it.

'I'm glad you are open with me André. Howard is a very sharp salesman, but I believe that he may have overstepped the mark a few times and I will need to have a very serious conversation with him shortly. Before that, any help you can give me', he looks at my file and pauses, 'would be most useful.'

I'm not sure where this is leading. Is he using me to play divide and rule to get himself off the hook? I can't let him do this. Howard is not the root cause. It's something more.

I decide to have it out. 'And the split salaries into offshore bank accounts. Are they legal and ethical and in line with our code of conduct? It is rumoured that even you have one.'

I can tell he was not expecting this. 'André. Let me tell you something.' He moves closer. 'We will never get the quality people we need in this company if we pay them normal salaries regulated by oppressive tax regimes. If we pay them a salary which gave them the net income they needed they would sink the company. That's why we look for legal, but innovative schemes so that we can go outside of the normal system and find loopholes in the laws to make it possible to obtain the people we need at a fair price.

People who can implement our code of conduct, André.' He looks like he feels he is on safe ground now.

'With all due respect, sir, I don't believe you even know what you meant when you just said that? I'm an accountant and I know that avoiding taxes of the countries where people work is not legal, and in my view unethical.'

I have touched a raw nerve, but I'm not sure which one.

'Do you have any more grievances about the company that pays your salary, and the person that has supported your career?'

He's now dispensed with all politeness. Despite his condescending tone I know that if I don't raise this last issue with him, I might not get another chance. I can't dance around the subject anymore.

'Have you received money from companies like Thornbird?' I need to know.

He was not expecting this, but still remains calm and collected. He pauses, looks out of the window and then straight into my eyes. 'Never heard of the name, what did you say it was again?'

'Thornbird Investment Holdings Inc, to give it its full name.' I repeat the question. 'Have you taken any money out through this company?'

'Before I answer this question I should like to say one thing in our defence. N-Trex is a corporation, André, and our primary duty is to make profits for our owners. That's how we keep ourselves gainfully employed. Now you could, if you want, push your campaign to the limits, but if you do that then what would you achieve?'

I shrug.

'Let me tell you,' he continues, 'You will trigger a plummeting share price, endless bad press and redundancies. You could even have my head if you wanted it. None of us are perfect. Now, do you really want that responsibility on your shoulders?'

If that was a disguised confession I am not sure how to respond. I force a smile but don't say anything. I hadn't anticipated this happening in the interview and now I don't know what to expect.

John stands up, indicating to me that the audience is over. 'If that's it then I thank you for bringing these matters to my attention,' he says rather formally, 'I will discuss the issues you have raised with the board. In the meantime, I want you to put a hold on any further enquiries until we have made a decision as to what happens next.' Then he unnerves me by looking directly into my eyes and saying in a very even voice, 'André, I like you and what you want to do for this company. You yourself said that I have supported you on your controls and anti-fraud crusade. Just be careful to not overreach yourself.'

'Thanks for the advice.' I leave, taking my file and blank notepad with me.

Chapter 10

I spend the next few days tidying my office, catching up on the last three-months travel expense claims and filing papers and notes.

The first Health Checks are uncovering more and more red flags, and the training programmes are rolling out with the knock on effect of more and more feedback. At this point I don't know what to do.

I can't get excited about any of the findings at the moment because my conversation with John hangs over me like a dark cloud. Unlike my turbulent rows with Howard news of what happened in John's office does not seem to have spread anywhere. In one way this is good, but in another I am left with a feeling of emptiness because I feel until something is resolved I am operating in a vacuum. I am also very uneasy at what I took to be a veiled threat as we ended our conversation, or was I just imagining it?

I haven't seen John since our meeting but thankfully Cedric has been more cheerful than usual. I decided not to tell him about the true purpose of my meeting with John. If he knows anything Cedric is not giving much away either. I can't work out whether he is looking forward to my imminent departure from N-Trex and if this is the case what shape or form it will take. With hindsight I realise that I probably should have been better prepared for John than I was. Since then I have given a copy of my most recent investigation file to some dental friends of Marilena to keep in their safe.

Mirabel has been away giving a paper at a conference, or at least I haven't seen her, and I don't want to disturb Max. The poor chap needs a rest too. I tell Rob and Jamie as little as possible other than that there will probably be another meeting.

As the days pass by without me hearing anything, I begin to seriously doubt that anything at all is going to happen. I think that John has realised that it is one thing to have an anti-fraud and -corruption strategy, but it is a whole new ball game to actually have to live and breath it. He is probably looking for a way to put a lid on the Pandora's box which I have opened before he too becomes a victim. The corporation is an uncaring beast and just like me, he has a board to answer to as well.

I decide to discuss my dilemma with Suzy, who has been pestering me about what happened in my meeting with John. I tell her about how disappointed I am with John's response.

'I don't see much point in carrying on here. It's really demotivating when the boss clearly doesn't support you any more. I'm going to start looking at the job adverts before they have time to sack me,' I say, turning to the back pages of this morning's newspaper.

'That was a really pathetic thing to say you know,' she retorts

I am taken aback by her response and am about to tell her that I wish I had not said anything to her when Mirabel pokes her head around the door.

'Am I interrupting something?' she says.

I make a sign with my hand that I will be two minutes but Suzy is not taking any of it.

'This cowardly idiot told me he wants out,' she says, almost shouting. I don't know what has got into her. It's only a job after all.

Her full frontal onslaught shakes me for a moment. 'They were only thoughts. I shouldn't have told you any of my thoughts,' I say quickly.

Mirabel comes in and shuts the door behind her. 'But you are thinking of giving up aren't you? Tell me what happened. No Suzy,' as Suzy starts to leave, 'you stay, you are as a much a part of this as I am.'

Nobody dares disobey Mirabel when she is in this sort of mood.

I bring Mirabel up to date on my last conversation with John.

'Sounds like he bought himself some time to think,' she says.

'But if he's involved why doesn't he admit it?' I ask.

'It's not that easy André. He has a lot of hard choices to make. No, I'm not defending his behaviour, just trying to make sense of it. As the CEO he is answerable to the board and they probably want results and want them yesterday. He has some belief in the Code of Conduct and in Corporate Responsibility, but he has to balance them up against some hard facts of life.'

'That's what he said too. Maybe you two would get along well Maribel,' I say, deliberately mispronouncing her name; but I overdo the sarcasm and am immediately sorry for it.

'André, you are very prickly today. You know you cannot change things overnight or do it alone. Just look at what we all have achieved in twelve months. Even the external auditors are taking their responsibilities and you more seriously.'

She has a point there; we have achieved a lot and John has been our chief backer.

'If we continue, think how much more we can do. Eventually John will have to support you as he was the leading proponent of the Code of Conduct. He can't turn back now, so stop getting all bitter and twisted.'

I'm about to say something in my defence but Suzy, who has been keeping quiet, adds, 'And working for you until now has been very inspiring André. Rob and Jamie agree with me on this. If you give up now what sort of signal does that send to us and all those other potential Andrés out there?'

I'm not entirely convinced that being a potential André is a good thing. Even if we change things here at N-Trex, it probably will not make any difference to the big picture; it will be like pissing on a forest fire. All the same, Suzy's and Mirabel's passion for the cause is rather touching.

'You know, Suzy's right,' adds Pete, who has just walked in without me noticing. 'Sorry, am I gate-crashing the party?'

'No come in, the more the merrier. Stacey here was just having a fit,' says Mirabel.

'Thought you might want to see this then,' he says as he passes around copies of an email.

From: John.Thornbury-Stevens@N-Trex.com
To: Mailing list Company Internal
Re: Organisational changes
Date: 15/06/20XY

With immediate effect, N-Trex's Sales and Marketing Director, Mr Howard Jackson will be stepping down, for health reasons, and will be leaving the company as from today. Tim Crispin has kindly agreed to stand in for Mr Jackson as we initiate external recruiting procedures.

Mr Allan Smythe, a leading city attorney and long-time advisor to N-Trex will be replacing Mr Harald Schmidt as Chief Legal Counsel at N-Trex this week. Mr Schmidt will be assigned to certain special projects reporting currently to the CFO, Mr Cedric Watkins.

Should anyone have any questions about the above or if there are any external enquiries as to the reasons for these changes please refer to my office.

Regards

John Thornbury-Stevens

Chief Executive Officer, N-Trex

'Wow,' says Mirabel.

'What do you make of that?' I ask.

'Either you're a hero or the next one in the firing line,' muses Pete.

'Thanks for the reassurance, Big P.'

Just then the phone rings. It's Cedric. 'Can you come upstairs André. John wants to see you.'

'I saw the email. Is it firing-squad time?'

'Just get up here, stupid.' His tone is light-hearted, friendly.

Cedric accompanies me in to John's office.

'I've been reflecting on our recent chat André. I have to rush to the airport to catch a plane to Vienna in five minutes but I wanted to see you and put your mind at ease.'

I have nothing to say yet so I keep my mouth shut.

'You've seen the email I presume.' I nod in agreement, 'And you of all people can read between those lines.'

'That wasn't too difficult,' I say as I catch a hint of a smile on his face.

'Your passion to fight fraud and corruption simply caught me off guard the other day. When I looked into things I found out that … ' He pauses for a moment and glances at Cedric, '… that I had a Head of Marketing and Sales who would never implement the principles against bribery and a Head of Legal who felt that it was in my own best interests that I was kept in the dark about some of the doings in N-Trex. He used the phrase plausible deniability. I want an open and transparent company. Everything needs to be above board and where the people at the top, and that includes the people in this room, provide an example of the sort of behaviour which reflects our code of conduct.'

I don't know what to say. It's a good speech. He doesn't mention his own behaviour but maybe that is going to change. Somehow I think it is best for me, him and N-Trex that I agree with him.

'That's fantastic,' I say with as much enthusiasm as I can muster.

He grabs his leather case and bag. 'We'll talk more when I get back André. I just want you and Cedric to know that you have my full support, as always. It is on the agenda for the next audit committee.'

And then, he is gone.

A few days later I am leaving early to pick up Timmy. From the car I remember to make a social call to Max. I am sure that Max has been dying to get involved again but heard that his wife has put her foot down and grounded him. However she is happy to put my call through to his bedroom.

Max already knew about the reorganisation. The old fox has persuaded me to meet him in a park this afternoon near his house on the pretext of getting some fresh air.

I know the park and am going to take Timmy. He'll be thrilled to meet his hero, special agent de Gras who has been the object of my mythical bed-time stories of late.

He looks quite well. I expected worse. 'Just wanted to see how you are doing, bean-counter boy.'

Timmy is thrilled to meet a real detective and pesters Max with questions like 'Where do you keep your gun?' and 'Do you have a different girl with you on every assignment?' I find out later that he has been watching James Bond movies at a friend's house.

Max is gracious until he says, 'Nature calls.'

As he heads for the public toilets, Timmy and I instantly look at our watches to time how long he will be. I had told him the story.

The reorganized Anti Fraud and Corruption Team is meeting today. On the agenda for which I am responsible are just a number of questions like: How good are we at managing the risk of fraud and corruption in N-Trex?, Where are the key risks? and How effective are N-Trex's policies and training and awareness programs?

We have assembled and are just having morning coffee with Cedric who has joined for the first hour when Suzy comes in with a few sheets of paper.

'Thought you might find it useful to look at this before you start. It just came into the U-Count mailbox.' She hands out copies.

From:	John.Smythe278@hotmail.com
To:	U-Count@N-Trex.com
Re:	Environmental fraud ?
Date:	15/06/20XY

Dear U-Count

I am an employee of N-Trex working in one of the countries where you have significant production. I am using a pseudonym primarily because I would like to have direct contact with a senior person in N-Trex who can receive the information I have. I want to minimize the risk of possible local retribution where I live so was reluctant to take chances by using my name and company e-mail address.

I am a technical person who has worked with highly respected environmental consultants who work on and off for N-Trex. Some time ago decisions were taken, ostensibly for cost reasons to install sub-standard equipment and filters at selected sites. This has resulted in abnormally high levels of pollution. If the authorities discover what we have done we could face penalties in the region of up to $700 000, for this year alone. We took this up six months ago with local management and members of the technical steering group but have had no reaction. Now we suspect a cover-up. It is also rumoured that the supplier who installed the equipment is in collusion with our own technical manager.

To me this seems like a gross breach of the N-Trex Code of Conduct. I completed the training a month back. In addition the relationship between our technical manager and the supplier looks like fraud.

Since management are not listening what I am looking for is advice as to what to do next and who to tell.

If you can reply to this hotmail address, which I apologise is a pseudonym, expressing an interest to make contact and also who the name of the person I need to contact, I will call back in person tomorrow.

I have heard that you take these matters seriously.

Regards

John Smythe

'André, do you want to reply or should I,' asks Cedric.

'I guess I should since it's implied in my mandate,' I reply. Here we go again I think.

Epilogue

Surprisingly I have to admit that life has become smoother since my run-in with John half a year ago. I am at home more and have recruited four new staff to my team: two to bolster Rob's internal audit arm plus an assistant risk manager and a new administrator. Although I tried to persuade Suzy to stay at N-Trex she has taken up a post as a trainee controller on the other side of the city. We still keep in touch by mail and we are having lunch at Il Franco's in 11 days.

With the risk of being complacent our fraud and corruption management strategy is working and although I am expecting another backlash shortly, I am confident we can handle it. Today's lunch is hosted by Cedric. He has invited Mirabel, Katja, Pete and me out to mark a new era of cross-functional teamwork, as he puts it. He has been smiling a lot more recently and even goes home early a couple of times a week. The décor, menu and fairytale atmosphere in Alice's Brasserie is not exactly what I expect from Cedric until he tells us about childhood fascination with Lewis Carroll's *Alice in Wonderland*. Since the others are equally enthusiastic I decide not to let on that I never really connected with Mr Carroll.

As we begin our starters the first notes of 'Spring' from Vivaldi's *Four Seasons* burst forth from Cedric's personal digital organiser. He fumbles with his new toy trying to find the right button to take the call. Katja points discreetly to the anti-mobile phone signs and Cedric shuffles towards the door, organiser glued to his ear, mouthing the word John. He's still Cedric.

The conversation drifts back to the reasons for this lunch.

'So you really believe we are making a difference?' asks Katja, looking at me.

Pete replies before I can. 'Who cares if we are? Most of the time we are all doing what we want now without the red tape and gibberish and enjoying it too.'

'But how long will it last before we all get slapped down again?' asks Katja.

'I don't know but at least you will be more prepared this time. We have learnt things the hard way.' Pete looks at me. 'Well you have anyway Stasi-boy.'

The joke doesn't hurt me anymore. 'I really thought I'd thrown my career away when I yelled at him but Suzy and you guys kept me from completely losing it.'

Pete and the others raise their glasses in a mock toast to Suzy and me.

'As for John Thornbury-Stevens,' says Pete, spitting out John's name, 'everything may look fine now but the man's a complete leopard and he is not going to change, André. You're safe for now but something's got to give sooner or later.'

'André's got to have some options,' interjects Katja looking concernedly at me.

Mirabel has been a silent observer up until now. 'I've been thinking about this for a while. OK then guys, we're all in this together, so it's not just André in the

firing line. We should concentrate on what we can do about it. As I see it we have three options.'

'Go on then,' says Pete.

'Option one, we fulfil our mandate and keep on cleaning this company and digging and stay as minor heroes not daring to deal with John. If we do, then we look for new jobs. Option two,' continues Mirabel, 'we make John realise he can't get rid of us so easily and he makes us all offers we can't refuse.'

'You wouldn't be bought off would you André?' starts Katja as Pete just laughs.

'Option three,' concludes Mirabel, 'we find a way to beat John at his own game.'

After a reflective pause Katja says, 'And how would you do that?'

'We need to understand the animals we are dealing with. N-Trex is like hundreds of other large organisations and John is like most of their chiefs. I honestly do not believe he is an evil person, egocentric, misinformed and greedy as he may seem to us at times. He has after all publicly set a standard and to an extent puts his foot where his mouth is. It's John who will eventually sell our ideas in this company once we convince him it is in his best interests.'

'As long as he can make money and take all the credit, that is,' adds Pete the cynic. But Mirabel is not deterred.

'You are absolutely right, and that's where we need to start. The primary aim of a corporation is to make profits, and John just happens to be in the driving seat. Therefore he can make the decisions about how we go about doing it. He's given us part of the steering, so let's use our chance to help him go in the best direction for all of us, himself included. He knows as well as we do that really preventing fraud and corruption is far, far better for profits than just doing autopsies.'

'I'm still not sure I trust him,' says Katja.

'I agree. You surprise me Mirabel. You sound like an idealist,' says Pete.

'You don't have to trust him, and for your information I was offering some practical advice, Peter. Once you understand where he's coming from and that what he wants, even more than you, is to be seen as the hero, you can just let him believe that he is leading the fight against fraud and corruption. That's what I mean about playing his game and winning.'

'That's what you mean about playing his game and winning,' I muse. 'You know that international conference on Corporate Crime Resistance which you are on the organising committee for. Why don't you put John forward for the keynote address?'

'Good thinking Stasi,' says Pete.

'Not a bad idea at all,' says Mirabel just as a harassed-looking Cedric wanders back. 'And what's more let's talk about what we have done at N-Trex, and let John take a role in pushing things forward even more. Wasn't it him that told you, André, that none of us are perfect?'

'So what you are saying is that as long as there is genuine improvement and a will to reform then we should spend more energy cleaning up the future rather than hunting down everyone's past misdemeanours?'

'Are you talking about me behind my back?' says Cedric.

'Not really,' I say. 'We were just contemplating what brought us all together over the last two years.'

'And we never found the guy who wrote that letter which started the whole thing either, did we? You know I reckon it was one of the guys in Human Resources working for Amanda who got fed up of her turning a deaf ear to the people in this company.'

'What if this guy of yours Pete was in fact, a lady?' says Katja.

If you have found this book useful you may be interested in other titles from Gower

Best Practice in Corporate Governance
Adrian Davies
0 566 08644 1

Commercial Due Diligence
Peter Howson
0 566 08651 4

Constructive Engagement
Nicholas Beale
0 566 08711 1

Data Protection in the Financial Services Industry
Mandy Webster
0 566 08662 X

Due Diligence
Peter Howson
0 566 08524 0

Understanding and Managing Risk Attitude
David Hillson and Ruth Murray-Webster
0 566 08627 1

For further information on these and all our titles visit our website – www.gowerpub.com
All online orders receive a discount

GOWER

About the Authors

Nigel Iyer

Nigel Iyer is a Director and founder member of Hibis Scandinavia and a Director of Hibis Europe Ltd.

He worked on his first fraud case at the age of 16 and developed a keen interest in the subject. Since graduating from the University of Manchester in 1985 and subsequently training and qualifying as an English Chartered Accountant, his career has focussed on the prevention and investigation of fraud and corruption, initially working for large corporations, then as a consultant for UK-based Network Security Management.

In 1999 Nigel Iyer co-founded the Hibis Group (www.hibis.com) to specialise in the prevention of fraud and corruption. The Hibis Group now comprises four independent companies in the UK, Nordic Countries and Australia.

Nigel Iyer believes that investment in prevention has a far greater return than reactive investigation and therefore has invested considerable time in training managers to implement techniques to raise awareness and put in place detection programs. He lectures widely and is co-author of *Fraud Resistance: a Practical Guide* published by Standards Australia in 2003.

Nigel Iyer currently resides in the UK and Scandinavia.

Martin Samociuk

After graduating from university, Martin Samociuk worked in a copper smelter in Africa, before joining UK-based Network Security Management in 1981, initially specialising in the investigation of fraud and computer hacking.

In 1988, Network Security Management became a subsidiary of Hambros Bank and grew to become one of Europe's leading fraud investigation and prevention companies. Martin became firstly Managing Director and then Chairman and Chief Executive. In 1999 he co-founded the Hibis Group before moving to Australia to form Hibis Consulting in Sydney in 2001.

Martin is the lead author of *Fraud Resistance: a Practical Guide* and contributing author to the book *The Protection of Computer Software: Technology and Applications* published by Cambridge University Press, and the *Computer Security Reference Book* published by Butterworth Heinemann.